MODULARITY AND CONSTRAINTS IN LANGUAGE AND COGNITION

The Minnesota Symposia
on Child Psychology

Volume 25

MODULARITY AND CONSTRAINTS IN LANGUAGE AND COGNITION

The Minnesota Symposia
on Child Psychology

Volume 25

Edited by
MEGAN R. GUNNAR
MICHAEL MARATSOS
University of Minnesota

LEA LAWRENCE ERLBAUM ASSOCIATES, PUBLISHERS
1992   Hillsdale, New Jersey   Hove and London

Lawrence Erlbaum Associates, Inc., Publishers
365 Broadway
Hillsdale, New Jersey 07642

Library of Congress Cataloging in Publication Data

Modularity and constraints in language and cognition / edited by Megan
R. Gunnar, Michael Maratsos.
    p. cm. — (The Minnesota symposia on child psychology : v.
25)
    Papers presented at the 25th Minnesota Symposium on Child
Psychology, held Oct. 25-27, 1990, at the University of Minnesota.
    Includes bibliographical references and index.
    ISBN 0-8058-1175-3
    1. Cognition in children—Congresses. 2. Language acquisition-
-Congresses. 3. Modularity (Psychology) in children—Congresses.
4. Developmental psychobiology—Congresses. I. Gunnar, Megan R.
II. Maratsos, Michael P. III. Minnesota Symposia on Child
Psychology (25th : 1990 : University of Minnesota) IV. Series:
Minnesota symposia on child psychology (Series) ; v. 25.
BF723.C5M63 1992
155.4'13—dc20

91-39523
CIP

Printed in the United States of America
10 9 8 7 6 5 4 3 2 1

Contents

v

Preface

Megan R. Gunnar
University of Minnesota

This volume contains chapters based on the papers and discussant comments presented at the 25th Minnesota Symposium on Child Psychology, held October 25-27, 1990, at the University of Minnesota. As has been the tradition for this annual series, the faculty of the Institute of Child Development invited internationally eminent researchers to present their work and to consider problems of mutual concern.

The theme of this volume is modularity and constraints in language and cognition. The major goal of the symposium was to bring together researchers from differing perspectives to present data and to discuss the values and limitations of the concepts of modularity and constraint to our understanding of language and cognitive development. Students of language and cognition are increasingly adopting the notion that developmental processes in these domains are governed by intraorganism constraints. That is, the human organism is seen as biologically predisposed to abstract information in particular, highly determined ways relative to a wide array of options available in the input. These constraints are seen as governing the form that knowledge takes and therefore the outcomes of the developmental process. Furthermore, it is increasingly being argued that the constraints on the way information is abstracted are modularized. Modularity variously refers to aspects of brain organization that are seen as highly canalized for the processing of input (e.g., perceptual mechanism underlying the parsing of phonemes), or in Fodor's analyses, the discrete packaging of input within functional domains. Although modularity and constraint perspectives have been gaining influence, these perspectives are not universally accepted as useful or accurate. Indeed, the conjunction of these perspectives defines an area of intense controversy driving many and varied research programs. A focus on this controversy provided a mechanism in the 25th Minnesota Symposium for identifying the research and theoretical concerns that are at the cutting edge of work in language and cognitive development.

To this end, we are fortunate to have as contributors to this volume some of the most outstanding current scholars in this area. The contributors are, in alphabetical order, Thomas Bever, Frank Keil, Ellen Markman, and Laura Ann Petitto. Carol Malatesta-Magai and Bruce Dorval also contributed a chapter allowing an extension and critical analysis of the applicability of the modularity concept to the study of the interface between language and emotional expression. We were also fortunate to have three discussants at this symposium, all of whom have provided written comments for this volume. Michael Maratsos, who served as the co-organizer and co-editor of the symposium, presents an overview chapter outlining the issues and noting their relations with each of the presentations. Then both Jacqueline Goodnow and Robert Siegler provide insightful and thought-provoking discussant chapters at the end of the volume.

In all, the chapters in this volume provide a rich discussion of the concepts of modularity and constraint as they apply to the study of language and cognition. They, however, reflect only part of the richness of the symposium held in October 1990. We wish to thank all of the individuals who took part, speakers, discussants, and members of the audience, for making the 1990 symposium a great success. Thanks are also due to LuJean Huffman-Norberg, who served as my secretary for the symposium, Helen Dickison, who organized many of the symposium events and saw to many of the administrative details, and Teresa Smith, who helped with copyediting of the manuscripts.

The job of organizer and editor of the Minnesota Symposium is typically a 5-year assignment in the Institute. With this volume I come to the end of my 5-year stint. The role of organizer and editor has been an interesting and challenging one. I have learned a great deal about many of the current "cutting edge" areas of our field. I have also met or gotten to know better many wonderful and talented researchers. I would like to thank all of the contributors to this volume and to Volumes 21 through 24 for an enriching, if sometimes mildly exasperating, experience.

Finally I would also like to acknowledge financial support for the 25th symposium from the National Institute of Child Health and Human Development, R13 HD 21906.

1 Constraints, Modules, and Domain Specificity: An Introduction

Michael Maratsos
University of Minnesota

The general topic of the 1990 Minnesota Symposium was modules, constraints, and domain specificity. This chapter is an introduction to some general ideas and problems in this area.

A GENERAL BACKDROP

At its broadest, the problem of modern developmental psychology does not just reflect differences in investigator's beliefs about particular hypotheses regarding psychology and the development of children. It also reflects a clash between two major approaches or attitudes to scientific investigation.

A first goal is one of the oldest goals of science: the uniting of a wide range of apparently diverse phenomena by the positing of a relatively small set of general underlying principles. Indeed, achievement of this goal has been one of the time-honored closest-to-the-heart characteristics of science since ancient times. With the inception of Newtonian physics, it achieved such successes as to become a paradigm goal. To explain why the phenomena that the planets do *not* fall into the sun really comes from the same reasons that objects *do* fall onto the earth is the kind of triumph toward which all sciences have since aimed.

This goal is reflected by the attempts of behaviorists to find a few elementary principles and processes by which all behavior could be explained. In more modern times, it is reflected in a search to explain the mind by highly general principles that can be posited to underlie all the diverse areas of cognition. In developmental psychology, Piaget's theory

1

provides a general model of this kind. More recently, most work of the information-processing school (e.g., Anderson, 1976) seeks a set of explanatory principles that apply equally well to all domains of thought, including language, problem solving, arithmetic, and any other sub-species of the cognitive processes.

On the other hand, in recent years, another kind of idea about cognition has emerged. Perhaps a great deal of cognition consists of special-purpose systems each designed for particular tasks, such as learning language, or dealing with quantity, systems that reflect the diverse sets of tools that given species evolve in order to find, or create, a particular niche. This kind of thought stresses its continuity with evolutionary biology, in which the idea of species-specific, particular systemic properties of organisms is a natural one. As Mayr (1980) said, much of current evolutionary thought stresses the diversity present within species; the diversity provides the food of evolution.

According to Mayr, the two ways of thought about organisms—underlying generality versus underlying diversity of organization—have indeed clashed before in the history of biological thought. He said that attempts to gain an analysis like that of physics was one of the hindrances to a development of evolutionary theory. For development of evolutionary theory requires taking as basis the very great diversity of behaviors and systems within species; a concentration upon achieving description in terms of a few relatively simple, abstract underlying elements and principles thus impeded at different times the development of evolutionary thought.

In some ways, of course, biology itself has come full circle. At the molecular level, it now seems possible to understand all of the different genetic messages as being arrangements in triplets of four relatively simple amino acids. Yet this analysis does not remove the usefulness of dealing with the behavioral diversity of organisms at the level of problems such as accounting for speciation, or niche-filling.

Generally speaking, it seems to me that psychologists have tended to look fairly exclusively to physics as a model of the goals and methods of scientific investigation. What the history of science seems to show is that no particular mode of analysis has always been the correct one for all problems. Indeed, as a digressive remark, it seems likely that for many problems that presently occupy psychology, the general model of scientific thought provided by biological evolutionary theories before the development of molecular genetics may well provide a more profitable mode.

To return to the original problem: It is unlikely that investigators will drop their search for general underlying principles to explain apparently diverse phenomena; nor should they. But the possibility that much of human cognitive and social organization is diverse at important underlying levels as well also is a serious competitor as a model of psychological organization. The differences between these two approaches and beliefs are real; they are not separated simply by misunderstandings of concepts and terminology, but by real differences in goals and ideal aims.

In this volume, the concentration is on current work pursuing possibilities and problems in the approach of more domain-specific, species-specific underlying cognitive systems. Work in this kind commonly turns up concepts like "constraint," "module," or "domain specific." Indeed, in language, the prototypical examples of such systems in higher cognitive functioning, these concepts seem to arrive as a package.

As is often the case, a prototype may put things together that analytically may be separated. Thus, attention to the prototype alone may serve to confuse understanding of the separable nature of what are indeed partly individual concepts. Thus, a primary goal of this chapter is to give an idea of what such concepts mean; but an equally important secondary goal is to show how they are potentially partly independent.

DOMAIN SPECIFICITY

Probably the key concept of all these three is *domain specificity*. This concept refers to a claim that the manner in which information is processed in one domain may be different from the manner in which it is processed in another. This stands in opposition to systems like behaviorist associationism, for example, in which association of stimulus to stimulus, or stimulus to response, occurs in the same fashion for any kind of stimulus or response.

Domain specificity by itself, however, does not simply mean there is something specific about some domain of functioning in the behavior of the organism. An organism might learn to make specific types of responses in one domain, such as arithmetic, and in ordinary language terms, this would correspond to some degree of domain specificity in the organism's responses.

But in current usage, domain specificity means there is something *innate* in the organism that causes responses in that domain to be different in some important way. Such systems of response are now easy to document in animals. For example, a general rule of conditioning is that the animal will associate two stimuli with each other only if they are temporally contiguous, that is very close in time. It is accordingly a classic finding of modern psychology that in at least one domain, this rule does not hold. For Garcia (Garcia & Revusky, 1970) has shown that a rat will associate a novel taste with induced sickness (induced by the experimenter) if the novel taste precedes the sickness by 30 minutes; if the taste occurs right before the rat sickens, the rat does not make any association. Only in the first circumstance of a delay of some time does the rat avoid the novel taste later on.

Evolutionarily, this makes sense. It takes food some time to make one sick. So a system for learning food avoidance would do far better to associate a novel taste from a while ago with illness than a novel taste that occurs just before. But obviously this special rule of conditioning violates the general rules. Thus, there is something specific to the domain of association of taste with illness in the rat, and this domain specificity is innate.

Garcia's studies of illness and taste association in the rat thus provide prime examples of what is meant by a domain-specific learning system. In the study of higher cognition, it has been customary to think that the laws of learning and theory construction by the child are essentially the same in all domains of thought, such as language or logic (e.g., Piaget, 1970). Domain specificity refers to the hypothesis that there is instead something different among different domains in how they deal with information; they may have restrictions on what kinds of information are dealt with, or in what conclusions can be drawn from the information.

What counts as a domain? Essentially, any discernible body of functions that can be discriminated from another in some aspect of its content is a potential domain. Nor should it be expected that domains that are convenient for us to think of as separate will turn out to be different; or conversely, domains we think of as unified might turn out to be made up of separable domains upon further study. For example, arithmetic and logic are seen in the work of many 20th-century logicians and mathematicians as being essentially part of the same domain; but it might be that psychologically, aspects of the mind have developed to treat materials in the two fields in characteristically different ways. So a "domain" means any organized content area in which one might imagine or propose there being innate, specific distinctive mechanisms or ideas.

CONSTRAINTS AND DOMAIN SPECIFICITY

Constraint is a term that has an ordinary language meaning, but is developing a more specialized meaning in its current uses. Again it is obvious that in its widest sense, constraint would apply very broadly to what organisms do, and how they think. Organisms are constrained in their behaviors by systems of social rewards, punishments, and motives.

Humans are constrained in how they can think by the presence or absence of education in some subject.

But constraint in current discourse in modern psychology is intended to mean something more specific than this. It is intended to mean that because of innate structural specification, the organism does not process information in some fashion that one might logically imagine it could. Thus, some limitation in one's behavior that arises from education or training (or the lack of it) would not comprise a constraint.

Even adding innateness, however, does not capture the modern use of constraint. In broadest terms, no account of behavior or learning system has ever proposed that organisms are totally unconstrained in how they can process or construe incoming data. Any proposed processing system has proposed to specify what the organism does; it must thereby, by implication, specify things the organism does not do.

Behaviorist views of human behavior thus were, and were meant to be, highly constrained: For example, it was claimed that much of human functioning may and should be captured simply by analyzing the associations made between stimuli and responses under various conditions; all such stimuli and responses and conditions were supposed to be clearly physically observable; stimuli and their associated responses were stipulated as having to be temporally contiguous. These stipulations are very strong constraints indeed, and the ferocity of the constraints was customarily portrayed as a distinct advantage of the theory.

Important aspects of other, more current theories of human cognition also clearly comprise some kind of constraint. For example, modern information-processing theories generally claim that there is a short-term memory and working space distinct from long-term memory. This short-term working space is typically said to be able to hold only a limited number of items (Miller, 1956), or to have only a limited amount of attentional focus available to it.

But in current usage, it is very doubtful that either behavioristic constraints upon the association of stimulus and response, or information-processing constraints on short-term memory, are the kind of thing that is meant when someone uses the word "constraint" in discussing cognition. But, if "constraint" does not mean any possible innate constraint upon the organism's processing of information, then, what does it mean? In most current uses, "constraint" refers to something the organism does not do that it might because of something innately specific to a particular domain. Thus, in Garcia's experiments with rats and the conditioning of novel tastes and sickness, one might expect the rat to associate a novel taste and an immediately following illness, given that the rat typically (or at least often) associates temporally contiguous stimuli. But the rat does not. Therefore, something must constrain the rat from doing so; this is the specific mechanism that, in the domain of taste and illness, associates novel tastes with illness that follows some time later.

In current work in cognition, "constraint" refers to some constraint placed by a domain-specific structure that affects the organism's processing of cognitive information. The notion of a constraint in modern cognitive work developed with certain central connotations derived to a large degree from some of its initial uses in the study of linguistics. I thus attempt to develop here at some length some of the logic of one of these initial usages. I then present more briefly some of the further, much wider uses "constraint" came to have in linguistic work.

The central initial example of a constraint in linguistics emerged in the analysis of a rule often called *wh*-movement, one of the transformational rules of Chomskyan grammar (Chomsky, 1957, 1965). This rule is the central operation in the transformational machinery for producing *wh*-questions like "what will he eat?" or "when can he come?" In the transformational description of such sentences, the *wh*-term appears initially in a declarative-like position in the sentence. Thus, the initial form of "what will he eat?" is "he will eat what?" in which "what" appears as the direct object of the verb "eat." Indeed, in this sentence, "what" is a constituent that asks for information about that which was eaten, and so this initial form put it in a sentence position that indicates this direct object function more clearly. The *wh*-movement then moves "what" to the front of the sentence:

he will eat what?

wh-movement

$\Longrightarrow$

what will he eat?

(A second rule is responsible for the movement of the auxiliary verb *will* from after the grammatical subject to in front of it; this rule is not important for discussion here.)

So in the transformational description, *wh*-terms frequently begin in one position in the sentence, then move to the front. In the following examples, I put "3/M" in a fully formed *wh*-question, in order to indicate the position from which the *wh*-term was moved by the transformation. Thus "what will he eat 3/M" indicates that "what" was moved from the position after "eat."

A central property of English and many other languages is that *wh*-terms can be moved from a very great variety of positions to the front. Basically, any noun phrase constituent can be questioned by replacing it with a *wh*-term or phrase and moving the *wh*-constituent to the front. Indeed, in theory, *wh*-terms can be moved from an infinite variety of contexts. For one of the central properties of language is that sentences may be embedded inside other sentences. For example, the sentence

"John thinks that Mary likes Tom" has a full sentence "Mary likes Tom" embedded as the grammatical direct object of the verb "think." (In this sentence, the word "that" is an introducer for the embedded sentence.) The structural rules of natural languages allow such embedding to go on forever, or in practical terms, for as long as a speaker's memory allows. One can say "John thinks (Mary convinced Sam [that Hillary likes Tom])," which has two sentence embeddings; or one can say "John thinks (Mary convinced {Sam that Hillary said [that Margaret likes Tom]})," which has three embeddings, and so on, in theory *ad infinitum*.

What is of interest here is that *wh*-movement can extract a *wh*-term from a position as far down in any of these embedded sentences as one might like; the following pairs illustrate this (in part, of course):

1. John thinks Mary convinced who that Hillary likes
   Tom   *wh*-movement
                                                =====>

   Who does John think Mary convinced _____ that Hillary likes Tom?

2. John thinks Mary convinced Sam that Hillary likes
   who(m)   *wh*-movement
                                                =====>

   Who does John think Mary convinced Sam that Hillary likes ____?

If sentences can be embedded, in theory, infinitely, and a *wh*-term can be extracted from any such level of embedding, it is impossible to state the entire set of particular contexts for their extraction. Rather, it is best to say the rule can apply to any *wh*-term anywhere, and allow such terms to be removed from any context. The rule is thus a very powerful one, applicable in theory to a potentially infinite variety of sentence contexts.

Yet left in this necessarily general form, it is also too powerful. Consider the following sentence pair:

3. John likes dogs that eat what?   *wh*-movement
   What does John like dogs that eat ____?   =======>

The first sentence of Example 3 certainly has an interpretable meaning. Yet application of *wh*-movement to it in the usual fashion results in an ungrammatical sentence that speakers quite typically also find incomprehensible.

The ungrammaticality of this result is not a function of the kinds of lexical meanings, involved, for example. Rather, there is a systematic, structural exception to the generalization that *wh*-terms can be moved from any embedded sentence position. Although they can be moved from embedded sentences from an infinite number of positions, they cannot be moved from an embedded sentence that comprises a relative clause (Ross, 1967).[1]

Thus, on the one hand, the grammar needs a *wh*-movement rule that must be stated in a very general and powerful way to extract *wh*-terms freely in general from main clauses and embedded sentences. This very general rule must simultaneously be stated to have a specific negative constraint upon it. Thus, the constraint is one that acts upon a very powerful process. It is a negative prohibition, rather than a positive statement of something that can be done. Furthermore, it has been argued (as is discussed shortly) to be specific to the domain of language, to grammar in particular.

This particular constraint is quite well-known because it has figured prominently in arguments about the innate, specifically programmed nature of human language. The arguments go something like the following: All speakers of English seem to have formulated or learned this constraint. No one disagrees on the ungrammaticality of the relevant sentences, a striking fact. Yet as far as is known, it is not the case that children produce such sentences and then receive corrective feedback, to tell them that such sentences are not possible. Nor obviously, do children or adults receive overt instruction that tells them not to produce such sentences. The presence of such exceptions to the general patterns of *wh*-questions was not even known until about 25 or 30 years ago.

But one might say that no one hears such sentences in the first place. There are two problems with this argument. First, a central point of language competence is that it allows people to produce and comprehend sentences that no one has said or heard before. So the general argument that one has ever heard such sentences before is not quite right.

But, one could say, no one hears this *type* of sentence. This is essentially an argument from similarity and dissimilarity. It is an argument that such sentences are not similar enough to sentences one has heard, to be included in the class of possible English sentences.

But what does "similar enough" mean here? In fact, these un-grammatical *wh*-questions certainly are similar in many respects to grammatical English sentences. They can be analyzed as sentences in which a *wh*-term is taken from an embedded sentence, and as such they are certainly similar to the many (in principle) inexhaustible sets of sentences in which *wh*-movement does work. What one could say is that they are similar in some respects to grammatical sentences one has heard,

---

[1] As anyone with specialized knowledge of linguistics would quickly see, I am often giving only approximately correct descriptions of technical matters throughout these discussions. The actual constraint formulated by Ross (1967) to cover this case was not in terms of "relative clauses," but a formal syntactic configuration that also applied to certain kinds of noun phrase complement constructions. For purposes here, the difference is not very important, and relative clause is probably more accessible to a general reader than Ross' more formal and general analysis.

and not similar in other respects.

But typically when something is similar to something else in some pointed respects, but not similar in others, people will disagree in their judgments. Some in effect say "it's similar enough," and so judge whatever it is, to be something of the same kind. Others say "it's not similar enough, the differences are too great," and so it is judged to be different. People disagree in this way about moral and social situations all the time, for example.

But in the case of these judgments of the grammaticality of *wh*-questions, people do not disagree. It is not that some people are more struck by the similarity to grammatical cases, and others are more struck by the dissimilarity. Rather, the determining force or this particular dissimilarity is agreed upon spontaneously by everyone who speaks English as a native speaker. This unanimity of agreement about what is, so to speak, the appropriate property for stimulus discrimination, must be taken as very striking, whatever one's eventual analysis of why people converge so well in their judgments on these sentences.

At this point, then, it seems likely that there is some underlying property of the mind at work, which so constrains these judgments. There does seem to be some kind of powerful constraint upon the applicability of *wh*-movement, and it is plausible to argue this is a given, rather than acquired property.

This does not in itself, however, demonstrate that the relevant constraint is one that is indeed peculiar to language, rather than following from some more general property of the mind. The Chomskyan argument that this constraint is language specific, is in the end one about the lack of successful competition to the linguist's description: A linguist can make a language-specific statement of this constraint; that is, the statement itself is in terms of operations such as *wh*-movements, relative clauses, and other constructs apparently specific to language itself. No one has proposed a description, alternatively, of some more general property of the mind that produces this set of constraints for *wh*-movement, and that also is evidenced by sharply analogous constraints in the functioning of some nonlinguistic domain. Thus, by default, the only available theory is a language-specific one, and the constraint can be proposed to be an innate language-specific one. It is frustrating that the argument, put in this way, is not presently essentially an empirical one; it is one of theoretical noncompetition. Yet if no plausible mind-general proposal emerges, this failure of emergence must be at least taken seriously.

Suppose we take the *wh*-movement constraints largely as given above (in fact, modern linguistic formulations of these phenomena have changed in a number of important ways; but our purpose here is partly historical, and so reference to the original proposals is appropriate).[2] Like constraints on stimulus–response associations, or short-term memory, *wh*-constraints are thus proposed to be innate properties of thought. They innately constrain what kinds of conclusions the organism can draw from the data.

But *wh*-constraints are furthermore claimed to act within a domain-specific system of abstract, specific articulated operations. The elements on which the relevant operations take place are highly specific to the domain of language and within language, the domain of syntax. Furthermore, they are "superprototypical" constraints, because they serve to constrain a general rule process that is already actually part of the system (*wh*-movement) and so does produce highly related outputs. Finally, one might add, the phenomena to which the constraints refer, and the constraints themselves, are surprising; they are not the sort of thing one would have suspected ahead of time. (This is part of what makes them feel unlikely to be derived by general processes of thought, in fact, they are surprising because they do not resemble other things one is familiar with.)

It might seem attractive to define *constraint* as referring to the specific cluster of properties given earlier. In fact, however, even within linguistics itself, the concept of constraint is used over a much broader range of situations and rule types. For example, the *wh*-movement constraint is an explicit negative prohibition, which serves to restrict the operation of a rule that is already part of the system. Other times, however, linguists speak of the necessity of "constraining" the language learner from formulating certain logically possible rules at all, and this may be done by a positive principle rather than a negative prohibition. In current Chomskyan theory, for example, every sentence has a grammatical subject at some level of analysis, even if none appears in the apparent form of the sentence (e.g., an imperative like "eat your dinner") is described as having an underlying grammatical subject, even though none appears in its overt form. Thus, the language learner must be constrained from making an analysis of imperatives in which a particular one has no subject. This could be done by negative prohibition: Do not allow grammatical underlying sentence forms that have no subject. But in fact, it is done by a positive principle: The underlying form of every sentence has a grammatical subject. This positive principle thus implicitly, rather than explicitly, rules out any hypothesis that a sentence might lack an

---

[2] The reasons for these changes are quite important: Languages do not observe the same set of constraints on *wh*-movement. Thus, current theory endows the child with knowledge of the limited numbers of ways in which these constraints on *wh*-movement can vary, and with a procedure, "parameter setting," for quickly deciding what kind of language the child is still exposed to. This of course comprises a partly new structural type of constraint (see Chomsky, 1981, for discussion).

underlying subject. (It also implicitly rules out any hypothesis that an underlying sentence form might have two or more separate subjects.) Thus, rather than "don't do X" the constraint takes the form "do Y." Rather than restricting the output of some rule, the positive principle simply does not allow certain rules as possibilities in the first place.

In other cases, the relevant constraint is achieved by having the output of a rule in one subsystem conflict with a principle of another. For example, in current Chomskyan linguistics, some *wh*-movement outputs are generated, which are later marked deviant because the resulting structures cannot be given a coherent semantic-referential interpretation by another subsystem of the grammar. Having one positive subsystem remove part of the output of another comprises one of the major types of constraint in current grammar. Still other constraints, called *markedness constraints*, are essentially preference rules: "Assume X unless there is evidence against it." [3]

At the most general level of description, the notion of "constraint" in modern linguistics thus really corresponds to fairly straightforward notions, like "Do X" (and therefore do not do not-X); or, "do Y except in situation A"; or, "mark outputs of 'Do X' deviant if they do not fit the requirements of 'Do Y.'" Constraint simply means *some* formal means of preventing the language learner from formulating a system that might seem possible on various interpretations of the input data, but that will produce incorrect output.

But as has been seen, other systems, such as behavioristic associationism, or short-term memory components in information processing, also place severe constraints on children's analysis of input. The differences, then, lie in various more specialized aspects of the proposed constraints. These include, to recapitulate:

1. the innate constraints and principles are specific to some domain, like language: They are not applicable to any domain of cognition, nor are they interpretable as a subcase or a more general principle of mind; they typically specify elements peculiar to the domain;
2. the constraints are both abstract and specific.

Finally, as mentioned earlier, a "good" constraint or constraining principle has, properly presented, a kind of surprising quality to it: One is surprised that the system cannot produce certain output, given some of

---

[3] Actual, parameter-setting models like those referred to in footnote 2 correspond to giving the child a limited number of choices; they might be described in this fashion: "Do X, or Y, or Z (but not anything else)," in which X, Y, and Z lie along a gradient of greater or lesser freedom of output for some specified construction.

the output it does produce; or one is surprised the language learner does not consider the data in a certain light, given how reasonable it would be to do so. This, however, is obviously not a required property; it is simply a property of many of the proposed constraints that have given the concept of constraint much of its associated interest.

MODULARITY AND CONSTRAINTS

Another concept that has acquired much conceptual cachet in current thinking is that of a *module*. Again, the notion of module in cognitive psychology arose in a specific context, and so took on specific properties established by its initial prototype; and again, this initial prototype was, for many purposes, Chomskyan linguistic theory. It also turns out that module has possible meanings not confinable to this initial prototype, from which it can borrow connotations or denotations that are not definitionally necessary.

A reasonable first approximation of many of the ideas of Chomskyan modules that have since become "prototypical" or modules more generally, is the theory of language presented in the book *Aspects of the Theory of Syntax* (Chomsky, 1965). This theory differs in many serious ways from current work in Chomskyan generative grammar. But for many years it was the "standard" theory of grammar (so called, at least, in what was claimed to be a purely nonevaluative way by Chomsky himself); it did comprise the standard representation of linguistic theory for most psychologists.

The theory had four main modules: a base component, a transformational component, a semantic interpretive component, and a phonological component. These can be schematized roughly as in Fig. 1.1.

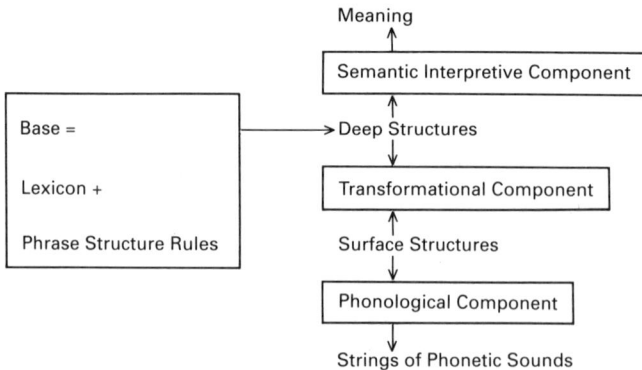

FIG. 1.1.   Four main modules of the aspects linguistic model.

It would be an impossible task here to describe the working of these components, or their justification, in anything like sufficient detail to show how or why the system came out in this way. All that is done here is to review some of the central properties of this system, as reminders or guides to the reader. After this brief review, a few of the properties of the system that are central to this discussion are highlighted.

The aspect of the system that captured the most interest was the way in which the relationship between deep structures and surface structures was mediated by transformational rules. For example, two sentences like "John eats eggs," and "Eggs are eaten by John," have an intuitive relation between them despite the surface differences in the sequences of words and details of verb and noun phrase marking. This relationship was captured in the grammar by supplying them in deep structure with highly similar phrase structures; essentially, both had the same underlying deep structure (see Fig. 1.2).

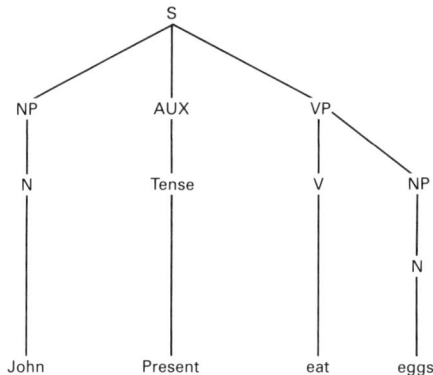

FIG. 1.2 .   Deep structure for "Eggs are eaten by John" and "John eats eggs."

This structure captures the information that for both sentences, the noun phrase (NP), "John," is the underlying subject of the main verb "eat," and "eggs" is the underlying NP object of "eat." To produce the passive form, a transformational rule of passivization then interchanged "John" and "eggs." The same rule also added a form of "be" and changed the verb to past participle form. [4]

Deep structures themselves comprised the output of the base

---

[4] Again, I am approximating important details of the description. The description I am referring to for the passive here is actually more like the description in Chomsky's earlier work (1957) *Syntactic Structure*. In the *Aspects* model, a dummy prepositional phrase was present in the base structure already to receive the to-be-moved underlying subject, and there were other differences among actives and passives. Again, however, it is not clear these differences are important for the discussion here.

component module. This module consisted of two main parts: phrase structure rules that produced deep structures, and the lexicon, which contained information for individual lexical items as to which syntactic deep structures they could appear in. For example, the information that "eat" is a transitive verb that can take both a syntactic underlying subject and object is stored in the entry for the verb "eat" in the lexicon.

The semantic interpretive component and phonological components each had limited access to some level of analysis of sentences to perform particular tasks. The semantic interpretive component was a component that read off the meaning of the sentence using information from the deep structure and information from the lexicon. For example, from the deep structure "John eat Present eggs," the component could read that "John" is the underlying subject of "eat." Given this information, and information stored in the lexicon about "eat," it could then supply the interpretation that the referent of "John" is therefore an animate being that put into its mouth, chewed, and sent to its digestive organ through some channel, the referent of the direct object of "eat." A central point for the discussion here is that the semantic component, in the 1965 version of the grammar, had access *only* to deep syntactic structures; it had no access to any syntactic structure that resulted from the operations of transformations.

The phonological component had the task of supplying the actual sound representations of the sentence, such as stress patterns. It also was limited in what kind of information could enter it. It could receive as syntactic input only the surface structure that comprised the output of the transformational component. It received no semantic information, for example, nor any information from syntactic deep structure.

An important property of this system that has probably entered into many people's understanding (and misunderstanding) of modules more generally, is what was called the *autonomy* of the syntactic module. Obviously this does not mean that the syntactic module (the base plus transformational rules) has no connection with other components. What it means is that the elements referred to in the syntactic rules are hypothesized to be purely syntactic elements; they are not semantic, conceptual, or any other kind of nonsyntactic element. This is so despite the fact that in popularizations of the system, the deep structures were often explained as being the "meaning of the sentence." In fact, deep structure had the same relation to the meaning of the sentence that a blueprint has to a building: The meaning could be read off of the deep structure, but the deep structure itself was a purely syntactic structure that itself had no meaning. The fact that the NP, "John," refers semantically to a conceptually animate, human individual plays no role in the operation or specification of the syntactic rules; it is only the semantic interpretive component that is supposed to have access to this information. In effect, there is a division of labor among the components in their attention to the various aspect of words and sentences.

It is worth noting, however, that the interpretive components are true modular components, yet *do* mix syntactic representations with other kinds of representations. The semantic interpretive component, for example, registers the fact that "John" is a syntactic deep structure subject of "eat" to interpret "John" as an agentive doer of the eating action. Thus, only the syntactic components were "autonomous" in this sense of being homogeneously composed of component-specific elements of an unmixed kind.[5,6] A component can be modular without being "autonomous," contrary to the impression given by Chomskyan syntactic modules.

Chomsky's model of linguistic structure was thus probably the first well-known modular model in higher cognition. It also, of course, had another well-known property: It was (and is) claimed to be innately specified that languages in general have this kind of particular modular structure.

FODORIAN MODULES

Chomskyan modules are a claim about mental structure; but their relation to real-world general measurement properties is often fairly abstract (even though, of course, they have some very close relationships to some such properties; e.g., sentences have meaning, sound, and sequential

---

[5] Whether syntax is indeed autonomous in this sense has for a long time been one of the major disputes within both linguistics and psycholinguistics. Many would claim that the Chomskyan systems make syntax autonomous by purely formal means; that in reality, syntax is partly determined by semantics or pragmatics, but in the formal description, these aspects of the syntax-semantics codetermination are always farmed out to some other component of the grammar in order to keep the syntactic component apparently purely syntactic. Or devices may be used such as calling semantic properties like animacy syntactic ones if they play clear roles in determining grammatical choices of various kinds (as in Chomsky, 1965). I, for example, agree with those who hold that the autonomy of the syntactic component is largely a contrived property rather than a real one. This is not to deny, however, the possibility that some elements involved in syntactic rules are indeed peculiar to the syntactic domain; it is simply to say that it is not necessarily therefore the case that *all* elements involved in syntax are peculiar to the syntactic domain. Whether any syntactic elements are indeed purely syntactic, or are constructions from other systems also remain a highly debated issue, it should be noted.

[6] In this volume, Frank Keil proposes that biology may be autonomous because there might be some domain-specific elements in biological thought. It is worth keeping in mind that this is not the same as the use of "autonomous" in "autonomous syntax," which means that in the relevant component, there are *nothing* but domain-specific elements.

form). In the past years, Jerry Fodor has put forth an influential account of modular organizations. His account has some general common ground with Chomskyan description; it also has closer ties to general behavioral measures, and is more explicit about certain aspects of modular organization. At the same time, an exposition of some properties of his accounts again indicates how some properties of a concept such as module are less rigidly specified than is sometimes understood from their particular instantiations; as always, key properties are more general and independent than might appear to be the case.

Fodor proposed four properties of modules in general:

1. they are encapsulated;
2. they are evidenced by, and built to give, fast processing of material;
3. they are "hard-wired," that is, built in biologically rather than assembled over time; furthermore, they are localized in a particular region (particular to each module) in the brain; and
4. they are domain specific, and form "vertical" rather than "horizontal" domains.

Each of these points is discussed in turn.

Encapsulation.   As just mentioned, encapsulation corresponds to one of the central properties of modules: Modules have only limited access to each other. It is important to note, again, however, that unlike the impression often given by reference in particular to Chomskyan syntax as "autonomous," this does not mean that modules are completely closed to one another, or cannot sometimes use material of overlapping types. Rather, it means that the kind of materials one module can receive from another is strictly specified.

Fodor supplies a classic example of encapsulation, that of optical illusions such as the Muller–Lyer illusion. This illusion was also, noncoincidentally, studied by Piaget, for it displays in classic form the conflict between perception and higher cognition. In the Piagetian form, the subject is first shown two lines that are clearly equal in length:

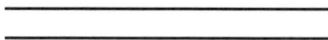

Arrows are then drawn as here and the subject is asked if the lines are still of the same length:

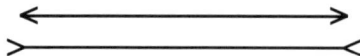

To most people, although it is cognitively clear that the lines must still be of equal length, the lines now *look* different in length.

Piaget's interest in the procedure lay in its demonstration of the opposition of cognition and perception. Fodor pointed out that if systems were completely open to one another, one might expect that the perceptual system could be "persuaded" by the cognitive system that the lines are indeed still equal. But the perceptual system in dealing with this particular problem appears to go about its own business with not much influence here from what the cognitive system knows. The perceptual system is here extremely encapsulated in its workings; at least this is so in its dealing with illusions like the Muller–Lyer illusion.

Again, however, it is necessary to point out that this "classic" example may mislead in its useful extremity. For this is an example of what appears to be complete "autonomy" of one system. But as noted earlier, *complete* lack of access is *not* a concomitant of encapsulation. Rather, it is restricted access that is what encapsulation refers to; complete lack of access is simply the limiting case of restricted access that might form an unfortunately vivid prototype because of its clarity.

Of the four attributes of Fodorian modules listed here, only encapsulation is a necessary definitional concomitant of modules in the most general sense. The other three attributes form part of a hypothesis about how modules might be instantiated, or about a useful definition of them, but are not necessary attributes of modular systems in general. They are nevertheless, worth discussing as examples of how a modular proposal can be filled out, and again, have come to become prototypically representative, at least in part, of how the concept of a module has come to be used.

Fast Processing. According to Fodor, fast processing is the characteristic of some systems that first inspired his interest in making an extended analysis of modular systems. In particular, he made a plausible argument that when various time delays specific to the task implementation of sentence shadowing comprehension tasks are allowed for, sentence comprehension in adults is essentially instantaneous. Considering the indubitable complexity of sentence structure, this is a remarkable finding. Many aspects of perception have similar properties: essentially accurate and very fast processing of information.

The natural explanation for this, Fodor held, is that systems such as language and perceptual analysis are modularized. That is, they are highly organized, modularized sets of operations. Encapsulation serves to aid fast processing because the systems need only consider a fraction of the available information, in a specified way. A system that can, and does, consider information from every possible other part of the cognitive system, in an unbounded variety of ways, must in contrast—or so it can be argued—operate more slowly. Thus, encapsulation serves, and results in, fast processing.

In responses in a later article, Fodor (1981) acknowledged another possible explanation for fast processing in a domain—that of automatization. It is a familiar phenomenon that something that is learned may initially proceed slowly with a great deal of conscious effort, yet eventually through practice become automatic and quick. Learning to drive provides a useful example of this. Fodor's response to this possibility, (e.g., that language processing is fast through being automatized, not through being modularized) is that automatized processes can be slowed down voluntarily. One can pay attention to one's driving and go through the motions slowly; or one can type slowly. On the other hand, it is seemingly impossible to slow down one's comprehension of a sentence. One does it quickly or not at all.

Hard-Wired.   Another property Fodor claimed for modules is that they are hard-wired, that is, assembled not by induction from experience, but instead given by evolution as part of the biology of the organism. Furthermore, they are hypothesized to be localized in a particular region of the brain, such as the occipital lobe for vision, or the left temporal lobe for language.

Both of these conjectures—hard-wiring, localization—are again not part of the *definitionally necessary* makeup of modules, but rather hypotheses about how a central class of modules are realized in human cognition. The hypothesis about biological innateness rests partly upon evidence from empirical study, and also accords with the fact that perceptual and language processing are very robust faculties. In the case of localization, the conjecture again partly rests upon extent evidence, but is also made to fit some empirically investigatable concreteness to the modular concept. The hypothesis of localization is interesting because it is in fact not necessary. One could easily imagine a neurological system that is structured to act as a module, but has its actual input, processing, and output locations in different parts of the brain. Because modules can receive input from other systems, for example, their relevant input locations might be located near those systems, just as corporations may locate factories for various steps in processing raw materials near the materials, even though the entire manufacturing process is in fact highly "modularized."

Domain-Specific Vertical Modules.   Finally, Fodor proposed that modules refer to domain-specific "vertical" modules, rather than "horizontal" modules that cut across various domains. For example, he noted that one might propose there is a memory faculty that cuts across domains like perception, language, and other realms of higher cognition, but is essentially the same faculty. This would comprise a horizontal module. Instead, he proposed that essentially each domain has its own memory storage, even if there have to be routes of access from one domain-specific module to another to exchange memory and other information. In this, Fodor essentially followed a Chomskyan approach. In fact, it is clear that even a highly structured, innately set up modular organization does not have to be domain specific. Piagetian operational structures, for example, such as those of concrete operations or formal operations seem to have been module-like systems of operations that were open to access from various domains. What Fodor's proposal brings out, and exemplifies, is the strong current association of modularity with innateness and domain specificity in most of its current uses.

Big and Small Modules

The types of modules discussed by Fodor and Chomsky are essentially large systems of groups of operations within a domain; certainly a Chomskyan modular system implies within each subcomponent a highly articulated set of such operations with only limited access to and from other submodules.

In fact, however, the usual definition of a module is simply a processing unit with some degree of self-containment (not complete self-containment, because modules must transmit information to other parts of the cognitive organization). This partial or high degree of self-containment is gained by limiting access to the module, and in limiting its output paths to other units.

But it follows from this that in fact, any domain-specific processing unit, however small, to some degree has a modular quality. For if it is domain specific, it by definition limits the input that can enter it. Thus, such a module might be a very small processing unit indeed, with only a couple of internal operations upon data.

As can be seen, the prototypical Chomskyan–Fodorian modules refer to large systems; thus they do not definitionally coincide with any domain-specific processing operation. But there is no formal current requirement in the use of module in the literature that the module be of any particular internal complexity or size. The limit of this lack of formal definition is that any domain-specific processing trivially implies some degree of modularity. This is perhaps unfortunate, because the connotation given by prototypical instances thus conflict with possible uses; at present there is no particular resolution to this referential problem. [7]

INNATENESS, MODULES, CONSTRAINTS, AND
DOMAIN SPECIFICITY: VARIATION AND EXTENSIONS

As can be seen from the previous discussion, current prototypical uses of concepts like "innateness," "constraint," "domain specificity," and "module" imply considerable referential intertwining of the concepts. A learned module in a particular domain, like a particular way of doing topographical algebra, is not what is meant by usual current uses of module, for it lacks innateness. A constraint imposed by social forces or education is not an innate, domain-specific constraint of current use. An innate requirement to associate temporally contiguous stimuli in any domain is not what innateness or constraint in the current codes mean.

Despite this degree of intertwining, it is necessary not to lose sight of the degree of variation also allowed even within these current uses. As seen earlier whether or not a domain-specific operation comprises a prototypical "module" depends on how big a size one requires in a module. A domain-specific unit or operation necessarily restricts what input it accepts, so it itself is a kind of "small" module. But it is therefore not equivalent to a large massed bloc of interconnected operations to which there is a restricted access. A module, especially of the second, "large" type, is in turn necessarily a constrained system. But the kind of constraint involved could involve explicit negative prohibitions (like the original form of *wh*-movement constraints), or simple positive principles about what kinds of material can be acted on, or default principles, or some other form of internal constraint. Or consider the notion of domain specificity of an operation or module. This could mean, as in the Chomskyan "autonomous" syntactic rules, that all the elements of a relevant operation or set of operations are claimed to be specific to a particular subdomain. Or it could mean that the relevant component has at least some parts that are characteristic of it alone, but also allows

---

[7] Keil's reference to biological systems as being likely to be "modularized," in this volume, strike me as not differentiating between "small" and "large" modules in this sense. He seems to mean that biology has specific principles of interpretation that are innate and peculiar to it. As discussed here, however, this does not entail that biology form a highly organized large module organization; it could be that it is a system largely formed of units from other domains, or with highly free access to them, which also has a small number of domain-specific operating units. The latter could be seen as forming small modules, but do not entail a highly organized major relatively self-enclosed system. Without a fairly specific proposal about the organization of biological knowledge, which Keil reasonably states not to be available at this time, one cannot tell what degree of "modularization" is implied by the particular proposals he puts forth. And if biology turns out to involve content-specific rather than domain-specific "constraints" (see discussion toward the end of his chapter and also the end of this chapter), then some kind of highly organized, modular organization for biology becomes still less plausible.

operations to refer to elements of other types, as does the Chomskyan semantic interpretive component, which states operations on both syntactic and semantic elements, and is thus not autonomous in the same sense. To take another point of variation, operations within a component may differ in structural nature from those of another component, as in Chomskyan modules; or operations in different modules might just differ in the types of materials on which the operations work, without the operations being different in structural kind.

Thus, although these concepts have various prototypical instantiations, there is considerable range of variation even within the centrally defined range. Furthermore, all of these are concepts that are currently part of changing development in the field of cognition and cognitive development. The range of delimitations outlined previously may prove an inadequate guide to newly developing uses of these concepts.

Indeed, one can both find uses of the same words in related fields that do not have quite the same meaning, and uses within the current developing shape of cognitive development that already are starting to diverge from the definitional-conceptual core sketched out in the previous pages. Some of the chapters in this volume offer some indications of variations that are currently developing in the definition of these concepts. Both Markman and Keil, for example, discuss the idea that various innate constraints might consist of positive principles about how to handle particular kinds of contents. But a given type of content might in fact occur in different domains, and so what we would have is content specificity, not necessarily domain specificity. Keil, for example, proposes that children may have the innate principle that something with heterogeneous parts has some kind of purpose, which is not the same as an intentional goal. As he writes at the end of his chapter, this principle may be especially targeted for, or nested in, biological thinking, and thus would comprise a domain-specific constraint or principle. Or, it might be that it applies to objects with heterogeneous parts in any domain, among which biology is especially prominent.[8]

Markman considers a related notion of domain-specific constraints, among the many possibilities discussed in her chapter. Specifically, this proposal is that word-learning principles may choose among general analyses and principles available from other systems. For example, she says that children apply a principle in word learning that word concepts

---

[8] At this point, one could always propose that any such "content" that has some innately structured principle involved in its nature or processing, in fact thus comprises a "domain" of its own sort; this would retain the association between domain specificity and constraints. But it would do so at the cost of attenuating the definitional focus of the idea of a domain, or at least make necessary some way of distinguishing between larger, more familiar domains and these new types of "domain."

are taxonomic rather than thematic in nature. (See her chapter for discussion of the differences among these.) But taxonomic and thematic concepts are also to be found used, or not used, in other domains of cognition as well. It might be, she writes, that different domains are naturally specified as using one or the other, so that access of a domain to each type of principle is restricted; but the principles themselves are not restricted to a particular domain. Thus, domain specificity here means restricted access to a general type of analysis, on the part of some domain of functioning, but not exclusive association of some principle and one particular domain.

In still other sections of her chapter, Markman considers the possibility that some of the constraints she has proposed for word learning might actually result because of principles in other domains. Thus, children's assigning whole-object analyses to new words (rather than textures, or parts of novel objects) might result from whole objects being the foundational process for analyzing events more generally. As can be seen, this weakens the prototypical conceptual definition that a constraint in some domain of functioning is actually part of the functioning of the domain itself. What is kept of the meaning of constraint is that the child does not think about some kind of content in a way that seems otherwise possible.

It is clear from reading these and other current papers that the manner in which concepts like constraint and module are used, is indeed changing even now. To some degree this reflects necessary flexibility of non-mathematical concepts as the problems being considered change. In any case, this means that a reader of new work needs to both have some sense of how the concepts have been used, which already covers a wide range, and the fact that their developing uses may change in important ways still.

As Mayr (1980) has written, developing a clear set of concepts is in fact important for the progress of most fields. Thus, the fact that such concepts are in flux has both its good and bad points. The general ordinary language sense of "constraint," as has been seen, is so broad as to be effectively non-communicative. If "constraint" is stretched far enough, it will eventually become as lacking in meaning as "stimulus" often became in the older stimulus–response psychology. Currently, it still retains some core of referring to some kind of innately caused constraint on how various contents are handled in a cognitive system, and the fact that some appear to be handled differently from others. It can be hoped that in the long term, there is again a sharpening in the meaning of idea of constraint or a sharpening in delineation of important subtypes of constraints, so that damage to discourse in the field is not caused by too great a conceptual spread in its key concepts.

In the meantime, however, probably what is most important about current developments are the developing attempt to look for particularity of structure and processing in central aspects of cognition outside of domains like grammar where these are better entrenched (although still being vigorously argued about). To this end, the chapters of this volume bring up important current evidence on the status of this quest in biology, word learning and symbol use, emotion, and in the older parts of language study itself. To the degree that this introduction gives some idea of the definitional-conceptual backdrop into which this work is now moving, it serves in helping to understand the goals, aims, and emerging preoccupations of the research in these domains.

REFERENCES

Anderson, J. R. (1976). *Language, memory, and thought.* Hillsdale, NJ: Lawrence Erlbaum Associates.

Chomsky, N. (1957). *Syntactic structures.* The Hague: Mouton.

Chomsky, N. (1965) *Aspects of the theory of syntax.* Cambridge, MA: MIT Press.

Chomsky, N. (1981). *Lectures on government and binding.* Dordrecht: Foris.

Fodor, J. (1981). *Modularity of mind.* Cambridge, MA: MIT Press.

Garcia. J., & Revusky, S. (1970). Learned associations over long delays. In G. Bower (Ed.), *The psychology of learning and motivation: Advances in research and theory.* New York: Academic Press.

Mayr, E. (1980). *The history of biological thought.* Cambridge, MA: Harvard University Press.

Miller, G. (1956). The magical number seven, plus or minus two: Some limits on our capacity for processing information. *Psychological Review, 63,* 81–97.

Piaget, J. (1970). *Genetic epistemology.* New York: University of Columbia Press.

Ross, J. R. (1967). *Constraints on variables in syntax.* Unpublished doctoral dissertation, Massachusetts Institute of Technology, Cambridge, MA.

2 Modularity and Constraints in Early Lexical Acquisition: Evidence From Children's Early Language and Gesture

Laura Ann Petitto
McGill University

THE ONTOGENY OF LANGUAGE AND GESTURE

Only one explanation of human language ontogeny fully accounts for over a decade of findings in my laboratory concerning signing and speaking children's use of early lexical and gestural forms: Humans are born with a predisposition to discover particular sized units with particular distributional patterns in the input, guided by innately specified structural constraints (e.g., Jusczyk, 1986; Petitto, 1984, 1985a, 1985b, 1987; Pinker, 1984; Pinker & Bloom, 1990). At birth, this nascent structure-seeking mechanism is sensitive to the patterned organization of natural language phonology common to all world languages (e.g., Fernald et al., 1989), be they spoken or signed (e.g., rhythmic, temporal, and hierarchical organization) and is particularly sensitive to structures in the input that correspond to the size and distributional patterns of the syllable in spoken and signed languages (e.g., Mehler & Fox, 1985; Petitto & Marentette, 1991a). Irrespective of whether an infant is exposed to spoken or signed languages, this nascent structure-seeking mechanism is capable of utilizing whichever channel (or modality) is receiving the structured input—and it will do so without any modification, loss, or delay to the timing, sequence, and maturational course associated with reaching all linguistic milestones in language acquisition (e.g., Petitto, 1984, 1985a, 1985b, 1986, 1987, 1988; Petitto & Marentette, 1990, 1991b), providing systematic language exposure begins very early (preferably at birth). For example, deaf children acquiring signed languages from birth and hearing children acquiring spoken languages from birth achieve all linguistic milestones on an identical time course (e.g., Petitto, 1984, 1985a, 1985b, 1986, 1987, 1988).[1] Even more surprising, "bi-lingual" hearing children in deaf or deaf and hearing homes, who are exposed to both a signed and spoken language from birth, achieve all linguistic milestones in both modalities at the same time (e.g., vocal and manual babbling, first words and first signs, first grammatical combinations of words and signs, respectively, and beyond), and on the same maturational time course as other monolingual hearing and deaf children (Petitto & Marentette, 1990, 1991b); indeed, their general pattern of language acquisition follows those reported in the literature for hearing children in bi-lingual homes acquiring two spoken languages (e.g., Genesee, 1987). One would expect that if speech were more suited to the human brain's maturational needs in ontogeny, this very group of children would attempt to glean every morsel of speech that they could get from their environment—perhaps even turning away from the signed input—favoring instead the speech input. But this is not what happens. Signed and spoken languages are acquired effortlessly by these children, and all of the children, including the deaf children of deaf parents, acquire signed languages in the same way, at the same time, exhibiting the same linguistic, semantic, and conceptual complexity (stage for stage) as hearing children acquiring spoken languages (see also Petitto & Charron, 1987).

Such findings compel the conclusion that all infants initially attend to and seek to discover very particular aspects of language structure at birth, irrespective of the modality of the input. Indeed, linguistically structured input—and not modality—is the critical factor required to trigger human language acquisition. This early template or structure-seeking mechanism constitutes the initial contents (or, "representation") of the nascent human language capacity at birth, which matures throughout development. At birth, it is initially blind to modality; it is "amodal" (i.e., it is capable of seeking specific structures in multiple modalities). When specific structures in the input correspond with those in the infant's nascent template, a tacit decomposition of the elements of the match begins. The product of such decompositions can then serve both as the units over which infants discover the permissible segments and combinatorial rules of their target language, and as the basis from which systematic motor production programs of early language units are

---

[1] One group of researchers has claimed that first signs are acquired earlier than first words (e.g., Bonvillian, Orlansky, & Novack, 1983). However, see Petitto (1988) for a critique of why these claims are unfounded. See also Bellugi and Klima (1982), Meier (1991), Newport and Meier (1985), and Petitto and Marentette (1990, 1991b) for a review of the early lexical and later grammatical milestones in signed language acquisition; these studies demonstrate that signed and spoken languages are acquired in surprisingly similar ways and on a similar time course, despite the modality differences.

derived: Hence, witness the existence of vocal and manual babbling. Each completed analysis permits the child to extract larger and larger components of language structure from the input, thereby propelling very early linguistic development from one period to the next. Again, this entire process is not special to speech. Importantly, the infant's structure-seeking mechanism permits him or her to begin the language acquisition process through very early tacit analysis of particular structures in the input—especially the general prosodic and sublexical phonological structures of language—well in advance of the infant having to know either the meanings or the grammar of the target language.

It follows from my arguments that the means by which the language capacity can be expressed *in ontogeny* need not be restricted (a priori) to exactly two modalities, spoken and signed. For obvious reasons, any productive system of language must be (a) perceivable, (b) producible by the human body, and (c) potentially segmentable (a restricted set of segments must be capable of multiple combinatorial possibilities). In principle, properties of the human body that satisfy these constraints could serve as language articulators (i.e., a means for expressing the contents of the language capacity). Although the oral-aural (speech) and manual-visual (sign) modalities are clearly best suited for language transmission and reception in ontogeny, it is possible that—under certain extraordinary circumstances—other units (perhaps the lower limbs in combination with facial markers) could serve as a vehicle by which the contents of the language capacity can be expressed. Note, however, that motor production systems alone do not constitute knowledge of language, as one essential feature of language is its underlying structure, and the structure of language is not wholly derived from the organization of any given motor production system—be it the hands, face, or mouth—although, clearly, a given modality does exert some influence on language structure. This fact is immediately apparent when considering the structure of signed and spoken languages: Both signed and spoken languages are produced with radically different articulators (both are subserved by different neurological motor substrates in the brain), yet both exhibit identical levels of language structure (e.g., phonological, morphological, syntactic, semantic, discourse). Moreover, both signed and spoken languages are acquired in highly similar ways, with babbling serving as one particularly revealing example: The *common* syllabic organization observed both in the vocal babbling of hearing infants and in the manual babbling of deaf (and hearing) infants exposed to signed languages, despite radical modality differences, could only be the product of a *common* brain-based structure seeking mechanism (e.g., Petitto & Marantette, 1991a).

The claim, then, is that humans are born with a nascent structure-seeking mechanism, blind to modality, which initially attends to and seeks to discover particular units with particular distributional patterns in the input, corresponding in size and organization to the phonetic and syllabic units common to all languages (spoken or signed). The saliency of particular types of patterns over others in the input is entirely commensurate with what we know about other brain-based biological systems, such as the visual system. For example, the specialization of particular cells to particular patterns of visual stimuli (e.g., form, size, and orientation) is a well-known system of this sort (Hubel & Wiesel, 1959). However, the nascent human language capacity can seek particular linguistic patterns in multiple modalities (e.g, the pursuit of particular patterns is neither restricted to visual nor to speech stimuli). Implicit in this theory is the claim that the infant's tacit structure-seeking analyses are the product of innately specified mechanisms that respond to specific patterns unique to world languages (i.e., units possessing phonetic and syllabic size and organization, as well as the phonological and prosodic markers specified earlier), and not to general perceptual, or general cognitive dimensions. In this way, they are domain-specific pattern analyzing mechanisms. Particularly dramatic support for this claim comes from the study discussed here in which young deaf infants consistently differentiate between signs (identical to words) and gestures throughout development, even though signs and gestures reside in the same modality, and even though some signs and gestures share formation and referential properties. The infants' failure to confuse signs and gestures suggests that gestures must violate the structural requirements of the nascent structure-seeking mechanism and that a structure-seeking mechanism exists, sorting through the input and searching for a particular structure and no other. Thus, as is shown here, *aspects* of human language acquisition must be driven by language-specific knowledge—knowledge that is not wholly derived from infants' general cognitive capacities (see also Petitto, 1984, 1985a, 1985b, 1987, 1988).

A clear implication here is that, in ontogeny, humans can acquire language in either the spoken or signed modalities, be they hearing or deaf. Once the child is exposed to structured linguistic information in one modality (e.g., the verbal modality in hearing children), the alternative, "unused" modality (e.g., the gestural–visual modality in hearing children), can then serve secondary signaling and augmenting functions. However, signaling and augmenting functions are "piggybacked" onto the child's emerging linguistic and conceptual capacities and not vice versa.

Like other biological phenomena, mastery of a target competence—in this case, a target language—depends on the organism's ability to receive and maintain a steady sample of input despite a constantly varying environment (e.g., Mayr, 1982; Shatz, 1985). Young infants' early gestures (e.g., pointing), provide them with a mechanism by which they can attract a caretaker's attention, who then responds with a communicative exchange that invariably contains linguistic content. Indeed, it is widely known that young children's gestures elicit rich linguistic input from caretakers, especially names for things (e.g., Shatz, 1985). This use of gesturing constitutes a "mechanism of self-control" (e.g., Shatz, 1985; see also Petitto, 1985b, 1988). That is, early gestures ensure that the young infant receives and maintains ample linguistic input. This input constitutes the "data" over which the child tacitly performs his or her language structure-seeking analyses that will ultimately yield "knowledge of language" (e.g., Chomsky, 1975; Gleitman & Wanner, 1982; Petitto, 1987, 1988; Pinker, 1979, 1984).

Children's later gestures (e.g., 12–24 months) serve an important augmentative function. They are used to augment (through emphasis) the child's failed communicative interactions, which, at first, typically involved only their primary linguistic system. As is shown in this chapter, support for this claim comes from a variety of observations, including: (a) Symbolic gestures (empty-handed gestures that "stand for" or "represent" referents) in hearing and deaf children occur only *after* children are able to first comprehend and/or produce the corresponding primary linguistic form (i.e., the word or sign, respectively). The reverse ordering was never observed. (b) Young children (from around 11 months old and beyond) produce even their *earliest* lexical forms in constrained ways that correspond to different word/sign types (object names, property words, event words, etc.; Carey, 1982; Huttenlocher & Smiley, 1987; Keil, 1989; Markman, 1989; Petitto, 1988; Quine, 1969). However, their use of symbolic gestures within this same time period were used both within and across word/sign type boundaries; this revealing finding suggests that the knowledge underlying gesture and language is distinct, and provides key insights into the nature and type of linguistic and conceptual constraints underlying children's early lexicon. (c) Children use their symbolic gestures largely to augment their primary linguistic system (be it spoken or signed), often when a communicative interaction between adult and child fails and almost always to request objects rather than to identify or name them.

To review, once systematic input is received in a primary channel, the alternative channel can then assume global signaling and augmenting roles, drawing from and driven by the contents of the blossoming linguistic capacity. However, without systematic input, the "unused" channel—again, the gestural–visual modality in the case of hearing children—remains an unsystematic signaling device, which then takes on very different, but nonetheless useful, language-eliciting and language-augmenting functions. The distinction between primary linguistic systems and gestures is so powerful in ontogeny that the language–gesture distinction is maintained even in infants acquiring signed languages. Indeed, the child exposed to signed languages carves out this distinction even though the input channel contains both language and gesture in a single gestural–visual modality, and even though language and gesture in signed languages can be tantalizingly close in their formational and referential properties. That the language–gesture distinction is observed even in extremely young infants acquiring signed languages provides additional support for the claim that the human infant is predisposed to discover particular linguistic structures in the input, guided by innately specified structural constraints that have unique (domain-specific) representation and that can be mapped onto multiple production channels at birth—as signed language studies have clearly demonstrated that the newborn's specifically linguistic structural analyses of the input is not specific to the speech modality. Importantly, hearing children's very ability to produce gestures reflects their residual capacity to receive and produce language in the gestural–visual modality, should they have been exposed to it.

Thus, comparative analyses of gesture and language provide a clear window into the biological foundations of human language. Later, I focus on one type of gesture in language acquisition, the symbolic gesture, because the perceived similarities between this particular type of gesture and children's first words have been used to support extremely powerful theories of mind (e.g., Acredolo & Goodwyn, 1985, 1988; Bates, Benigni, Bretherton, Camaioni, & Volterra, 1979; Bates, Bretherton, Shore, & McNew, 1983; Goodwyn & Acredolo, 1991; Lock, 1978; Piaget, 1962; Shore, O'Connell, & Bates, 1984; Werner & Kaplan, 1963). Although a clear prediction of the theory that I have just outlined is that children's early lexical and gestural use will be similar on some dimensions, it clearly predicts that critical *differences* should also exist between them. Similarities will occur because augmentative gestural signaling is parasitic on the child's emerging linguistic and conceptual capacities. Differences will occur because aspects of language (e.g., the infant's structure-seeking capacity) constitute domain-specific knowledge.

However, current research on children's gestures has focused nearly exclusively on the similarities between gestures and language rather than on the differences between them. Indeed, many researchers compare young children's gestures and early lexicon, stressing the similarities between the two, and then conclude that gestural communication and language are fundamentally continuous because of these similarities. Aside from the fact that language is often defined in simplistic ways in the service of such comparisons (e.g., language exclusively in terms of its "communicative function"), the basic problem with this approach is that it makes the hypothesis that gestures are positively related to human language wholly *unfalsifiable*. What is the metric for counting similarities? How many must there be in order to conclude that the young child's gestures resemble the use of language in an interesting way (e.g., see Seidenberg & Petitto, 1987)?

That similarities exist between children's symbolic gestures and first words is not denied in this chapter; children's symbolic gestures and early lexicon do share referential and communicative properties. Nevertheless, I show here that despite these similarities, key differences exist that shed new light on the unique constraints that underlie human language acquisition in particular, as compared with other general cognitive and communicative capacities to symbolize. In the course of doing so, I hope to provide insights into the nature of gestures, the constraints that underlie early lexical knowledge, and, most importantly, the types of knowledge underlying human language acquisition.

Types of Gestures in Human Development

All humans gesture. An intriguing feature of human development is that infants also produce gestures well before the onset of their first words. Many children continue to gesture while producing their early words and beyond. Summarized here are the variety of gestural types common to most children.

Beginning around 9 months and continuing throughout the first 3 years, infants use indexical gestures ("pointing gestures") in a wide variety of contexts, performing various communicative functions, such as requesting and denoting. By 13 months, however, children display a fascinating ability to produce a variety of non-indexical gestures and other manual actions with and without objects in hand. For example, if presented with an empty cup, most children will bring it to their lips and produce drinking-like motions ("actions with objects"). Or, when desiring to be held, many children will raise their arms above their heads to be picked up; likewise, when desiring an object, many children will produce the classic "beg gesture," whereby they hold out their hand, often opening and closing it ("empty-handed instrumental gestures"). Further, children also produce a variety of culturally established gestures (e.g., waving "hello" and "bye-bye"; "yes" and "no" head nods) and routinized gestures in games (e.g., "itsy-bitsy spider") that are found in many societies ("social gestures"). Later, around 15 months, children produce empty-handed gestures for things and events in the world ("symbolic gestures"). For example, if presented with a closed jar, some children will spontaneously produce an empty-handed "twist" gesture.

The main distinction drawn among the various types of gestures involves the extent to which gestural types *symbolize* referents (e.g., object, person, place; what is referred to) and events in the world, rather than simply refer to them. Minimally, a gesture is a manual form that refers to or picks out a referent or event in the world. Gestures, however, can also be used to symbolize ("stand for" or "represent") a given referent or event. Although the pointing gesture can refer to (or pick out) referents and events, it typically does not symbolize them. Indeed, a single pointing form can refer to a potentially infinite class of referents. Further, there is a literal, physical identity between the form of "actions with objects" and what one does with a given object once in hand ("brushing" actions with brushes is what one does with a brush to realize its function). Similarly, the form of instrumental gestures appears to be part of the action associated with a given referent or event. For example, the form of the "beg" or "give me" gesture appears to be tied to the actual behavior used in the act of receiving (or taking), rather than a schematic representation of it (the child enacts rather than depicts). In contrast, the form of symbolic gestures involves some degree of representation. The child could, but does not, actually twist open a jar when producing the "twist" gesture. Symbolic gestures preserve partial information about actions that are associated with objects (e.g., twisting hand motions when opening jars), but they are not the enactment of the designated activity (e.g., children do not literally open a jar). In this sense, then, it has been argued that, for example, a form such as the "twist" gesture is a schematic representation for jars because they can be said to both refer to (pick out) and represent (symbolize) the referents (e.g., Bates et al., 1979; Bates et al., 1983; Werner & Kaplan, 1963).

Attributions of Lexical Status to Children's Gestures: When are Gestures Said to be Linguistic?

Little controversy exists over children's indexical gestures, social gestures, and other clearly nonlinguistic activities (e.g., scratching, reaching, grabbing). Most researchers studying the gestures of hearing children set aside these three types, as they are typically not judged to have lexical (linguistic) status. An analysis of instrumental gestures was provided earlier and in Petitto (1988). However, "actions with objects" and "symbolic gestures" remain the subjects of controversy, with the linguistic status of symbolic gestures constituting the most lively debate of all. Indeed, symbolic gestures and their referential and representational (symbolic) status have been directly compared to the referential and representational status of children's first words, with identical linguistic status (grammatical and semantic) attributed to both (e.g., Acredolo & Goodwyn, 1985, 1988, 1990; Bates et al., 1979; Bates et al., 1983; Goodwyn & Acredolo, 1991; Lock, 1978; Piaget, 1962; Shore et al., 1984;

Werner & Kaplan, 1963). Consequently, the existence of symbolic gestures has been regarded as providing critical insights into the knowledge that underlies the human language acquisition process.

Actions With Objects in Hand. Initially, some researchers made very strong claims about children's "actions with objects." Indeed, previous researchers referred to this type of manual activity as "gestures with objects," and they explicitly claimed that the 13-month-old's manual activities with objects did not constitute *pre*linguistic acts at all. Rather, they were said to be the gestural equivalents of linguistic names for things and were considered to be a kind of "noun or object name" (Bates et al., 1983). It was claimed that when a child produces an action with an object in hand (e.g., drinking motions with a cup), the use of this hand activity is *functionally identical* to the child's early use of words (e.g., saying *drink* upon noticing a cup). Similarly, the word "cup" is used with cups and not other objects. In the same way that a child uses the word "cup" to pick out a referent as being a member of a known class or kind, it was argued that the child's use of the *action* for cup is also showing that this gestural act is true of the objects that belong to the class or kind "cup." The presumption here is that children will not produce *function violations*. That is, children will not "drink" with, for example, a hammer, because this manual act is not "true" of the class or kind within which hammer resides.

I have argued elsewhere that the claims made here are most probably false (Petitto, 1985a, 1985b; see especially 1988). First, close examination of children's entire range and use of actions with objects (ages 9 through 20 months) reveals that they are not used in a way that is functionally identical to children's use of early words. Children (13 months and beyond) will produce methodical and repetitive sequences of actions with objects in hand with no apparent communicative function or intent. That is, they do not use "actions with objects" communicatively, whereas they do so freely with their corresponding first words occurring within the same time period. For example, children will produce the action for cup without any apparent communicative intent (eye gaze fixed at object rather than adult), but will use the word "cup" in rich and varied ways to identify cups, to comment upon liquid being added to a cup, to be given a cup, and so forth (with eye gaze to adult, and/or from object to adult or vice versa). Second, children (13 to 18 months) routinely begin by making function violations when producing actions with objects, suggesting that object functions must be learned, and are learned over time. Although 13-month-old children would pick up a spoon, place it in an empty cup, and "stir," they were equally likely to pick up other objects that shared certain critical physical dimensions with spoons and "stir" with them as well (e.g., hammer, mirror); importantly, children produced correctly many of the words for objects *prior* to producing the correct functions (or actions) associated with the same objects (Petitto, 1988). Thus, it appears that children's "actions with objects" in hand are not used identically to linguistic names or "nouns." Rather, they appear to be complex actions associated with objects, an observation originally made by Piaget (1962).

Symbolic Gestures. Children's empty-handed symbolic gestures are by far the most interesting type of gesture, and they are the focus of this chapter. Because there appears to be general correspondences between this type of gesture and children's early lexicon, they have recently received much attention. In general, some children produce symbolic gestures within the same time period when they exhibit a period of rapid vocabulary growth (15 to 18 months, or 18 to 24 months). Both symbolic gestures and words are used communicatively and intentionally; both are used referentially; both appear to have some representational component; both appear to be used in functionally correct ways. Thus, researchers have claimed that children's early *symbolic gestures* and early *words* are deeply equivalent; symbolic gestures are said to have lexical status, albeit in the gestural mode. Moreover, they are said to be parallel expressions of reference. Indeed, the single persistent assertion common to many current studies is that symbolic gestures and words have equal symbolic status, that is, gestures *mean* the same thing as words (e.g., Acredolo & Goodwyn, 1985, 1988, 1990; Bates et al., 1979; Bates et al., 1983; Goodwyn & Acredolo, 1991; Lock, 1978; Piaget, 1962; Shore et al., 1984; Werner & Kaplan, 1963).

Consequences for Theories of Mind

The previous interpretation of children's symbolic gestures and words has been used to support a very powerful theory of mind. Because both gesture and word are said to have equal symbolic status, it has been argued that the representation of language in the brain is routed in general cognitive capacities (cognitive–general model). Indeed, correspondences between early symbolic gestures and first words have been regarded as "... providing support for the hypothesis that strides in cognitive abilities such as memory, categorization, and symbolization underlie [the first symbolic gesture and first word] milestone in both modalities" (Goodwyn & Acredolo, 1991, p. 2). Although the identical data would also support the equally plausible hypothesis that similarities between gestures and words are driven by a specifically linguistic capacity, this possibility is not considered. Instead, the interpretation here has been used to challenge a major alternative theory of language representation in child development, one in which language is considered to be a distinct mental capacity, reflecting domain-specific knowledge that is not wholly derived from general cognitive capacities (domain-specific model). In this latter view, distinct representational structures underlie language but no other communicative capacity such as gesturing; we know this view as a "modular" model of the brain.

Thus, we have a situation in child development where very strong claims are being made about the brain-based knowledge that underlies human language acquisition, which, in turn, rely entirely on the claim that children's gestures and language are used in symbolically and functionally equivalent ways.

Existing Evidence.   None of the brain-based claims that gestures and words have equal symbolic status are based on *data samples* and/or *data analyses* that would support the claims (e.g., Acredolo & Goodwyn, 1985, 1988, 1990; Bates et al., 1979; Bates et al., 1983; Goodwyn & Acredolo, 1991; Lock, 1978; Piaget, 1962; Shore et al., 1984; Werner & Kaplan, 1963). For example, although Goodwyn and Acredolo (1991) employ very commendable criteria for what constitutes a symbolic gesture or word, the basic data sample of the children's *gestures* were collected from audiotaped telephone interviews containing mothers' *verbal* reports. That is, the gestures produced by the children were never actually seen or analyzed by the experimenters; this is true for the children's words as well. The data in this and related studies include:

1. lists of symbolic gestures and their English glosses, as well as their grammatical categories (e.g., common noun, proper noun);
2. the age at which the mother said that her child first produced symbolic gestures (as compared with first words); and
3. the manner in which the mother said the symbolic gestures were used (spontaneous, imitative, elicited) and acquired (directly taught by a parent, spontaneous imitation/parental actions, etc.) as compared with words.

In summary, use of mothers' reports—which involve a mother's attributions of meaning to her child's forms and are typically based on her memory of its use—makes it difficult to interpret these researchers' potentially important claims.

Mothers' reports cannot be used as a primary data in child language, either for words (e.g., Huttenlocher & Smiley, 1987) or gestures (e.g., Petitto, 1985a, 1985b, 1988). As Brown and Hanlon (1970) noted, parents pay far more attention to the meaning of their children's utterances rather than to the syntactic form. The identical phenomenon exists when parents evaluate their children's gestures (Petitto, 1985a, 1985b, 1988). Parents do not interpret children's gestures based on how they were used in the past, or whether there are consistent correlations between particular gestural forms and their referents. For example, in studies of parental attributions in my laboratory (e.g., Petitto, 1988), one parent, in the same taping session, attributed a *single meaning* to her child's gesture, even though the child used *multiple gestural forms*, in the identical context, at different times. Conversely, a *single gestural form* was interpreted as having *multiple meanings* at different times throughout the session; these findings are representative of the other mothers in our studies. In the same study, a deaf researcher was asked to transcribe a videotape of a *hearing* boy aged 10 and 11 months (see Petitto, 1988, for details). Based on the child's natural repertoire of gestures (e.g., reaching, grasping, banging, pointing gestures, and other motoric hand movements), she reported nearly 100 "sign" utterances, including complex sign combinations. Thus, parents and researchers alike, freely attribute a variety of complex desires, intentions, and knowledge to children's gestures, based on their interpretation of what they think the child means, rather than on the actual gestural form used to convey it.

In order to assess claims about the symbolic status of gestures, the appropriate data needs to be gathered. That is, children's actual gestures must be studied, rather than the researcher's English glosses of mothers' reports of their children's gestures. Once the data is gathered, the following types of analyses can be conducted: (a) identification of the gestural forms, relative frequency, and distribution of all forms both within and across children over time; (b) the range of referents over which the forms are applied (and vice versa); and (c) a comparison of the forms/range of referents for both gestures and words, and all other analyses detailed here.

Predications and Objectives

If symbolic gestures *mean* the same thing as words, it would follow that they are used in ways highly similar to children's use of early words, particularly their words for objects. Construed as a testable hypothesis about the language acquisition process, the prediction is that there will be consistent word and gesture use with regard to the same or highly similar range of objects in the world.

Studying the question in the context of signed languages offers a unique window into the knowledge that underlies human language acquisition. In signed languages, both gesture and language reside in a single modality, the gestural–visual modality. Thus, the existence of signed languages provides a "natural experiment" regarding the two conflicting models of the brain. For hearing children, gestures and words are produced using different modalities (gestural and vocal), which may clue them into any different referential properties of early gestures and words, should they exist. This is not the case with children acquiring signed languages. If children's gestures and early lexical items have equal symbolic status (mean the same thing), we might expect to see especially close correspondences between them in children acquiring signed languages. If, however, distinct knowledge structures underlie children's gestural and lexical use, then their use should differ. Indeed, when I first began this research, one question intrigued me most: Will the young signing children show *any* evidence of differentiating gestures from signs given that both are in the same modality?

In the remaining portion of this chapter, I focus largely on what I have learned about young hearing and deaf children's symbolic gestures. I provide the first analyses of the form of children's symbolic gestures, especially with regard to the range of referents over which the form(s) are applied. I also provide the first comparisons between the range of referents for symbolic gestures and the range of referents for early words in hearing children and early signs in deaf children. This makes it possible to determine whether symbolic gestures and early language have equal symbolic status.

SUBJECTS

To examine the questions asked earlier, I summarize the findings from one group of six children whose results are representative of all of the other children studied in my laboratory. The six subjects included three hearing children of hearing parents acquiring spoken languages (languages: two French, one English), and three profoundly deaf children of deaf parents acquiring signed languages (languages: two Langue des Signes Quebecoise, LSQ, one American Sign Language, ASL),[2] ages 8 through 20 months.[3]

---

[2] ASL and LSQ are two entirely distinct, natural signed languages. Further, neither language is the signed counterpart of the spoken majority language (e.g., English or French, respectively). Each signed language has its own grammar (linguistic units and rules for combining them).

[3] Videotaping and data analyses for all but two of the hearing children were conducted until the children were over 4 years old. However, ages 8 through 20 months capture the relevant period under question in the literature (the transition from prelinguistic to linguistic expression). See Petitto and Kampen (in prep.) for additional details.

METHODS

Procedures

Monthly videotapes of each child and a parent were collected (see Petitto & Kampen, in prep., for a full report on the procedures and analyses used in this study). After an initial warm-up period in which the child played with toys, four controlled elicitation tasks were administered to assess the child's production and comprehension of words and/or signs and gestures, including common gestures and those produced by the children themselves. Every videotaping session also contained a period with (a) the parent and child in free play and (b) the child alone in free play. Further, monthly reports of the child's lexical and gestural activity were collected from the parent using the Bates and Fenson assessment battery ("MacArthur Communicative Development Inventory: Infants and Toddlers"), and detailed experimenter reports were also made at the end of each taping session. Videotaped sessions served as the primary data in this study and parental and experimenter reports were used only to ensure that our samples were representative of the child's behavior at any given age.

Data Transcription

Detailed transcriptions of the entire content of each videotape were made by two independent observers and entered into a computer database. Transcriptions were entirely theory-neutral. In this transcription system, the precise physical form of the child's every manual activity is coded with diacritics that represent the internal and external features of the hand(s), such as its handshape, movement, and location in space; head, face, and body movements are also coded (see also Petitto, 1988; Petitto & Marentette, 1991a). Then, the precise manner of use is coded for each manual activity, including whether the form

1. was produced in a spontaneous, imitative, or elicited manner;
2. was used with or without objects in hand;
3. was used "referentially" (used in relation to a referent in the world; if so, the precise referent was specified);
4. was used "communicatively" (produced with clear communicative intent; e.g., involved eye gaze with an adult);
5. had "conventional meaning" (manual activity with established cultural meaning that was not the standard sign in either ASL or LSQ);[4] or
6. was a standard word or sign (or "lexical form"; more on this later).

---

[4]For example, the common form used to convey "quiet" (index finger to pursed lips while producing a "shhh" sound) is used by deaf and hearing children and adults to indicate "quiet," but the sign QUIET in ASL (and in LSQ) is produced with a different handshape and movement.

Information about the apparent function of the manual form for the child as well as detailed information about the context were also coded. Finally, mothers' manual activity was also coded. Mothers' reactions to the child's manual activity (mothers' apparent interpretation), and the child's reaction to the mother's manual activity were also coded. Children's verbal productions were coded in a similar manner, except that extremely detailed phonetic transcriptions were not made for each form; in particular, an unidentifiable vocalization would be coded as a "voc" and then the other information would be subsequently coded.

Unique Features of Transcription System.   Use of this transcription system permitted frequency and distributional analyses of all of the types of children's manual and verbal activities over time, and across thousands of contexts, in a way that has simply never before been provided in the literature. Moreover, it permitted within and across child comparisons of manual and verbal activities in a manner that has also never been provided before. Importantly, this transcription system permitted the following crucial analysis necessary to make attributions of meaning to children's forms: For every manual and verbal form, it was possible to identify the precise range of referents that it was produced in relation to. Conversely, for every referent, the exact manual and verbal form(s) that were used with it were also wholly identifiable.

Data Analyses

The overall behavioral patterns and their frequencies and distributions were identified within and across children over time, for example (a) empty-handed activity; (b) manual activity with objects in hand; (c) head, face, and body movements; and (d) lexical forms (including ill-articulated and proto-forms; see Petitto & Kampen, in prep., for details). Children's use of empty-handed activity was compared with their use of manual activity with objects in hand, and children's use of empty-handed activity was compared with their use of lexical forms. Of particular interest was the nature of the relationship between a given form and its referent—in other words, we were interested in a form's meaning as well as the range of meanings that children expressed through their use of gestures and lexical forms.

The Set of "Symbolic Gestures" and the Set of "Lexical Forms".   Similar criteria were used to determine whether a manual or verbal form was to be considered a candidate for inclusion in the set of "symbolic gestures" or the set of "lexical forms," respectively. Both manual and verbal forms minimally had to "refer." Operationally, this meant that a form had to be used in relation to a referent (e.g., eye gaze includes gaze to a target referent, and/or related referents if none existed in the world). There were also the following form requirements:

1. As was noted in the introduction, the form of symbolic gestures contains a representational component; thus, to be considered a candidate for inclusion in the set of symbolic gestures, in addition to referring, a manual form also had to contain a representational component; that is, the child may not have actually produced the manual form by physically manipulating a target referent.
2. To be considered a candidate as a "lexical form," a further requirement was that verbal or manual forms had to be produced according to the standard—or approximation to standard articulary constraints of the adult word or sign (respectively); importantly, the child did not have to produce the exact adult form (ill-formed and ill-articulated forms, baby words and signs, and proto words and signs were accepted), and the child did not have to demonstrate adult usage (adult meaning).

These criteria both capture the critical features used to identify children's symbolic gestures and words in the literature and, at the same time, they are over-inclusive relative to them. For example, a form did not have to be produced spontaneously in order to be considered a candidate for inclusion in the set of "symbolic gestures" or set of "lexical forms"; the analyses of possible symbolic gestures was also expanded to include forms produced nonmanually (i.e., on the face, head, and body). This procedure was adopted to "stack the deck against our hypothesis," that is, to find as many candidates for our analyses as possible, should they exist.

Attribution of Meaning: Do Symbolic Gestures and Lexical Forms Have Equal Symbolic Status?   The identical criteria were used to evaluate the symbolic status of the forms just discussed. In order to determine whether children's set of "symbolic gestures" and set of "lexical forms" had equal symbolic status (i.e., the *same meaning*), it was necessary to determine the child's grasp of the meaning of lexical and symbolic gestural forms.

The study of word meaning has a long, thorny history, and at least three critical distinctions must be made when studying it: (a) What is the meaning of a word? (b) What is an individual's grasp of the meaning of a word? and (c) How can researchers determine an individual's (a child's) meaning of a word? [5] In Petitto (1985a, 1985b, 1988), I attempt to answer these questions. I discuss cognitive notions of reference and argue that the meaning of, for example, a common noun, is the range of referents over which it could potentially refer (be applied). Like others, I argue that an individual's word meanings have both intensional and extensional referential properties, and that an individual's word meanings are conceptually constrained across kinds or types of words (e.g., kinds of objects, kinds of events, kinds of possessions, kinds of locations). I further argue that a revealing way to determine the child's grasp of the meaning of a word is to examine the range of referents over which a given word is applied. Here, I use similar analyses to examine the meaning of children's lexical and symbolic gestural forms.

In this study, meaning is determined by observing the relationship between a child's form (be it lexical or symbolic gestural) and the entire range of referents over which the form applied. Once this is done, the meanings of all of a given child's lexical forms and all of her symbolic gestural forms are compared, within the child and across children. Note that the more general problems associated with extensional (associationist, and/or behaviorist) theories of word meaning are not at issue here, nor do they detract from the value of using this particular method as an operational measure of children's competence (e.g., see Petitto, 1985a, 1985b, 1988; see also Huttenlocher & Smiley, 1987, for an excellent discussion of the controversy over determining word meanings in child language, and the database that is required in order to make attributions of meaning to children's lexical forms).[6] Once the sets of symbolic gestures and lexical forms were identified, the following analyses were used to assess their meaning: (a) was a given form used systematically (i.e., was it used in a stable manner across multiple contexts); (b) was a given form used in relation to a referent, was this use systematic, was this use restricted to a particular referent or was it applied over a range of referents; (c) if a form was applied over a "range of referents," did it constitute a restricted or unrestricted class? Whether a form was used in communicatively and semantically varied ways was also evaluated.

Children's symbolic gestures and lexical forms could—or could not— have been used in the ways detailed here. To be clear, these analyses were

---

[5] I thank Paul Bloom for pointing out the need to make this particular distinction explicit.

[6] Huttenlocher and Smiley (1987) stated that "Indeed, the data from mother reports are not highly concordant with independent observational data [refs]. Regular observations of a sufficient number of utterances, using a standard method of recording context, are essential in getting a proper data base" (p. 67). Though arrived at independently (e.g., Petitto, 1984, 1985a, 1985b, 1987, 1988), similar methods are used in the present study.

seeking to determine any shared pattern of use between the two sets, should they exist, and it was unbiased as to whether a given form was a standard lexical form in the adult language, a gesture, or otherwise.

Reliability

Reliability was assessed for both data transcription and data analysis procedures by two independent coders, with an overall reliability of 89.7% (see Petitto & Kampen, in prep.).

RESULTS

A select sample of the analyses conducted on the present data are provided here (see Petitto & Kampen, in prep., for a full report). There were 4,841 protocols collected from the six children over the course of 12 months. As is standard in the literature, 145 (2.99%) of the manual forms were excluded from further analysis because they either occurred one time only ($n=39$) or they were culturally established social gestures and/or routinized gestures in games ($n=106$); note, however, that symbolic gestures occurring one time only were not excluded from analysis. Manual forms occurred alone ($n=2,986$) and in combination with other forms ($n=1,133$); combinations were comprised mostly of points plus manual actions, or combinations of manual actions, as there were virtually no empty-handed, non-indexical gesture plus gesture combinations in the entire corpora. Most all of the children's manual activity with objects and empty-handed activity were produced spontaneously, which was also true of most of their tokens of lexical forms ($n=577$).

Here, I first provide an overview of the types and frequency and distribution of the gestures produced alone by the children; this information should provide a basis to interpret the findings regarding symbolic gestures, per se. Then, I provide an overview of how children used symbolic gestures as compared to their early lexicon. One striking finding of this study involved the constrained ways in which children used even their earliest lexical forms; the significance of this finding relative to children's use of symbolic gestures is discussed in the final pages of this chapter.

Gestural Types, Frequency, and Distribution

Types. Six types of manual activity were observed:
1. *motoric hand activity* (e.g., banging, scratching; beginning (b.) around 9 months (mths) and peaking (p.) 15–18 (mths);

2. *pointing* (e.g., to objects, locations, b. 7–9 mths, p. 18–24);
3. *social gestures* (e.g., waving "hello," "bye–bye," "yes–no" head nods; b. 12 mths and beyond) and other highly routinized manual forms common in parent–child games (e.g., patty-cake);
4. *actions with objects in hand* (e.g., brushing with a brush; b. 12 mths and beyond);
5. *instrumental gestures* (e.g., raising arms to be picked up; b. 12 mths, p. 15–18 mths);
6. *symbolic gestures* (e.g., empty-handed downward movements at side of head while gazing at a comb; b. 14–18 mths—save 1 form that appeared at 12 months in one child—p. 18–24 mths.).

The aforementioned represents the types and approximate developmental sequence of children's manual activities. These findings are entirely commensurate with other data reported in the literature (e.g., Bates et al., 1979; Bates et al., 1983; Zinober & Martlew, 1985)—although researchers typically do not provide type and frequency data as well as distributional analyses of types over time, especially with regard to children's entire range of manual productions over time (studies by Goldin-Meadow, e.g., Goldin-Meadow & Morford, 1985, constitute the only exception to my knowledge).

Frequency and Distribution of Types. The types of manual activity produced by the hearing and deaf children, as well as their relative frequency of occurrence, are shown in Fig. 2.1. What is most striking about Fig. 2.1 is that both the types and the frequencies of gestures are highly similar across the two groups of children.

Symbolic Gestures vs. All Other Gesture Types

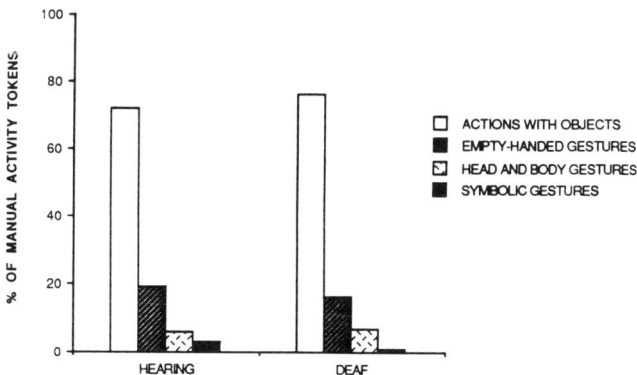

FIG. 2.1. Types and relative frequency of manual activity in the hearing and deaf children.

Figure 2.2 shows the relative frequency and distribution of gesture types over time for all of the children. Several important points to note are:

1. Actions with objects were by far the most frequent type found in all six children (*n*=44 types, 1,888 tokens). The 1,888 tokens were used mostly in noncommunicative ways, consisting largely of actions associated with playing with specific objects (e.g., hammering a peg, brushing hair with a hairbrush; 68%), followed next by nonrelevant motoric actions with objects (e.g., banging, swatting; 29%); the relatively few instances of communicative use involved some token of demonstrative "showing" (e.g., child offers object to an adult 1%), and "requests" (e.g., child holds up one object, such as a toy coin, to obtain a similar one in adult's hand; 2%).

2. Empty-handed activity (*n*=12 types: 485 tokens) included instrumental gestures (*n*=3 types), which were used almost exclusively to request referents, and empty-handed manual activity produced in play (*n*=9 types; e.g., stroking, patting, pressing); this "empty-handed activity" type of manual activity was significantly less frequent as compared with actions with objects, and they were even less frequent than pointing (*n*=509). Head and body gestures occurred less frequently than most of the other types (*n*=7 types, 104 tokens), but not less than symbolic gestures.

3. Symbolic gestures were the least frequent type to occur of all (*n*=6 types, 48 tokens). Thus, across all children, there were only 48 tokens of symbolic gestures out of 4,507 tokens, or (1.1%).

All Children -- Manual Activity Over Time

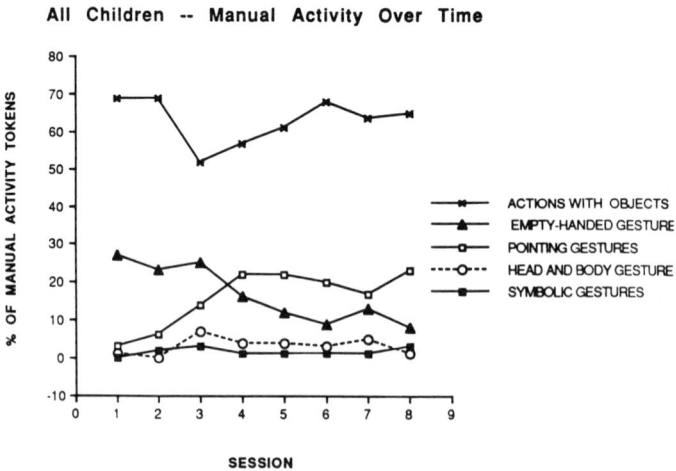

FIG. 2.2.   Distribution and relative frequency of manual activity by type for all children over time.

Although infrequent, symbolic gestures were nonetheless produced with apparent communicative intent, they appeared to be appropriate to the context, they were referential and contained a representational component. Are *these* forms fundamentally similar to the way children used their first words?

Use of Symbolic Gestures as Compared to Use of the Early Lexicon

The hearing and deaf children spontaneously used symbolic gestures in similar contexts (only in the presence of a referent) and with a similar communicative function (to request). Both groups of children extracted similar salient perceptual features from referents that were then produced in gestural form. For example, hearing and deaf children's symbolic gestures for a toy telephone all involved the feature of bringing the telephone receiver to the ear, although the specific forms of this (and other) symbolic gestures varied within and across children. Some symbolic gestures were used first by the child and some were used by parents and then subsequently used by the child. In either case, parents tended to produce the symbolic gesture themselves.

The hearing and deaf children produced their early lexicon on the same time course; deaf children do not acquire first signs earlier than hearing children acquire first words (see footnote 1). Indeed, deaf and hearing children achieved all early (lexical) and later (grammatical) linguistic milestones on a similar time course and sequence (see also Petitto & Marentette, 1990, 1991b). Furthermore, the children used their early lexicon with similar communicative functions (e.g., to name objects). Finally, the semantic and grammatical content of both groups of children's lexicon were strikingly similar (see also Petitto & Charron, 1987).

Thus, there were similarities between hearing and deaf children's use of symbolic gestures, and there were similarities between hearing and deaf children's lexical use. However, there were important differences between both groups of children's (a) use of symbolic gestures versus their (b) use of the lexicon that are described here.

Frequency of Symbolic Gestures Versus Words/Signs.   The children's symbolic gestures occurred infrequently relative to their words and signs. There were only 48 tokens of symbolic gestures (see Table 2.1) as compared with 577 tokens of lexical items (see Table 2.2). Three of the six types of symbolic gestures were used by all six children, and the three remaining types were used by one hearing child only; indeed, as is shown in Table 2.1, one hearing child (H2) produced all six types and the most tokens, revealing that there are individual differences in children's propensity to produce symbolic gestures.

TABLE 2.1
Number of Types/Tokens of Symbolic Gestures
Produced by the Deaf and Hearing Children

	Deaf			Hearing		
	D1	D2	D3	H1	H2	H3
Types	2	2	1	1	6	2
Tokens	7	4	4	2	17	14

TABLE 2.2
Number of Types/Tokens of Lexical Items
Produced by the Deaf and Hearing Children

	Deaf			Hearing		
	D1	D2	D3	H1	H2	H3
Types	22	8	12	11	57	2
Tokens	207	24	52	25	267	2

Distribution of Symbolic Gestures Versus Words/Signs.   Symbolic gestures enter the children's behavioral repertoire relatively late, around 14–15 months (save one form produced by one child that her mother used, i.e., smacking lips for cookies) and their frequency and distribution remains atypically constant over time. Conversely, children's vocabulary production begins around 12 months and continues a dramatic rise throughout the entire period when symbolic gestures maintain a constant pattern of infrequent use. Thus, although children's early lexical use climbs and increases in frequency, their use of symbolic gestures does not increase and remains infrequent. Symbolic gestures are indeed a non-robust phenomenon in child development.

Lack of Increased Complexity Over Time.   Unlike children's early lexical development, symbolic gestures exhibit a flat mean length of utterance (MLU; Brown, 1973). That is, there was no increase in the internal complexity of symbolic gestures—either formationally or referentially—over time, even though the complexity of children's words and signs increased steadily over time.

Although it is true that, unlike words and signs, children typically do not get systematic gestural models, parents do produce their children's symbolic gestures (as well as pointing, instrumental gestures, and actions with objects). Thus, it remains a puzzle why children would not use symbolic gestures more if they had equal symbolic status with lexical forms.

Inconsistent Forms.   An example of a symbolic gesture is as follows. One symbolic gesture—the "phone" symbolic gesture—was used in relation to a toy telephone and was produced by four of the six children (two deaf, two hearing). It was produced in relation to the same toy telephone but its form varied both within a child and across children: (a) a clenched fist at the side of the head, (b) a flat hand at side of head, (c) two flat hands at side of head. Interestingly, the form was typically accompanied by opening/closing mouth movements plus vocalizations, even in the deaf children who, clearly, could not hear, and whose parents used TTYs (a form of teletype machine). Note that variation of form was common for all of the 48 tokens of symbolic gestures reported here. However, we simply did not find a similar degree of variation in the form of children's early words across instances of use and/or contexts.

Restricted Communicative and Discourse Functions.   Symbolic gestures were used by the children largely in "request" contexts (n=36/48; 75%); for example, to get something from someone. Only three tokens (6.25%) of symbolic gestures were used to "comment upon" (or name) a referent, and eight tokens (16.67%) were produced as responses to questions (e.g., "what do you do with this?"). Conversely, the children's lexical items were used largely to "comment upon" or name referents.

Interestingly, children would spontaneously produce symbolic gestures in discourse contexts where use of their primary linguistic channel had somehow failed—either because they were misunderstood by an adult or because they did not have the corresponding word in systematic production (recall that comprehension–production asymmetries exist in early acquisition, e.g., Golinkoff & Hirsh–Pasek, 1987). That is, symbolic gestures were used in ways that *augmented* their primary linguistic channel.

Context Dependent.   All of the children's symbolic gestures were exceedingly context dependent and this did not change over time. That is, gestures (symbolic or otherwise) were used only when the object referred to was physically present. The referent was nearly always an object (as opposed to a person, location, attribute, etc.), and their forms always reflected some salient physical action associated with the referent. Although some early words/signs in our corpora were initially context dependent, their frequencies were greater than symbolic gestures, the forms were consistent, they were used with a broad communicative scope (they did not exhibit a restricted communicative function), and they ceased to be context dependent over time.

Order of Occurrence.   Symbolic gestures appeared only *after* the child was able to *comprehend* and/or produce the meaning of the word or sign to which the gesture corresponded. Said another way, words and signs were comprehended *prior* to the onset of such symbolic gestures. No child produced a symbolic gesture unless he or she first had the corresponding word in comprehension, and/or production, suggesting that children's use of symbolic gestures is dependent on their knowledge of language rather than the reverse.

Kind Boundaries.   To understand the meaning of the manual and verbal forms for the child, each form was examined in relation to the range of referents over which it was applied (form–referent pairings). Similarly, each referent was examined in relation to the range of forms that were used with it (referent–form pairings; see section on attribution of meaning). The analysis revealed that the form–referent (and referent–form) pairings observed with the children's lexical forms were different from those observed with symbolic gestures.

When the hearing and deaf children produced a lexical form, the range of referents over which it was applied formed particular word (sign) types or kinds, that is, type of object names, type of action/event words, type of property words, and so forth. For example, four of the six children produced the lexical form "open" (two deaf, two hearing). When "open" was produced by these children, it was used to refer specifically to the *action or event* involved in opening a variety of things (e.g., jars, refrigerator doors, boxes). Importantly, the lexical item "open" was not also used as the *name* for the object being opened; for example, "open" was not used as *the name* for jars—it was not used as the word or sign for glass containers with lids. "Open" was not used as a type of object name, nor was it used *to name* specific objects that are kept in jars (e.g., cookies; "open" was not used as the name for sweet round objects that are eaten). That is, "open" was never used both as a type of action/event word and as a type of object name. Instead, "open" and other action/event words (e.g., "give") were produced with proper extensions unique to the type "action and event words." This finding was true of all of the children's lexical forms, across all word/sign types. Each child's use of each lexical form was constrained along particular word/sign types from its first use and across many contexts over time.

Indeed, with few exceptions (3/577 tokens; 0.5%), the children used their lexical forms in ways that did *not* cross the boundaries of different word/sign types (see Petitto & Kampen, in prep., for details). Although the meaning of a given lexical item may have been under- or over-extended relative to its meaning in the adult language, it was not used in ways that violated the boundaries of its type. This finding corroborates those reported in a study of lexical use and meaning by Huttenlocher and Smiley (1987) in slightly older hearing children (range 11–30 months). However, the present study provides the first evidence that children's earliest lexical items are constrained along kind boundaries even when acquiring signed languages.

Unlike words or signs, when children produced a symbolic gesture, the range of referents over which it was applied did not always form particular types or kinds of object names, event words, property words and so on. It was common for a child to use a particular symbolic gesture in relation to, for example, a known type of related object in one context and, in another context, to use the same symbolic gesture in relation to objects from a different type. Variable use of the same or similarly formed symbolic gesture was common in the children.[7] For example, four of the children (two deaf, two hearing) produced a curved index finger pointed toward the far back of the mouth ("point-in-mouth"), and one hearing boy produced this form 12 times; his use of this gesture aptly captures the childen's use of their symbolic gestures. He produced the form (a) upon noticing the experimenter playing a toy flute, (b) when requesting a raisin, (c) when requesting a grape that was inside of a tightly closed jar after failing repeatedly to open it, and so on. Thus, the child produced one form with at least three different referents: flute, raisin, and grapes (we assume for the moment that the jar itself was not the referent in the third case mentioned). One interpretation of this symbolic gesture is that the child has used the form "point-in-mouth" in relation to object types, with the raisins and grapes constituting the object type "things one eats" (*form–object type*). In this view, the child's use of the form in relation to the flute would be a problem, because the flute, although an object, is clearly a different type of object from "things one eats." A second interpretation is that the child has used the form "point-in-mouth" in relation to action/event types (*form–action/event type*). In other words, the child's symbolic gesture could have been functioning in a verb-like manner. Here, too, the child's intended action/event type is not obvious. The form "point-in-mouth" may be conveying the action/event "eat" regarding the raisin and grapes, but the flute is still a problem. Thus, a problem for either of the two interpretations is that the child produced a form that has crossed type boundaries, and this did not occur with the children's lexical items.

Although it is always possible to argue that the "point-in-mouth" gesture is being used to convey a more general action/event type (e.g., "put in mouth"), the possible attributions are potentially infinite. For example, the second and third cases could also be further attributed to meaning "hungry," as in "I'm hungry" ("I want that raisin/grape").

---

[7] Even though the children's form of symbolic gestures were variable, there was no evidence that each variation of a form was a different symbolic gesture (e.g., similar to a different word or sign) in their repertoire of forms.

Although this is, in principle, true of attributing meaning to children's single words (e.g., Bloom, 1973), children do help narrow the possibilities through their use of actual lexical forms. In fact, a more parsimonious explanation of the "point-in-mouth" symbolic gesture—and other symbolic gestures—is that the children are producing stylized context-bound actions associated with referents (whose form implicitly contains other information such as the referent's location), and that these forms are not functioning as symbols that "stand for" (or represent) the referents.

Especially dramatic differences between language and gesture are uncovered when both types of information occur in the same modality. Two of the deaf children (age 20 months) produced the symbolic gesture "twist" in relation to jars at the same time that they produced the fully articulated adult sign OPEN.[8] Whereas OPEN was used exclusively to convey the action of opening (e.g., boxes, jars, drawers), the symbolic gesture "twist" was used in relation to the following range of referents: jar (the object itself), the specific objects in jars (e.g., cookies, raisins), to open (to get the jar opened), to close (to get the jar closed). Interestingly, the gesture was used only after the children's use of the lexical item OPEN had failed to get a response from an adult. That is, the "twist" gesture was used exclusively as an apparent last resort, to emphasize and augment primary linguistic information.

It could be argued that symbolic gestures violate Markman's mutual exclusivity principle (ME) (e.g., Markman, 1989).[9] Briefly, the ME principle postulates that young children assume that each object category has one category term: "A single object cannot be both a cow and a bird or a dog" (p. 187) (see also Gleitman & Wanner, 1982; Slobin, 1985). In the present study, recall that all symbolic gestures are produced only after the child first has the corresponding lexical form in comprehension and/or production. For example, the children who produced the symbolic gesture for the toy telephone first produced the lexical item "telephone." Because a single object appears to have at least two category terms—the gesture connoting the object (in some contexts) and the lexical sign—this situation may constitute an apparent violation of the ME principle, thereby revealing yet another way that early language and gesture differ.

To review, there were important differences between children's use of lexical items, be they words or signs, and their use of gestures. Children's use of lexical items was consistently constrained along word/sign type

---

[8] The "twist" gesture was also produced by the three hearing children.

[9] I thank Sandeep Prasada (Department of Brain and Cognitive Science, MIT) for first pointing this out to me.

boundaries, whereas their use of gestures was variable. Even when the lexical item and the gesture were in the same modality, the lexical item did not cross type boundaries, but the gestures often did.

No Gesture + Gesture Combinations. There were no combinations of symbolic gestures, even during the period when hearing and deaf children were producing two-word and two-sign combinations (respectively). That is, there were no symbolic gesture + symbolic gesture combinations, even though there were word + word combinations in the hearing children and sign + sign combinations in the deaf children.

Summary

Hearing and deaf children's use of symbolic gestures was similar. Hearing and deaf children's use of the early lexicon was also similar. However, the hearing and deaf children's use of symbolic gestures versus their use of the lexicon differed. Several factors differentiated children's use of symbolic gestures as compared to their use of words and signs. They were as follows:

1. The frequency of symbolic gestures was low (they constitute a non-robust phenomenon in child development).
2. The distribution of symbolic gestures remained uncommonly stead over time.
3. The forms and referential complexity of symbolic gestures did not increase over time ("flat MLU").
4. The forms of symbolic gestures were inconsistent.
5. Symbolic gestures were used with restricted communicative function (largely requests).
6. Symbolic gestures were far more context dependent than the children's words or signs.
7. Symbolic gestures were produced only after children first had the corresponding word or sign in comprehension and/or production and were often used to augment a failed communicative exchange involving their primary linguistic system.
8. Symbolic gestures were used in ways that crossed the boundaries of word/sign types in some contexts and did not do so in other contexts; however, children's use of words and signs were consistently used in ways that followed the boundaries of word/sign types.
9. There were no symbolic gesture + symbolic gesture combinations, even though children were combining their lexical items.

DISCUSSION AND CONCLUSION

On the Nature of Gestures

All manual activity termed *gestures* in the literature are not the same, and they occur with vastly different frequencies. Most of the manual activity that children produce are really actions—not gestures—with objects in hand, and the next frequent class to occur, empty-handed gestures, are used with grossly restricted forms and communicative functions. Symbolic gestures are the least frequent type of gestures to occur in spontaneous development, and they occur late relative to children's first words or signs. Once children begin to use symbolic gestures, its power is meager as compared to that of the word or sign.

That all children produce actions with objects in hand most frequently indicates that this information plays some role in the representation of objects as well as the corresponding words that symbolize them, particularly regarding the *functions of objects* (what one does with an object; what it is used for). However, it cannot be said that the functions of objects and the situational contexts within which they occur, make up the contents of children's early lexical representations (e.g., Bowerman, 1980; Nelson 1974; Snyder, Bates, & Bretherton, 1981). Indeed, the representation of human language involves much more than its communicative function, even in very young children. As is indicated in the present study, as well as other related studies (e.g., Petitto & Marentette, 1991a), specifically linguistic structural information regarding *language form*, and other *conceptual constraints* (e.g., constraints on word/sign types) also appear to be part of the young child's lexical representations.

As was indicated in the introduction, gestures serve a useful role in ontogeny. Early gestures (e.g., pointing) appear to be a primitive signaling device, on the same ontogenetic continuum with crying. They elicit language and attention. Gestures elicit language rich in referential information; they elicit names for things (e.g., Shatz, 1985). Also in the introduction is the observation that later symbolic gestures appear to serve a secondary role in language ontogeny—one that augments the child's primary linguistic system. Symbolic gestures appear to be parasitic on language rather than the reverse (e.g., see also Goldin-Meadow & Morford, 1989; McNeill, 1985); recall that words and signs occur first in comprehension and/or production in language ontogeny before the child produces a symbolic gesture.

Recent claims regarding the equal symbolic status of children's gestures are wholly unsupported by the present data (e.g., Acredolo & Goodwyn, 1985, 1988, 1990; Goodwyn & Acredolo, 1991). For example, Acredolo and

Goodwyn (1985, 1990), provide a case study of the first author's daughter, Kate Acredolo. The child was reported to have 40 symbolic gestures possessing the same symbolic status as words. In addition, they reported that Kate produced these symbolic gestures *prior* to age 19 months, that is, before her vocabulary spurt. Although these reports are interesting, the authors do not provide crucial information required to evaluate their claims. First, the authors do not report the relative frequency and distribution of the child's other gestures as compared with her symbolic gestures, thereby rendering the impression that her production of 40 symbolic gestures was more robust than it may have been. As was seen in the present study, once the relative frequency and distribution of symbolic gestures was compared to the full range of gestures produced by a child, we find that symbolic gestures are a nonrobust phenomenon in child development. Second, and most importantly, approximately 95% of the child's types of symbolic gestures were either directly taught to the child or "encouraged" (e.g., "Once Kate's interest in such gestures were noticed, the adults around her began to encourage the development of new gestures by pairing discrete actions with objects and conditions," Acredolo & Goodwyn, 1990, p. 18).

Given that symbolic gestures were directly taught or encouraged, it is of little surprise that the child in the study, as well as those in other studies (e.g., Goodwyn & Acredolo, 1991), produced symbolic gestures in a manner resembling early words and, at times, earlier than their words. Indeed, what I believe these researchers are picking up is an *artifact* of the fact that humans can learn either a signed or spoken language with no loss or delay in the timing and sequencing of language milestones.[10] When taught specific symbolic gestures (especially those used by the parents themselves), the child is merely learning lexical, or quasi-lexical, items in another modality—and, in the case of hearing children, a modality that could have been used for acquiring signed languages.

A final puzzle is this: Given that adults both teach and use symbolic gestures, why don't we see *more* symbolic gesturing in children? Why aren't there greater similarities of use between children's early symbolic gestures and early words? In understanding the answer to these questions, the essential features of early language representation are laid bare. Gestural input to children lacks critical regularities in structure, both sublexically and syntactically. The forms of parents' symbolic gestures vary, and parents do not produce combinations of symbolic gestures. In other words, gestures are not formed from a restricted set of combi-

---

[10] See especially Petitto and Marentette's (1990, 1991b) study of hearing children in bilingual signing and speaking homes who acquire both signed and spoken language milestones on the same maturational time course.

natorial units and are not hierarchically organized; indeed, they lack phonology, prosody, and syntax. Gestures do bear meaning and communicative information. However, proposals in child language that offer either the semantic or the communicative functions of language as being the exclusive explanatory mechanism that drives very early language acquisition are not supported by the present research. As seen here, meaning and/or communicative function alone, although important, are simply not adequate to support the use of a gesture as a form that possesses equal status with the word or sign.

The basic units of language structure that infants need in the input are not present in symbolic gestural input. Specifically, sublexical, phonetic, and syllabic organization as well as other phonotactic information (prosodic cues that bind segments into phrasal, clausal, and lexical bundles) are absent. The innate predisposition to discover these particular linguistic structures in the input is so strong that the child does not systematize symbolic gestural input, even though it shares similarities of reference and meaning with words. Without syllabic and phonotactic information, infants cannot set up the nascent representations of *language form* that I would argue are part of the very early representation of language, and are required before children can progress to adult linguistic competence. Like words and signs, children use symbolic gestures meaningfully. Unlike words and signs, the internal formational and referential complexity of symbolic gestures does not increase over time, demonstrating both the strengths and the limits of a referential system without structured input.

Constraints on Early Lexical Knowledge

Looking across individual meanings of words and signs, as compared to symbolic gestures, certain commonalities characterize the words and signs, but not the gestures. Children did not use particular words or signs across the bounds of different word/sign types (e.g., object names, property words, event words; e.g., Huttenlocher & Smiley, 1987), but did so with gestures. These results indicate that children's first lexical use is constrained along the bounds of word/sign types—even in signed languages (for other discussions of constraints on early lexical acquisition see Carey, 1982; Gelman & Coley, in press; Keil, 1989; Macnamara, 1982; Markman, 1989; Quine, 1969; Waxman, Shipley, & Shepperson, in press).

Knowledge Underlying Language Acquisition

There are similarities between symbolic gestures and language in human development. However, critical differences exist between them that have not received much attention in previous research on this topic. The child's clear differentiation between language and gesture in ontogeny suggests that distinct forms of knowledge govern their use. Indeed, young deaf infants' differentiation of language and gesture—even though both reside in the same modality—provides dramatic support for this analysis.

My claim, then, is that aspects of the structural and conceptual underpinnings of children's knowledge and use of language are fundamentally distinct from their knowledge and use of gesture. Knowledge of language is not wholly derived from a general cognitive capacity to symbolize. Instead, the findings from this and related studies compel us to conclude that domain-specific knowledge is involved in the human language acquisition process. Specifically linguistic and conceptual constraints are at work from birth to help the child discover particular structures in the input and not others.

ACKNOWLEDGMENTS

I am especially grateful to Kevin N. Dunbar for discussing the issues in this chapter with me and for his insightful comments on earlier drafts of the chapter. I also thank Marta Meana, Paul Bloom, and Susan Goldin-Meadow for comments on an earlier version of this work. This research was supported by Natural Sciences Engineering Research Council of Canada, McGill IBM Cooperative Project, and McDonnell-Pew Center Grant in Cognitive Neuroscience.

REFERENCES

Acredolo, L. P., & Goodwyn, S. W. (1985). Symbolic gesturing in language development: A case study. *Human Development, 28,* 40–49.

Acredolo, L. P., & Goodwyn, S. W. (1988). Symbolic gesturing in normal infants. *Child Development, 59,* 450–466.

Acredolo, L. P., & Goodwyn, S. W. (1990). Sign language in babies: The significance of symbolic gesturing for understanding language development. *Annals of Child Development, 7,* 1–42.

Bates, E., Benigni, L. F., Bretherton, I., Camaioni, L., & Volterra, V. (1979). *The emergence of symbols: Cognition and communication in infancy.* New York: Academic Press.

Bates, E., Bretherton, I., Shore, C., & McNew, S. (1983). Names gestures and objects: Symbolization in infancy and aphasia. In K. Nelson (Ed.), *Children's language* (Vol. 4). Hillsdale, NJ: Lawrence Erlbaum Associates.

Bellugi, U., Klima, E. (1982). The acquisition of three morphological systems in American Sign Language. *Papers and Reports on Child Language Development, 21,* 1–35. Stanford, CA: Stanford University.

Bloom, L. (1973). *One word at a time.* The Hague: Mouton.

Bonvillian, J. D., Orlansky, M. D., & Novack, L. L. (1983). Developmental milestones: Sign language acquisition and motor development. *Child Development, 54,* 1435–1445.

Bowerman, M. (1980). The structure and origin of semantic categories in the language—learning child. In M. L. Foster & S. Brandes (Eds.), *Symbol as sense.* NewYork: Academic Press.

Brown, R. (1973). *A first language: The early stages.* Cambridge, MA: Harvard University Press.

Brown, R. & Hanlon, C. (1970). Derivational complexity and order of acquisition in child speech. In J. R. Hayes (Ed.), *Cognition and the development of language.* New York: Wiley.

Carey, S. (1982). Semantic development: The state of the art. In E. Wanner & L. Gleitman (Eds.), *Language acquisition: The state of the art* (pp. 347–389). Cambridge: Cambridge University Press.

Chomsky, N. (1975). *The logical structure of linguistic theory.* New York: Plenum Press.

Fernald, A., Taeschner, T., Dunn, J., Papousek, M., de Boysson–Bardies, B., & Fukui, I. (1989). A cross-language study of prosodic modifications in mothers' and fathers' speech to preverbal infants. *Journal of Child Language, 16,* 477–501.

Gelman, S., & Coley, J. (in press). Language and categorization: The acquisition of natural kind terms. In S. A. Gelman & J. P. Byrnes (Eds.), *Perspectives on language and thought: interrelations in development.* Cambridge: Cambridge University Press.

Genesee, F. (1987). *Learning through two languages.* Cambridge, MA: Newbury House.

Gleitman, L., & Wanner, E. (1982). Language acquisition: The state of the state of the art. In E. Wanner & L. Gleitman (Eds.), *Language acquisition: The state of the art* (pp. 3–48). Cambridge: Cambridge University Press.

Goldin-Meadow, S., & Morford, M. (1985). Gesture in early language: Studies of deaf and hearing children. *Merrill Palmer Quarterly, 31,* 145–176.

Goldin-Meadow, S., & Morford, M. (1989). Gesture in early child language. In V. Volterra & J. Erting (Eds.), *From gesture to language in hearing and deaf children* (pp. 249–262). Berlin: Springer–Verlag.

Golinkoff, R. M., & Hirsh–Pasek, K. (1987, October). *A new picture of language development: Evidence from comprehension.* Paper presented at the 12th Annual Boston University Conference on Language development. Boston, MA.

Goodwyn, S. W., & Acredolo, L. P. (1991, April). *Symbolic gesture versus word: Is there a modality advantage for onset of symbol use?* Paper presented at the Biennial Meeting of the Society for Research in Child Development, Seattle, WA.

Hubel, D. H., & Wiesel, T. N. (1959). Receptive fields of single neurons in the cat's visual cortex. *Journal of Physiology, 148,* 547–591.

Huttenlocher, J., & Smiley, P. (1987). Early word meanings: The case of object names. *Cognitive Psychology, 19,* 63–89.

Jusczyk, P. W. (1986). A review of speech perception research. In K. Boff, L. Kaufman, & J. Thomas (Eds.), *Handbook of perception and human performance* (Vol. 2). New York: Wiley.

Keil, F. (1989). *Concepts, kinds, and cognitive development.* Cambridge: MIT Press.

Lock, A. (Ed.). (1978). *Action, gesture, & symbol.* New York: Academic Press.

Macnamara, J. (1982). *Names for things.* Cambridge, MA: MIT Press/Bradford Books.

Mayr, E. (1982). *The growth of biological thought.* Cambridge, MA: Harvard University Press.

Markman, E. (1989). *Categorization and naming in children: Problems of induction.* Cambridge: MIT Press/Bradford Books.

McNeill, D. (1985). So you think gestures are nonverbal? *Psychological Review, 92,* 350–371.

Mehler, J., & Fox, R . (Eds.). (1985). *Neonate cognition.* Hillsdale, NJ: Lawrence Erlbaum Associates.

Meier, R. (1991). Language acquisition by deaf children. *American Scientist, 79,* 60–70.

Nelson, K. (1974). Concept, word and sentence: Interrelations in acquisition and development. *Psychological Review, 81,* 267–285.

Newport, E., & Meier, R. (1985). The acquisition of American Sign Language. In D. Slobin (Ed.). *The crosslinguistic study of language acquisition* (Vol. 1, pp. 881–938). Hillsdale, NJ: Lawrence Erlbaum Associates.

Petitto, L. A. (1984). *From gesture to symbol: The relationship between form and meaning in the acquisition of personal pronouns in American Sign Language.* Unpublished doctoral dissertation, Harvard University, Boston, MA.

Petitto, L. A. (1985a, October). *On the use of pre-linguistic gestures in hearing and deaf children.* Paper presented at the 10th annual Boston University Conference on Language Development. Boston, MA.

Petitto, L. A. (1985b). *"Language" in the pre-linguistic child* (Tech. Rep. No. 4). Montreal: McGill University Department of Psychology.

Petitto, L. A. (1986). *From gesture to symbol: The relationship between form and meaning in the acquisition of personal pronouns in American Sign Language* (pp. 1–105). Bloomington, Indiana: Indiana University Linguistics Club Press.

Petitto, L. A. (1987). On the autonomy of language and gesture: Evidence from the acquisition of personal pronouns in American Sign Language. *Cognition, 27*(1), 1–52.

Petitto, L. A. (1988). "Language" in the pre-linguistic child. In F. Kessel (Ed.), *Development of language and language researchers: Essays in honor of Roger Brown* (pp. 187–221). Hillsdale, NJ: Lawrence Erlbaum Associates.

Petitto, L. A., & Charron, F. (1987). *Semantic categories in the acquisition of Langue des Signes Quebecoise (LSQ) and American Sign Language (ASL): A comparison of signing children's first signs with speaking children's first words* (Tech. Rep. No. 7). Montreal: McGill University, Department of Psychology.

Petitto, L. A., & Kampen, D. (in prep.) *The ontogeny of language and gesture: Are early symbolic gestures names for things?*

Petitto, L. A., & Marentette, P. F. (1990, October). *The timing of linguistic milestones in sign language acquisition: Are first signs acquired earlier than first words?* Paper presented at the 15th annual Boston University Conference on Language Development, Boston, MA.

Petitto, L. A., & Marentette, P. F. (1991a). Babbling in the manual mode: Evidence for the ontogeny of language. *Science, 251,* 1493–1496.

Petitto, L. A., & Marentette, P. F. (1991b, April). The timing of linguistic milestones in sign and spoken language acquisition. In L. Petitto (chair), *Are the linguistic milestones in signed and spoken language acquisition similar or different?* Symposium conducted at the Biennial Meeting of the Society for Research in Child Development, Seattle, WA.

Piaget, J. (1962). *Play, dreams and imitation.* New York: Norton.

Pinker, S. (1979). Formal models of language learning. *Cognition,* 217–283.

Pinker, S. (1984). *Language learnability and language development.* Cambridge, MA: Harvard University Press.

Pinker, S., & Bloom, P. (1990). Natural language and natural selection. *Behavioral and Brain Science, 13,* 707–778.

Quine, W. V. (1969). *Ontological relativity and other essays.* New York: Cambridge University Press.

Seidenberg, M. S., & Petitto, L. A. (1987). Communication, symbolic communication, and language in child and chimpanzee: Comment on Savage–Rumbaugh, McDonald, Sevcik, Hopkins, and Rupert (1986). *Journal of Experimental Psychology, General, 116*(3), 279–287.

Shatz, M. (1985). An evolutionary perspective on plasticity in language development. *Merrill–Palmer Quarterly, 31,* 211.

Shore, C., O'Connell, B., & Bates, E. (1984). First sentences in language and symbolic play. *Developmental Psychology, 20*(5), 872–880.

Slobin, D. (1985). Crosslinguistic evidence for the language-making capacity. In D. Slobin (Ed.). *The crosslinguistic study of language acquisition Vol. 2: Theoretical issues* (pp. 1157–1256). Hillsdale, NJ: Lawrence Erlbaum Associates.

Snyder, L., Bates, E., & Bretherton, I. (1981). Content and context in early lexical development. *Journal of Child Language, 8,* 565–581.

Waxman, S., Shipley, E., & Shepperson, B. (in press). Establishing new subcategories: The role of category labels and existing knowledge. *Child Development.*

Werner, H., & Kaplan, B. (1963). *Symbol formation.* New York: Wiley.

Zinober, B., & Martlew, M. (1985). The development of communicative gestures. In M. D. Barrett (Ed.). *Children's single-word speech.* New York: Wiley.

3

Constraints on Word Learning: Speculations About Their Nature, Origins, and Domain Specificity

Ellen M. Markman
Stanford University

Word learning is an inductive feat accomplished by the 2-year-olds of our species. To explain how such young children with limited information-processing abilities can so readily figure out what words mean, investigators have hypothesized that children are predisposed to elevate some hypotheses about word meanings over others. By greatly reducing the hypothesis space, these constraints on hypotheses help render the inductive problem soluble. Although the focus of this chapter is on three specific word-learning constraints: the whole-object, taxonomic, and mutual exclusivity assumptions, my goal is to consider broader fundamental questions about the nature of constraints on learning.

To begin, I briefly review the evidence for the three word-learning constraints. I then address misconceptions about the nature of biological constraints that pervade recent discussions of constraints on word learning where word-learning biases are interpreted as implying rigid, hard-wired, innate mechanisms that are immune from input. I argue that such constraints should be thought of as default assumptions, as probabilistic biases that provide good first guesses but not final solutions. Another misconception is to interpret these biases as necessarily being language specific. Analyses of other domains reveal, however, that all three assumptions appear in contexts other than word learning. This is not to say that they are completely general because, although some domains are governed by very similar principles, clear, important exceptions can readily be found. Domain specificity bears on questions about the origins of these constraints in that if comparable principles are found in other domains they may well be recruited for word learning. As for questions about the origins of the constraints, this complex and subtle set of issues is sometimes reduced to a simple contrast between innate versus learned. I show how this dichotomy can obscure rather than clarify the issues. For one, claims about the universality of constraints have been conflated with claims about innateness. Moreover, the innate-learned formulation seems to presuppose that a given constraint is a single homogeneous ability with a simple developmental history. Insights from an ethology of learning reveal that the innate-learned dichotomy further oversimplifies the issues in failing to acknowledge that learning itself is an adaptation. I conclude by suggesting that this ethological perspective be applied to the problem of word learning.

EVIDENCE FOR THE WHOLE-OBJECT, TAXONOMIC, AND MUTUAL EXCLUSIVITY ASSUMPTIONS

To provide a framework for speculating about the nature and origins of word-learning constraints I selectively review the literature, highlighting illustrative cases of children limiting their hypotheses as expected. For more comprehensive reviews of the literature and for attempts to reconcile the argument about word-learning constraints with some conflicting evidence, see Markman (1991) and Merriman and Bowman (1989).

The claim examined here is that constraints on hypotheses are needed to help children solve the inductive problem that word learning poses. On the most extreme formulation of this hypothesis, a baby would be unable to learn even a single word by any other means. However, there is reason to believe that word-learning constraints could be necessary for language acquisition, and yet still appear only after some language has been acquired. The reason for this claim is that somewhere around 18 months of age, the character of children's language learning appears to change dramatically (Bloom, Lifter, & Broughton, 1985; Corrigan, 1983; Dromi, 1987; Goldfield & Resnick, 1990; Halliday, 1975; McShane, 1979; Nelson, 1973). At this point, children start acquiring words at a very fast pace—in some cases several new words a day. This "naming explosion" or "vocabulary spurt" may mark a qualitatively new way of acquiring language. Such fast learning must be a constrained form of learning. Before the onset of the naming explosion, however, "word" learning might occur through a more brute force paired-associate kind of learning. Children may well acquire the first 50 or so words in their vocabulary by some slow associative mechanism, but this would account for only a tiny fraction of their language. As a working hypothesis, then, the prediction is that word-learning constraints should be available to babies by the time they are capable of fast word learning—at least by 18 months of age on the average.

The Whole-Object and Taxonomic Assumptions

When an adult points to an object and labels it, the novel term could refer to an object category, but it could also refer to a part of the object, or its substance, or color, or size, weight, position, texture, or pattern, among other things. Yet, children do not wait until enough evidence has accumulated to decide among the alternative hypotheses. Instead, it has been argued that one way children initially constrain word meanings is to assume that a novel label is likely to refer to the whole object and not to its parts, substance, or other properties (Macnamara, 1982; Markman, 1991; Markman & Wachtel, 1988; Soja, Carey, & Spelke, 1991).

Once children decide a term refers to the whole object, they still need to decide how to extend it to other objects. The term could refer to some external relation between two objects. Spatial relations, causal relations, possessor-possessed are some examples of common relations between objects that a term could in principle label. More generally, objects can be related through the variety of ways in which they participate in the same event or theme (e.g., cats eat mice; people read books; birds build nests). Many studies of classification in children demonstrate that children often find thematic relations particularly salient and interesting (see Gelman & Baillargeon, 1983; Markman, 1989; Markman & Callanan, 1983, for discussions).

If children are attending to thematic relations between objects, how is it that they so readily learn labels for kinds of objects instead? To answer this question, Markman and Hutchinson (1984) proposed that children constrain the possible meanings of words to refer to objects of like kind. This taxonomic assumption leads children to rule out thematic meanings. That is, children reject thematic relations as a first hypothesis about what a novel label might refer to, despite finding such relations to be salient and interesting. Markman and Hutchinson conducted a series of studies that compared how children would organize objects when an object was referred to with a novel label versus when it was not. When presented with two objects, such as a dog and cat, and a third object that was thematically related such as dog food, children would often select a dog and dog food as being the same kind of thing. If, however, the dog was called by an unfamiliar label such as *dax* and children were told to find another dax, they now were more likely to select the cat. This illustrates the basic phenomenon: When children believe they are learning a new word, they focus on taxonomic, not thematic, relations. These findings have been extended and refined in a number of studies (Baldwin, 1989b;

Hutchinson, 1984; Landau, Smith, & Jones, 1988) and Waxman has a series of studies documenting both the effectiveness and the limits of the taxonomic assumption and how it interacts with the hierarchical level of the category being named (Waxman, 1990, 1991; Waxman & Gelman, 1986; Waxman & Kosowski, 1990).

The main limitation of these studies is that most of them provide evidence for children 2 and older. One exception is a study that Backscheider and I conducted with 18- to 24-month-olds (Backscheider & Markman, 1990). Our results replicated the original Markman and Hutchinson (1984) findings with these younger children. In the absence of a label, the children tended to select thematic associates to the target. In marked contrast, when an object was given a novel label these 18- to 24-month-old children interpreted the novel label as referring to objects of the same taxonomic category the clear majority of the time. Thus the taxonomic assumption is used by children by 18 months of age.

Huttenlocher and Smiley (1987) have evidence from children's very early word use that further confirms that early language learners honor the taxonomic assumption. They examined the language use of children they followed from the time of their first word (around 13 months for most of the children) until the children were 2 or 2 1/2 years old. Their goal was to determine on what basis children extend words beyond their original context and to test whether early on children extend words complexively. A complexive use of a word would be tantamount to what we referred to as a thematic use—extending the word to a spatial, temporal, or causal associate of an object, rather than to objects of like kind.

Previous researchers have reported finding that children's early word meanings were sometimes complexive (Nelson, 1974; Snyder, Bates, & Bretherton, 1981), but Huttenlocher and Smiley argued that some of the previously reported instances of apparent complexive extensions of words by children may actually have been nonreferential uses of language by children. For example, a child who says "cookie" while reaching toward a cookie jar isn't necessarily labeling the jar as "cookie." Instead the child might know that cookies are kept in the jar and, being in the one word stage, about the only way to formulate a request for a cookie when no cookie is visible would be to say "cookie." Huttenlocher and Smiley set forth criteria to differentiate between that and other communicative uses of language from genuine complexive extensions. They found that even from the onset of language production, children were not using words to refer to complexively (thematically) organized objects. Instead, early language learners generalized object labels in ways that fit the whole-object and taxonomic assumptions.

Baldwin and Markman (1989) looked at what might be considered a precursor of the whole-object assumption, namely, does labeling an object for a baby cause the baby to attend more to that object than if it weren't labeled. We argued that if infants are biased to attend more to objects when they hear them labeled, then that could help them to notice word-object pairings. To test this, a first study compared how long 10- to 14-month-old infants looked at unfamiliar toys when a novel label was provided, versus when no label was offered. As predicted, labeling the toys increased infants' attention to them.

A second study examined whether labeling increased infants' attention to objects over and above what pointing, a powerful nonlinguistic method for directing infants' attention, can accomplish on its own. Infants ranging in age from 10 to 20 months were shown pairs of unfamiliar toys in two situations: (a) in a pointing alone condition, where the experimenter pointed a number of times at one of the toys, and (b) in a labeling and pointing condition, where the experimenter labeled the target toy while pointing to it. While pointing occurred, infants looked just as long at the target toy whether or not it was labeled. However, during a subsequent play period in which no labels were uttered, infants gazed longer at the target toys that had been labeled than at those that had not. Thus, labeling can increase infants' attention to objects beyond the time that the labeling actually occurs. This tendency of language to sustain infants' attention to objects may help them learn the mappings between words and objects. It could also serve as a precursor or component of the full-blown whole-object assumption.

The Mutual Exclusivity Assumption

If the whole-object assumption were all that children were equipped with they would not be able to learn terms that refer to substances, parts, or properties of objects. The mutual exclusivity assumption, which leads children to expect that each object will have only one label, helps children override the whole-object assumption, thereby enabling them to acquire terms other than object labels.

To see how mutual exclusivity overrides the whole-object assumption and helps children acquire property terms, suppose a novel term is applied to an object for which a child already has a label. In order to adhere to the principle of mutual exclusivity, the child would have to reject the novel term as a label for the object. The child could simply reject the term as a label for the object without coming up with an alternative meaning. Rejecting one meaning for the term, however, leaves the child with a term without a referent. This in itself may motivate children to try to find some meaning for the novel term. The mutual exclusivity principle does not speak to how children select among the potential meanings, but they might analyze the object for some interesting part or property and interpret the novel term as applying to it. Markman and Wachtel (1988) demonstrated that 3- and 4-year-old children can use mutual exclusivity to learn terms for parts and for substances. When a novel label was mentioned in the presence of an object with a known label, children rejected the term as a second label for the object and interpreted it instead as a label for a part of the object or its substance.

Mutual exclusivity could further contribute to word learning by helping children to narrow overextensions (Barrett, 1978; Clark, 1983, 1987; Merriman & Bowman, 1989). Suppose a child has overextended *dog* to apply to sheep as well as dogs, but then learns the correct name for sheep. The child would then need to stop calling sheep *dog* in order to avoid having two names for the same object.

Clark (1983, 1987) postulated another related principle to help account for semantic acquisition. (See Markman, 1989, for a comparison of lexical contrast and mutual exclusivity.) She argued, following Bolinger (1977), that every word in a dictionary contrasts with every other word and that to acquire words children must assume that word meanings are contrastive. Mutual exclusivity is one kind of contrast, but it is a more specific and stronger assumption: Many terms that contrast in meaning are not mutually exclusive. Terms at different levels of a class-inclusion hierarchy, such as *dog* and *animal*, contrast in meaning in Clark's sense because obviously the meaning of *animal* is different from that of *dog*. Yet, these terms violate mutual exclusivity. In fact, this points out one disadvantage of the mutual exclusivity bias: It impedes children's ability to learn class-inclusion relations (Markman, 1987, 1989).

Merriman and Bowman summarized the literature by outlining four ways in which children can act in accord with mutual exclusivity.

1. if a new term is used in a context in which it could either refer to an object with a known label or one whose label is not yet known, children should avoid interpreting the term as a second label for the known object and interpret it instead as referring to the object they cannot name.
2. alternatively, when presented with a second label for an object, a child could correct the old label, replacing it with the new one.
3. another option would be to simply reject the second label, either by explicitly denying that the term is appropriate (e.g., "No, that's not a . . .") or by just ignoring the second label.
4. finally, in order to preserve mutual exclusivity, children should avoid generalizing a new label to already named items.

Which option is selected for maintaining mutual exclusivity is argued to depend on the situation. If the reference of the second label is ambiguous, the child is likely to map the label onto an object without a known name. If the child is uncertain about the old name, he or she may correct it, replacing it with the new one. In a series of studies, children 2 1/2 and over were found to use mutual exclusivity in accord with these predictions.

As for children closer in age to the beginning of the naming explosion, Merriman and Bowman failed to find any evidence for the use of mutual exclusivity in 2-year-olds. However, Woodward and Markman (1991) pointed out several methodological flaws in Merriman and Bowman's (1989) procedures. Their measures of mutual exclusivity were overly taxing and thus overly conservative measures of very young children's use of mutual exclusivity. Although 2 1/2-year-olds were capable of maintaining mutual exclusivity despite these problems, 2-year-olds were not.

I now describe two lines of work in progress that are providing evidence for mutual exclusivity in children younger than 18 months of age. The first addresses whether mutual exclusivity can be used by babies about the age of the naming explosion to infer the referent of a novel label. One advantage of mutual exclusivity is that it allows children to acquire words for objects through indirect means, without anyone actually pointing to and labeling an object. Suppose, for example, a child sees two objects, one of which has a known label, say a ball, and another whose label is unknown, say a whisk, and hears someone say "Can you hand me the whisk?" A child who attempts to preserve the mutual exclusivity of terms should reject a second label for ball and thus infer that "whisk" must refer to the whisk given it is the only other object around. This ability to infer the appropriate referent has been documented in studies of children 2 or 2 1/2 and older (Au & Glusman, 1990; Dockrell & Campbell, 1986; Golinkoff, Hirsh-Pasek, Bailey, & Wenger, in press; Hutchinson, 1986; Markman & Wachtel, 1988; Merriman & Bowman, 1989).

Recently, however, Merriman and Bowman (1989) argued that these results could be obtained without recourse to mutual exclusivity, if children had a bias to fill lexical gaps. The lexical gap hypothesis states that in the presence of an object that as yet has no known label, children are motivated to discover its name (Clark, 1983, 1987). Thus, in the tests of mutual exclusivity just described children could map the novel word to the novel object because they have a novel object that they want to name rather than because they were reluctant to acquire a second label.

Work in progress (Markman & Wasow, in preparation) is designed to address both whether mutual exclusivity is available to children around 18 months of age and whether it can be differentiated from a propensity to fill lexical gaps. The lexical gap explanation is that upon seeing an object whose label is unknown, children are motivated to find out what it is called. To rule this out, we did not allow babies to view novel objects at the time the novel labels were heard. Babies heard a novel label in the presence of a familiar object with a known label, but no novel object was visible. Mutual exclusivity should lead children to reject second labels for objects and to search for an object whose name they do not yet know as a referent for a novel label. Both of these predictions were supported. Babies as young as 15 months old were found to honor the mutual exclusivity assumption, unaided by a bias to fill lexical gaps. Use of mutual exclusivity in these babies is particularly impressive because the situation was stripped of all other cues to a word's meaning. There was no object visible as a potential referent nor were there any of the typical cues that the speaker provides such as eye gaze toward the relevant object, pointing, or touching, or any other contextual cue as to the intended referent. Fifteen-month-olds thus relied heavily on mutual exclusivity to guide their search for an appropriate referent.

A second source of evidence that mutual exclusivity is used by very young children comes from studies of second-label learning (Liittschwager & Markman, 1991). Mutual exclusivity should lead children to reject second labels for objects thereby interfering with their ability to learn second labels for words. There have been several experimental studies of second-label learning in young children but all of these studies were undertaken for other theoretical reasons and did not systematically compare first- versus second-label learning (Banigan & Mervis, 1988; Taylor & Gelman, 1989; Tomasello, Mannle, & Werdenschlag, 1988; Waxman & Senghas, 1990). We focus on Banigan and Mervis' (1988) study that was designed to compare the effectiveness of several training methods for teaching 2-year-old children second labels for objects. Because some of the methods were successful, Banigan and Mervis concluded that children this young do not yet expect terms to be mutually exclusive.

Although Banigan and Mervis have shown that children are capable of violating mutual exclusivity, this is not tantamount to demonstrating children lack the mutual exclusivity bias. In fact, closer inspection of Banigan and Mervis' findings suggest that their study might be providing evidence in favor of mutual exclusivity. In particular, they found that it was rather difficult to teach children second labels for things. They included four different kinds of teaching methods. In one condition they simply pointed to the object (e.g., a unicorn that children called "horse" and said "this is a unicorn."). There was no learning at all in this condition. Yet this is a very common way of teaching object labels to young children. Had this been a *first label* for the object children may well have readily learned the new label. There was still no learning when labeling was supplemented by a description (e.g., "see it has a horn"). There was a small amount of learning when labeling was supplemented by a demonstration (having the unicorn butt with its horn). It was only when labeling, description, and demonstration were all included that appreciable learning took place. Again, this is unlikely to be needed for first-label learning. It may have been that such extensive training was needed because children are reluctant to accept second labels for objects.

To test this, Liittschwager and I attempted to teach 16-month-olds a novel label and then assessed their comprehension of the newly taught term. There were two conditions. In the first-label condition, babies were taught a term for an object for which they had no known label. In the second-label condition, babies were taught a term for an object for which they already knew a label. As predicted by the mutual exclusivity hypothesis, the babies readily learned first labels for objects but failed to learn the second labels.

These very recent findings, then, document the use of mutual exclusivity by babies 15–18 months of age. As predicted, these young babies are led by mutual exclusivity to reject a novel label as a second label for an object which (a) impedes their ability to learn second labels (Liittschwager & Markman, 1991), and (b) allows them to infer that a novel object is the more likely referent of a novel label (Markman & Wasow, in preparation).

In summary, although there are disadvantages to assuming that object labels are mutually exclusive, the advantages are that by assuming mutual exclusivity, children could avoid redundant hypotheses about the meanings of category terms, narrow overgeneralizations of terms, infer the correct referent of a term without anyone explicitly pointing it out, and override the whole-object assumption. At least some of these uses of mutual exclusivity are available to children from 15 months of age, and possibly earlier. Thus, there is evidence suggesting that all three postulated word-learning constraints could contribute to very young children's ability to quickly figure out a word's meaning. With this as background, I now turn to consider questions about the nature of these constraints.

CONSTRAINTS ON LEARNING AS DEFAULT ASSUMPTIONS

Recently, investigators have made explicit what has been implicit in many treatments of word-learning constraints, namely that they should be treated as default assumptions—as probabilistic biases that can be overridden (Merriman & Bowman, 1989; Woodward & Markman, 1991). In the absence of information to the contrary, these biases provide good first guesses as to a word's meaning. In summarizing this position, I borrow heavily from arguments presented in Woodward and Markman (1991).

There has been a good deal of controversy about whether postulating constraints on word learning is a useful way to conceptualize the problem (Gathercole, 1989; MacWhinney, 1989; Nelson, 1988). One source of disagreement is about the nature of the postulated constraints. Nelson (1988) argued that constraints must be absolute and that any deviation in a child's performance is evidence against a constraint operating. For example, she criticized the Markman and Hutchinson (1984) evidence for the taxonomic assumption on the grounds that children in these studies were not scoring 100% correct. Nelson's view is that to argue that there are constraints on word learning requires that these biases be absolute, admitting of no variance. This is certainly not the position of researchers who have proposed constraints on learning for domains such as conceptual development (Keil, 1979), causal reasoning (Brown, 1990; Gelman, 1990), counting (Gelman, 1990), object knowledge (Spelke, 1990), and language acquisition (Markman, 1987, 1989, 1990, 1991; Markman & Hutchinson, 1984; Markman & Wachtel, 1988; Merriman & Bowman, 1989; Pinker, 1984; Soja et al., 1991; Waxman, 1991; see also Keil, 1981, 1990; and Gelman, 1990a, 1990b). Moreover, the notion of constraints as default assumptions is widely held by ethologists arguing for biological bases of learning (cf. Marler & Terrace, 1984).

One way in which biases are not absolute is that they may be ordered into a hierarchy such that one bias overrides another. The extraordinary ability of migratory birds exemplifies such a case. Keeton (1974) summarized some of the most impressive of the documented feats of such birds. A manx shearwater, for example, migrated over 3,000 miles in 12 1/2 days to return to its burrow (Matthews, 1953, as cited in Keeton, 1974). Keeton concluded, for homing pigeons, that when the sun is visible, the pigeons use it as a compass. On overcast days, however, the pigeons are still able to find their way home. Thus, the birds have some alternative means of navigation that serve as a back-up system. Keeton reviewed the controversy about whether pigeons could be using the earth's magnetic field as one such system. Although this hypothesis was first put forward in 1882 and revived in 1947 there was so much contradictory evidence that it fell into disrepute. The reason for the failures to find that pigeons could navigate by geomagnetism is that it is not the birds' preferred strategy. Only when the preferred cue for navigation (the position of the sun) is unavailable do pigeons resort to relying on magnetism.

Imprinting provides a good example of a system of substantial plasticity that is nevertheless governed to some extent by innate predispositions. A given species of bird can be sexually imprinted onto a different species or even, in the case of hand-reared birds, onto humans. The birds will later show mating displays toward the foster species. Immelman (1972), on the other hand, documented that, despite this plasticity, there are preferences for a member of a bird's own species. In a test of whether zebra finches imprint most easily on their own species, male zebra finches were raised by a mixed pair of foster parents, a zebra finch and a Bengalese finch. Although there was equal opportunity for imprinting on either species, the birds nearly always had a sexual preference for their own species. Furthermore, imprinting onto a member of a bird's own species occurs more quickly, is more rigid, and is less likely to be reversed than imprinting onto a different species. Thus, the ease of learning and the quality of learning through imprinting is governed in part by the species–specific biases of the animal.

This point that constraints should be thought of as probabilistic biases was made repeatedly in a recent conference designed to consider issues of constraints on learning in biology (Marler & Terrace, 1984). Here is an example from Gould and Marler (1984) who argued:

> Indeed, it is tempting to place a default value interpretation on the associative biases of animals. Although bees, for instance, can learn that a flower is any color from yellow to ultraviolet, it learns the color of purple flowers far more quickly than any other color of flowers (Gould, 1984). At the same time, bees prefer purple silhouettes to all other colors on a spontaneous preference test. It is as though purple is the default parameter—a probabilistic bias which helps guide bees when they experiment with various flowers while searching for food. (p. 65)

And from Gould (1984), "In a very real sense, many cases of selective learning should be thought of as mechanisms by which experience serves to tune an animal's behavior from the default distribution of alternatives to the actual odds in the world around it" (p. 153).

Among ethologists, constraints are postulated as one means of helping the organisms to solve the inductive problems they face. In many cases, these biases could not provide absolute guarantees of correct answers because the environment is too unpredictable for absolute biases to be adaptive. Rather, the organism must be capable of learning—of extracting information flexibly from the environment. These biases give the organism a good first guess—a head start in solving the problem, compared to if it were sampling randomly from an extraordinarily large number of options.

It is in this way that constrains may be useful for young children trying to figure out what words in their language mean. The constraints that have been postulated, such as the whole-object, taxonomic, and mutual exclusivity assumptions, give the young child good first guesses about the meaning of a novel term. They provide powerful means to begin word learning, but not at all the final solutions.

Take the whole-object assumption, for example: Without evidence to the contrary, children should interpret a novel term as a label for an object—rather than a part or substance of the object or its color, size, shape, weight, action, and so on. Children must, however, be able to override this assumption in order to learn terms for parts, substances, properties, and events. Several different kinds of information could provide evidence to the contrary. If there were no salient object around at the time a novel term was introduced, the absence of a candidate object could override the whole-object assumption. For example, Soja et al. (1991) found that when presented with a blob of stuff rather than a discrete object, children will interpret a novel label as a substance term.

Baldwin's (1989a) work on how infants contribute to the establishment of joint reference points out another interesting factor that affects how children apply the whole-object assumption. Even if children honor the whole-object assumption, they still need to decide which object in their environment is the appropriate referent of a novel term. One solution could be to treat the label as referring to whatever object they happen to be viewing at the time they hear the label. If so, then errors would be expected on those occasions when the adult labels something other than what the child is attending to. Although vocabulary is acquired more quickly when parents tend to label what their children are attending to (Tomasello & Farrar, 1986), there is no evidence suggesting that wrong mappings occur when joint focus of attention is not achieved. One way that such errors could be avoided is if children monitor the speaker's focus of attention, through eye gaze, posture, or some other cues. To investigate this, Baldwin (1989a) taught 16- to 19-month-olds a novel word in two conditions. In the joint labeling condition, the experimenter labeled a toy at which the baby was looking. In the discrepant labeling condition, the experimenter labeled a toy other than the one at which the baby was looking. This was accomplished by having the experimenter look into a bucket, presumably at an object contained there, while she provided the novel label. The results indicate that babies do not simply map a novel label onto the object they are attending to. Even though the babies heard the label as they were looking at and playing with a novel toy, they only treated the term as a label for that toy when the speaker was also looking at the same toy. Children did not mistakenly treat the term as referring to the toy they were looking at if the experimenter was looking in the bucket. Instead children throughout this age range avoided errors. The 16- to 17-month-olds simply failed to learn the new term, whereas the 18- to 19-month-olds correctly inferred that the label referred to the (unseen) toy in the bucket. When that toy was later revealed, the older babies treated it as the referent of the novel label. Thus, children monitor the speaker's focus of attention before concluding that a given object is the referent of the term. The whole-object assumption is moderated by babies' requirement for a joint focus of attention.

Lack of joint focus of attention might, therefore, provide another means of overriding the whole-object assumption. Moreover, the absence of a joint focus of attention coupled with certain rhythmic cues might further discourage treating a term as an object label. Imagine, for example, an adult repeatedly lifting a baby overhead while saying "whee!" A child could, of course, find some object in the room to label. But the absence of ostensive cues from the adult along with the synchronizing of the "whee" with the swinging motion would lead the child to interpret "whee" as part of the event rather than as a label for an object. This rhythmic and synchronous use of "whee" or peek-a-boo and other games becomes part of the activity itself. This coordination of language with an activity is very different from saying, for example, "Let's do whee" and then silently lifting a baby. The absence of a salient object, the absence of joint focus of attention, and the rhythmic synchrony of language and events could work together to block the whole-object assumption in such cases.

As Markman and Wachtel (1988) demonstrated, the mutual exclusivity assumption can be another source of information in conflict with the whole-object assumption. By rejecting a novel term as a second label for an object, children will then search for a part, or substance, or other attribute of the object to label. Thus, children will violate the whole-object assumption in order to preserve mutual exclusivity.

As children learn more about their language, grammatical form class can serve as further means of overriding the whole-object assumption. If for example the novel word is clearly recognizable as a verb, that would cause children to override the whole-object assumption.

In sum, the whole-object constraint serves as a first hypothesis that can be overridden in a variety of different ways ranging from lack of environmental support (e.g., when there are no salient objects around), to lack of joint focus of attention on an object (as when an adult fails to attend to a candidate object), to its coming into conflict with other word-learning constraints (e.g., mutual exclusivity) to its conflict with other aspects of the linguistic system (e.g., grammatical form class).

One implication of viewing constraints as default assumptions is that violations of a constraint found in a child's lexicon are not necessarily evidence against the existence of the constraint. Yet such counter-examples constitute much of what has been taken as evidence against constraints (Banigan & Mervis, 1988; Gathercole, 1987, 1989; Merriman, 1987; Mervis, 1987, 1989; Nelson, 1988). Instead of treating such violations simply as negative evidence, we could look to such violations as information about how children go about overriding the constraint when needed. Merriman and Bowman (1989) approached the literature on mutual exclusivity from this perspective and argued that there is flexibility in how it can be manifested. Even when mutual exclusivity is preserved, children are not restricted to one set response, but, rather, are able to make use of different aspects of the situation to maintain mutual exclusivity.

This view of word-learning biases as default assumptions implies that violations of a constraint in a child's lexicon do not necessarily invalidate the constraint. The existence of violations is not sufficient to show that children lack the bias. How the interpretation was arrived at is what is at issue, not only what was acquired. For example, by postulating the whole-object assumption, one is not committed to a position that says children are incapable of learning property terms and that if one finds an adjective in a child's vocabulary the constraint is disproved. Rather, the argument is that object labels will typically constitute children's initial hypotheses upon hearing a novel word, and in order to learn property terms children must override that initial bias. Similarly, to claim that children are biased to treat object labels as mutually exclusive is not to claim that they can never learn more than one label for the same object. The test of the hypothesis requires examining the order of hypotheses children consider to determine whether they resist violating mutual exclusivity on first hearing a novel word. If a child's initial hypothesis reveals an attempt to preserve mutual exclusivity, then that would argue in favor of mutual exclusivity as a constraint on word learning even if the child is ultimately successful at overriding the constraint. For this reason, examining children's lexicons for counterexamples is not the appropriate test of whether children are guided by these assumptions. The lexicon reflects the conclusion of some process of word learning and not the process itself. We cannot judge what hypotheses children may have begun with when the only record is the end product, the words they have learned.

DOMAIN SPECIFICITY

In terms of the general theme of this volume, one question that arises is whether word-learning constraints are specific to language or whether they are common to other cognitive domains. This question of domain specificity very likely bears on questions about the possible origins of the word-learning constraints. If comparable constraints operate in other fundamental cognitive domains they may have been recruited for word learning. Word-learning biases might, therefore, arise out of more general cognitive biases. To date, we know so little about these issues that we can only begin to speculate. Also, there is no reason to believe that the word-learning constraints are necessarily equivalent in their domain specificity. Some may be unique to language, or more precisely unique to lexical acquisition, whereas others may apply more widely. Some very general biases may operate to reduce the hypothesis space across a variety of domains, whereas others may operate only in the case of word learning. However, if the criteria for domain specificity were to be that the bias appears in no other domain, then none of the lexical constraints discussed so far would qualify. On the other hand, Keil (1990) suggested a weaker criterion, namely that constraints are domain specific if they are content dependent, meaning that they apply only to types of knowledge that meet certain structural descriptions. This leaves open the possibility that a given constraint could be applicable in more than one domain, yet still not be domain general. From this perspective, Keil (1990) wrestled with this same question of whether the lexical constraints that have been postulated should be considered domain specific and found it hard to decide. With these caveats in mind, I comment on the domain specificity of each of the three lexical constraints discussed in this chapter, the whole-object, taxonomic, and mutual exclusivity assumptions, and conclude that none of them are domain specific in the strong sense of applying only to word learning.

The Whole-Object Assumption

Do children interpret novel labels as referring to whole objects because objects are in general very salient or is their attention to objects heightened in the presence of a novel word? Clearly, objects are perceptually salient. Moreover, Spelke has demonstrated that infants have a richly interconnected set of beliefs about physical objects including the expectations that objects are cohesive, bounded, and spatiotemporally continuous (Spelke, 1988, 1990). For example, in one study, 4-month-old babies were habituated to a partly occluded object whose ends were visible behind a screen (Kellmann & Spelke, 1983). In one condition the ends appeared to move together behind the screen. After habituation, babies were shown two displays: One corresponded to the perceptual display they had seen, namely an object with an interrupted center, whereas the other corresponded to a whole, connected object. If babies were habituating to the surface display—literally what they had seen—then habituation should have generalized to the fragmented object, and babies should look more at the whole object. On the other hand, if babies had perceived the center-occluded object as a continuous object, then habituation should generalize to the whole object and babies should look more at the fragmented one. The results were that as long as the ends of the object moved together behind the screen, infants perceived the object as connected. Moreover, if the object moved it was perceived as a whole connected object even if it were asymmetric and heterogeneous in color and texture. Thus, babies use common motion to infer that objects are continuous.

From a large body of such experimental evidence, Spelke (1990) concluded that infants possess a primitive theory of the physical world that is guided by three constraints on the behavior of physical bodies: A cohesion constraint that states that objects move as wholes; a boundedness constraint that states that objects move independently of each other; and a spatiotemporal continuity constraint that states that objects move on connected paths. These constraints guide babies' perceptions or interpretations of scenes by serving as criteria against which to identify objects found embedded in complex, cluttered, and changing arrangements that are typical of real-world scenes. Thus, objects may have a privileged conceptual as well as perceptual status in very young babies. The whole-object assumption in word learning might, then, directly reflect this nonlinguistic status of objects.

In this vein, Gentner (1981, 1982; Gentner & Rattermann, 1991) argued that the reasons children learn nouns before verbs stems from conceptual differences between object reference and relational meaning. She argued that the representation of nouns is more "dense" than that of verbs, where density refers to the ratio of number of internal links and the number of components linked, including external links. This implies that the meanings of nouns are more redundant and overdetermined than the meanings of verbs. Objects are argued to be conceptually cohesive and readily perceived as wholes. Thus, determining the boundary of object reference should be straightforward. In contrast, relational terms such as verbs refer to concepts that are more abstract, less cohesive, and whose boundaries are less clear. Verbs are more likely to alter their meanings as a function of context than are object terms, whose meanings are more stable. Children about to learn language will have already parsed the world into objects. According to Gentner (1982) "since the language they are about to learn will have been constrained to make the same mapping between perceptual field and linguistic description, the child need only match these preconceived objects with co-occurring words." In contrast, "for verbs and other predicate terms, the child must come to discover which elements of the perceptual field can be combined and lexicalized."

The evidence from which Gentner drew these conclusions comes from a variety of different studies. In one study, the number of word senses was tallied for each dictionary entry for the 20 most frequent nouns and verbs. As predicted, there were more senses per verb than per noun. In a second study, subjects were asked to paraphrase metaphorical senses such as

"The lizard worshiped." In their paraphrase, subjects were more likely to change the meaning of the verbs than the nouns. In a third study, bilingual subjects were asked to translate English sentences into their second language, and other bilingual subjects then translated these sentences back into English. More of the original nouns than the original verbs reappeared in these second translations. On a variety of measures, nouns were found to be recalled more accurately than verbs. Most importantly, there is cross-linguistic evidence from languages as diverse as English, Mandarin Chinese, and Kaluli, that nouns are learned more readily than verbs and comprise more of children's vocabulary (Gentner, 1982).

Maratsos (1991) elaborated Gentner's position while considering how children acquire grammatical form class. He argued that nouns are a family resemblance category partly defined by semantic properties and partly defined by structural properties, and that concrete objects comprise the semantic core of the family resemblance definition. Maratsos further argued that nouns are the only candidate for a universal form class.

Adjectives may contrast with nouns in some of the same ways that verbs do. Adjectives may be more prone to adjust their meaning according to context than are nouns. For example, the meaning of "good" is adjusted to fit the category it modifies ("good person" vs. "good knife"; Katz, 1964). "Large" interacts with what it modifies ("large house" vs. "large mouse"), as does "red" ("red hair" vs. "red apple"). Bolinger (1967) argued that, in general, the interpretation of an adjective varies, sometimes dramatically, depending on the noun it modifies. For example, "criminal" means roughly "defending criminals" in "criminal lawyer" but "committed by criminals" in "criminal act." In these examples the noun refers to an object; the adjective presupposes that object for its interpretation.

Analogously, adjectives adjust their form in some languages, depending on the noun they modify. For example, adjectives in French must agree in number and gender with the noun they modify. In fact, it is a language universal that, of all languages in which the adjective follows the noun, all the inflectional categories of the noun will be marked on the adjective but might be absent from the noun (Greenberg, 1966). Again, this implies that nouns have a fixed form independent of any modifier they receive, whereas adjectives presuppose a noun and must adjust their form to correspond to the inflections of that noun. In Markman (1989), I summarized some experimental findings with nouns and adjectives that parallel some of those of Gentner's with nouns and verbs.

Another way in which object reference might be primary can be derived from work on holistic versus analytic strategies for determining category membership (Kemler, 1983; Kemler-Nelson, 1984; Smith, 1979). Children have been shown to be less capable of analyzing objects into their component features. Yet, this difficulty in analyzing objects could benefit children in a number of ways (see Markman, 1989). One is that it could simplify the induction problem in word learning. The problem is to understand how children can so quickly settle on objects as the referents for terms, given that a label could, in principle, refer either to an object or to its color, size, shape, and so on. To think of hypotheses such as color, size, and shape, however, requires analyzing the object into those dimensions in the first place. Thus, these competing hypotheses may not be so readily available to the young child. Another way of stating this is that a limitation on children's information-processing abilities may actually provide part of the solution to the induction problem. This is reminiscent of an argument put forward by Newport (1984) to explain how it is that children are so competent at acquiring language. Newport raised the possibility that some cognitive limitations of children may actually work to their advantage in learning language. Here too, in the domain of acquiring object labels, a limitation may work to children's advantage. Their limited analytic abilities may effectively narrow down the hypothesis space that they need to consider. The hypothesis space that children at first generate would not expand to encompass all of the possible features and Boolean combinations of features. By not generating the hypotheses in the first place, children do not have to subsequently rule them out. Thus, children's holistic processing could also contribute to the whole-object assumption.

There is a variety of evidence, then, suggesting that the conceptual status of objects is privileged relative to that of properties or relations. The whole-object assumption could then be a direct reflection of the nonlinguistic status of objects. In other words, children treat labels as referring to objects because typically objects are most salient. On the other hand, imagine a child watching a colorful pulsating neon object twirling around in an interesting way. Under these conditions, it is very likely that the color and motion of the object would be attended to as well as the object per se. If so, what would happen when the object was labeled? Would the child interpret the label as referring to the brilliant color, the pulsating rhythm, the interesting motion, or to the object itself? The whole-object assumption predicts that children should interpret the novel label as a label for the object even in cases where the nonlinguistic salience of properties is greater than that of the object. In other words, the constraint is presumed to operate in language learning even when it fails to coincide with what is salient nonlinguistically. Although the whole-object assumption has not yet been subjected to this stringent a test, Baldwin's (1989b) and Backscheider and Markman's (1990) studies suggest that in those cases where color or a dynamic activity are made salient to children, children will still interpret the label as a label for objects. Perhaps the whole-object assumption in word learning capitalizes on a cognitive bias to parse the world in terms of objects and that labeling objects may exaggerate this more general tendency, strengthening it enough to promote objects to the preferred interpretation of a novel label even in those cases where properties are otherwise more salient.

The Taxonomic Assumption

The taxonomic assumption is clearly not limited to word learning but, on the other hand, there are domains and situations where it is not readily used. At first sight, Markman and Hutchinson's (1984) evidence for the taxonomic assumption might suggest that this assumption is specific to word learning. In fact, the impetus for studying this word-learning constraint was the observation that children treat words as referring to objects of like kind although they often organize objects according to their thematic relationships in classification and other tasks. When the task involved word learning a different organizational principle was invoked. On the other hand, there is no question that children notice and use taxonomic relations in domains other than language learning. One important and very general domain where the taxonomic assumption appears is in inductive projections from one object to another. Children are almost certainly more likely to make inductive generalizations from one object to another of like kind than to one that is strongly associated with it. For example, after having learned that a poodle has incisors a child should be more likely to conclude that a collie has incisors than that a bone does, even though dog and bone are strongly associated. Such comparisons have not been made, but there is ample evidence that children draw inductive projections to objects of like kind, tempered by children's knowledge of the domains, the hierarchical levels, and implicit theories (Carey, 1985; Gelman, 1988; Gelman & Markman, 1986; Keil, 1979) and, to my knowledge, no evidence that children project properties to objects that are thematically related. Thus inductive inferences about object properties are also governed by a version of the taxonomic assumption.

The widespread use of the taxonomic principle in governing inductive projections might provide a possible account of the origins of the taxonomic constraint in word learning. Word learning might exploit the basic principles of inductive generalization. Here is a schematic description of inductive projection that might help to draw the parallel to word learning. (This sketch simply stipulates that generalization occurs and begs the central problem of induction which is why only a small set of the logically possible inductions are ever made; Goodman, 1955; Quine 1960).

- In *inductive projection*, a property is attributed to an object. Other objects of like kind are then assumed, with some degree of confidence, to also possess the property, whereas strong associates of the target object are not assumed to have the property.
- In *word learning*, an object is named. Other objects of like kind are then assumed, with some degree of confidence, to also have the same name, whereas strong associates of the first object are not assumed to have the same name.

If the taxonomic constraint in word learning is derived from the taxonomic basis of inductive projection, then that might help explain Premack's (1990) finding that language-trained chimps also show the taxonomic assumption. Chimps (language-trained and normal) were given a match-to-sample task where they could choose either a taxonomic or thematic associate of a target object. For example, if the target were a lime, then the two choices would be another lime (the taxonomic associate) and a knife (the thematic associate because these chimps enjoy cutting limes with knives). Juvenile chimps select the thematic associate (e.g., the knife) at above-chance levels. Young chimps, then, show the thematic bias seen in young humans. When the target object is labeled, either with a well-known word (e.g., the plastic symbol for lime) or a novel word (a novel plastic symbol), then the language-trained chimps now select the object of like kind (e.g., another lime) rather than the thematic associate. The chimps without language continue to select thematically.

One interpretation of these findings is that the taxonomic assumption is tied to word learning but that it is not species specific. Premack rejected this interpretation however. He argued that these chimps, who were only at the beginning stages of word learning, could not be said to have a real word, in the sense of understanding reference. Instead, they have learned some nonlinguistic contingencies, such as "in the presence of this symbol, one can obtain a lime." This then becomes generalized to something like "when a symbol is presented along with an object, one can obtain that kind of object in the presence of the symbol." Premack concluded that if a weaker explanation is possible for young chimps, it may also be possible for children and that this therefore undermines the evidence that children use word-learning constraints.

Suppose Premack is correct and that these chimps do not know words per se. One way of interpreting these findings is that the chimps have solved this discriminative learning task following more general inductive principles. The discriminative stimulus signals that objects of like kind will be available rather than associates. In other words, this could be an instance of the taxonomic basis for inductive generalization. What about

Premack's conclusion that this kind of task could not, then, provide evidence for word-learning constraints in children? Here I don't agree unless Premack means only that the taxonomic assumption is not limited to word-learning. More general constraints may enable children to figure out what words refer to as well as domain-specific constraints (if any exist). Word learning is governed by the taxonomic bias whether the bias is domain specific or not.

Although the taxonomic assumption is seen both in word learning and in inductive projection of properties from one object to another, there are important domains where taxonomic inferences are avoided. One of these is causal reasoning. In general, causes and effects are not thought to be similar. In inferring a cause from an effect or an effect from a cause, one would typically avoid looking for objects or events of like kind. Suppose for example, that someone saw a popped balloon and needed to infer what caused it to pop. Another balloon, popped or otherwise would be a very unlikely candidate for the cause. Conversely, if someone viewed a pair of scissors opening and closing and had to predict what they might do, causing another pair of scissors to open and close would be a very unlikely inference. Thus, one fundamental and pervasive domain, causal reasoning, eschews generalization based on the taxonomic assumption.

Classical conditioning provides an example of a kind of learning that relies on thematic rather than taxonomic associations. In classical conditioning, after repeated pairings with an unconditioned stimulus, a conditioned stimulus becomes capable of eliciting a conditioned response. Dogs salivate at the sound of a bell or the sight of a bowl after the bell or bowl has become associated with food. The conditioned stimulus is a temporal or spatial associate of the unconditioned stimulus. Although a bowl and meat, for example, are strongly associated, they are not things of like kind.

Petitto (chapter 2, this volume) compares the principles that govern the extension of signs that are words in sign language to nonlinguistic gestures. She reports that signs conform to the taxonomic principle, as expected, but that nonlinguistic gestures do not.

In summary, properties learned of one object are generalized to objects of like kind rather than to strongly associated objects. This widespread use of the taxonomic assumption in governing inductive inferences might be the origin of its use in word learning. Although the taxonomic assumption is clearly not limited to word learning, there are important domains, such as causal reasoning and classical conditioning, where inferences and associations are more likely to be based on spatial or temporal contiguity and causal relations rather than taxonomic relations.

The Mutual Exclusivity Assumption

The mutual exclusivity assumption resembles a number of principles that have been postulated in other cognitive domains. Whether this similarity is only superficial or whether it reflects a common source for these principles across domains is not yet clear. For now, however, mutual exclusivity appears to be the most likely of the constraints to qualify as domain general. Some examples of other domains in which biases comparable to mutual exclusivity appear are discussed next.

Other Linguistic Constraints

One possibility is that mutual exclusivity is not limited only to word learning but is used more broadly in language acquisition. Or to be more accurate, mutual exclusivity would result from a more general principle, either a one-to-one mapping principle (Slobin, 1973, 1977) or the uniqueness principle (Pinker, 1984; Wexler & Culicover, 1980) applied to word learning. Slobin's (1973, 1977) one-to-one operating principle of language acquisition is that children expect the organization of language to be clear. One way of accomplishing this is for languages to establish a one-to-one mapping between the underlying semantic structures and the surface forms. Although this principle was formulated for morphemes in a sentence, if it were extended to category terms it would result in the mutual exclusivity of the terms. That is, each category term would be referred to by only one category term.

The uniqueness principle (Pinker, 1984; Wexler & Culicover, 1980) is another related principle that has been hypothesized to help account for the acquisition of syntax. The motivation for this principle is to help account for how children can acquire grammatical rules in the absence of negative feedback (Pinker, 1984; Wexler & Culicover, 1980). If children are not informed that a given grammatical rule they have hypothesized is wrong, how could they reject erroneous hypotheses and settle on the correct grammar for their language? Pinker (1984) argued following Wexler and Culicover (1980) that, in some cases, the need for negative evidence can be eliminated if the child assumes the uniqueness principle. That is, when the child is faced with a set of alternative structures fulfilling the same function, he or she should assume that only one of the structures is correct unless there is direct evidence that more than one is necessary. The principle allows the child to reject structures even when there is no negative feedback indicating that they are ungrammatical. Languages do violate the uniqueness assumption to some extent. According to Pinker, the child requires more evidence to accept a construction with a uniqueness violation than a construction that does not violate the assumption.

Mutual exclusivity is consistent with the uniqueness principle as applied to category terms. As in the domain of syntax, if children start out biased to assume that terms are mutually exclusive, then they should require more evidence to accept a construction, such as class inclusion, that violates mutual exclusivity than a construction that is consistent with it. There is one major difference in the rationale for the uniqueness principle and that for mutual exclusivity. The major impetus behind postulating the uniqueness principle is the problem of lack of negative evidence in the acquisition of syntax. There is little evidence that parents or other adults explicitly correct children's ungrammatical sentences and even some evidence that they do not (Brown & Hanlon, 1970). A theory of the acquisition of syntax cannot depend on children getting explicit correction when their constructions are wrong. Moreover, even when children do receive negative feedback, there is still a serious problem left of interpreting what aspect of an utterance is being criticized (Bowerman, 1987; Gleitman, 1981). The situation is different for the acquisition of the vocabulary of a language. Children are frequently provided with corrections to wrong labels for objects or other mistaken use of terms (e.g., "It looks like a dog but it is a wolf." "That's not a dump-truck it's a fire-truck."). How widespread such corrections are for children, and how children make use of these corrections, is not yet known, but the situation is clearly different from that of the acquisition of grammar. Nevertheless, children may still be able to make use of the mutual exclusivity assumption in an analogous way to that of the uniqueness principle: Allowing them to reject certain hypotheses about a word's meaning because it would violate mutual exclusivity, even if no negative evidence were provided.

Essentialist Biases

Mutual exclusivity may not be limited to language, however. It could derive from children's beliefs about objects and not just their beliefs about object labels. Children might believe that an object has only one identity, that is, it can be only one kind of thing, and that its identity is revealed by object labels. The mutual exclusivity of object labels would then be derived from this more basic essentialist belief about objects. Similarly, Flavell (1988) argued that young children assume that each thing in the world has only one identity, an assumption that adults may share. Unlike adults, however, children do not understand that each thing may, nevertheless, be represented in more than one way. According to Flavell, this limitation on multiple representation is revealed in a number of diverse tasks, including visual and conceptual perspective taking and understanding the appearance reality distinction, along with assuming mutual exclusivity of category terms.

A Domain General Constraint on Systematization

A final possibility is that mutual exclusivity or some more general principle that subsumes mutual exclusivity is a domain general constraint—appearing widely in various manifestations across many diverse domains. Here are some examples from classical conditioning and social psychology.

Blocking and Overshadowing in Classical Conditioning. Two well-known phenomena in classical conditioning, blocking and overshadowing, are governed by some principle that appears related to mutual exclusivity in that animals seem best prepared to learn only one conditioned stimulus (CS) for a given unconditioned stimulus (US). Whether blocking and overshadowing are the results of attention, learning, or performance is still under debate (see Gallistel, 1990; Kehoe, 1987; Macintosh, 1975, for reviews and discussion). Whatever the process, its result suggests something akin to mutual exclusivity in that a previously learned or salient CS seems to preempt an animal's learning or use of another CS. In both blocking and overshadowing, a candidate CS, say a tone, that would ordinarily serve as a perfectly learnable CS is rendered ineffective by the presence of another CS, say a light. In blocking an animal is first presented with one CS until conditioning occurs. For example, a light would be repeatedly paired with a US until the animal shows signs of anticipating the US on seeing the light. In the blocking phase of the experiment, the first CS, the light, is now presented along with a second CS, for example a tone. The light and tone are then repeatedly paired with the US. In this situation, despite the repeated pairing of the tone with the US, the animal does not become conditioned to the tone. That is, the animals do not appear to anticipate the US when the tone alone is presented. Yet, animals have no trouble becoming conditioned to tones in a simple conditioning procedure. Having learned one CS appears to block learning of a second CS.

In an overshadowing procedure, from the start of conditioning two stimuli, for example a light and a tone, are presented together during training. Either one of these stimuli presented alone would readily be conditioned to the US. However, when both CSs are presented together and thus both paired equally often with the US, animals become conditioned to only one of them and show no signs of conditioning or diminished conditioning to the second. For example, animals who experienced repeated pairings of light and tone with a US, might learn that the light predicted the US but not show any signs of learning that the tone did. Presumably the more salient of the two CSs overshadows the other and reduces or prevents learning of a second CS to the US.

One extremely detailed and general model has recently been proposed by Gallistel (1990) to account for a wide variety of phenomena in classical conditioning including overshadowing and blocking. One component of the model consists of three constraining principles: "additivity," "inertia," and "uncertainty minimization." According to Gallistel: "The first two principles may be summarized by saying that unless it has to, the system does not entertain solutions in which CSs act interactively (conjointly) or in which different rates are ascribed to a CS during different epochs" (p. 425). The Uncertainty Minimization principle "comes into play in situations in which there is more than one way (usually an infinite number of ways) to apportion the observed rates of US occurrence to the influence of different CSs in a manner consistent with the first two constraints" (p. 426). The uncertainty minimization principle "drives the ascriptions to the solution that minimizes the number of CSs to which a nonzero influence on the rate is ascribed" (p. 426). Together then, these principles yield a bias toward simplifying the possible associations.

Attribution Theory: The Discounting Principle.   The discounting principle in attribution theory provides an example of a principle similar to mutual exclusivity operating in yet another domain. Here the problem domain is how people come to infer causes of their own or others' behavior. Kelly (1973) proposed that people reason about causes of behavior in accord with the discounting principle: "The role of a given cause in producing a given effect is discounted if other possible causes are also present " (p. 113). Similarly Kanouse (1971) concluded that

> individuals may be primarily motivated to seek a single sufficient or satisfactory explanation for any given event, rather than one that is the best of all possible explanations. That is, individuals may exert more cognitive effort in seeking an adequate explanation when none has yet come to mind than they do in seeking for further (and possibly better) explanations when an adequate one is already available. This bias may reflect a tendency to think of unitary events and actions as having unitary (rather than multiple) causes. (p. 131)

This analysis led Kanouse to conclude there is a "primacy effect" in the formation of attributions such that one stable attribution tends to preempt or preclude others by making individuals relatively unresponsive to new information (Kanouse, 1971).

The best known example of the discounting principle at work in children comes from the studies comparing intrinsic and extrinsic motivation and studies of overjustification (Kassin & Lepper, 1984; Lepper, Greene, & Nisbett, 1973; Lepper, Sagotsky, Dafoe, & Greene, 1982). This work has documented that extrinsic rewards can undermine a child's intrinsic interest in an activity. Under some circumstances, rewarding children for performing tasks they enjoy can reduce children's interest in the activity. The idea here is that children seek a cause for their behavior. When engaged in an activity, for example, coloring with markers, they could assume they color because they like to or that they color for some extrinsic reason. If children are provided with a salient, compelling external reason for engaging in an activity, then they will accept that as the cause for their behavior and discount the intrinsic value of the activity. For example, Lepper et al. (1973) selected children who showed a high level of interest in a given activity, such as coloring with markers, and assigned them to one of three conditions. In one condition, children were informed that if they performed the activity they would receive a "good player's award." This was the experimental condition. There were two control conditions. In both of the control conditions children were invited to engage in the activity and no mention was made of a reward. In one condition children were unexpectedly given the good player's award at the conclusion of the session and in the other they were not. Two weeks later the children were again observed at play in the classroom and the amount of time they spent engaged in the various activities was measured. The children who had expected a reward engaged in the activity significantly less than children in the other two conditions. Thus, providing children with a compelling external cause for their behavior reduces their intrinsic interest in the task. Although the discounting principle is revealed in children's loss of interest in a task, young children may not have an explicit awareness of the principle and may not predict or explain other children's performance in accord with the principle (see discussion by Kassin & Lepper, 1984). Given that many parents would find this principle counterintuitive and continue to reward their children in ways that often backfire, it is not surprising that young children fail on some tasks that require explicit knowledge of discounting.

Similarities and Differences Across Domains.   One similarity between mutual exclusivity in word learning and similar principles in classical conditioning and social attribution is that they are fallible. One objection raised against the argument that mutual exclusivity serves as a guiding principle of word learning is that languages do not completely conform to mutual exclusivity. Investigators have questioned why a child should be equipped with a principle that is wrong. Languages have synonyms, hypernyms, and overlapping terms all of which violate mutual exclusivity. I have argued that the advantages of mutual exclusivity outweigh these disadvantages. Although mutual exclusivity is not an infallible assumption, it is a useful one. Like mutual exclusivity in word learning, the simplifying principles used in classical conditioning and social attribution, although useful to the organism, are sometimes wrong. An animal in a blocking or overshadowing procedure is failing to learn about another reliable predictor of an event. People's motivation for doing things is multiply determined, yet given one sufficient explanation for someone's behavior we ignore others. In these domains as well as word learning the simplification may effectively discover and maintain simple relations at the expense of some loss of information.

Another similarity between mutual exclusivity in word learning and these related principles in other domains is that none of the principles is absolute or inviolate. When the evidence is irreconcilable with the simplifying assumption, animals and people will violate the assumption and construct a more complicated solution to the problem.

There are several differences in the way these simplifying principles are stated in other domains that suggest possible reformulations of the mutual exclusivity assumption. Mutual exclusivity in word learning leads children to prefer only one object label for a given object. Gallistel's model of classical conditioning leads animals to seek the fewest possible solutions, but not exactly one. Moreover, in both classical conditioning and in social attribution, the difference in learning is sometimes a matter of degree rather than complete rejection of a second solution. Thus, one may discount a second cause for behavior by underestimating it rather than ignoring it completely. Overshadowing and blocking sometimes diminish the strength of the association that is learned rather than preventing it completely. We have suggested that mutual exclusivity is a default assumption in the sense that it is a probabilistic assumption that can be overridden, but have proposed that children expect each word to have only one label (rather than a bias to minimize the number of labels) and that children will reject a second label, rather than learn it less well. These alternative formulations might be worth considering, however.

In summary, mutual exclusivity or some more general principle that subsumes mutual exclusivity, may be a widespread strategy for first systematizing a new domain of knowledge. Karmiloff-Smith (1979), Karmiloff-Smith and Inhelder (1975), and Carey (1978) have argued that children may begin acquiring knowledge in a domain by learning basic concepts in relative isolation, but after a while are driven to try to organize and systematize their knowledge. Mutual exclusivity is a simple, primitive form of systematization. Basically it works to keep relations between elements distinct and to maximize predictability from one element to another. Perhaps there is some very general oversimplification principle that operates across domains that serves to exaggerate regularities. Given limited resources, one way to impose order on a complex domain would be to ignore subtleties and complexity in favor of establishing some order and predictability. This would lead the learner to expect strong correlations between elements in a domain and to ignore or reject counterexamples and exceptions. Once regularities are discovered, they can serve as a scaffolding that can be elaborated and modified to incorporate exceptions and inconsistencies. The mutual exclusivity bias in language, then, could be one instantiation of a widespread attempt to find simple, regular, relations between elements in a domain. Mutual exclusivity, attribute discounting, blocking and overshadowing all cause animals and humans to overlook some regularity, to fail to learn something that could be useful. They are not flawless, but given limited resources may be highly adaptive.

In summary, the whole-object, taxonomic, and mutual exclusivity assumptions vary in their degree of generality across domains but none of them are specific to word learning. Knowing what other domains appear to be governed by principles similar to the ones postulated to guide word learning, may provide some insight into the possible origins of these constraints. I now discuss issues that arise in considering the possible origins of word-learning assumptions.

POSSIBLE ORIGINS OF WORD-LEARNING ASSUMPTIONS

The argument that I have made is that word-learning constraints such as the whole-object and taxonomic assumptions are what enable babies to acquire words so rapidly. They are expected to be universal: All babies, no matter what language they begin to learn would expect words to refer to novel objects unless given good reason to believe otherwise, and would generalize words to things of like kind rather than to strong associates. The argument includes the claim that extensive experience with language does not form the basis of the constraint. That is, these word-learning mechanisms are not learned generalizations from language input. Although such learning biases are argued not to be induced from language per se, this account leaves open the question of how they do originate.

Universal Versus Innate

It is important in considering questions about the origins of word-learning constraints, not to confuse claims about a principle being universal with a claim that it is domain specific or innate. Analogously, one should not confuse claims that such constraints are available to the beginning language learner as a claim that no learning or experience is required. A claim that a word-learning bias is universal and not a generalization induced from language does not boil down to a claim for a hard-wired domain-specific learning mechanism that is immune from input and operates independently of experience. Unfortunately, this question about their origins often is reduced to a question about whether the constraints are innate or learned. It is a truism in psychology that to dichotomize abilities into those that are innate and those that are learned oversimplifies the issues. The traditional response is that any given behavior or ability will reflect both genetic and environmental influences. But there are other ways in which this dichotomy is unsatisfactory.

Only Extreme Positions Considered

First, the innate-learned debate sometimes degenerates into caricatures of positions. An ability is considered as innate only if it is a hard-wired fixed-action pattern admitting of no variability and requiring no experience or input. Obviously, none of the word-learning constraints discussed so far fit this description, but this does not then warrant the extreme conclusion that they are therefore learned in the sense of being acquired from much exposure to language by an unbiased, all-purpose, inductive mechanism. There are many other possible ways in which to consider possible biological basis for learning.

Take the taxonomic assumption as an example. There are many possible accounts of its origins as a word-learning constraint besides the extreme views of either being hard-wired or being acquired by an unconstrained learning mechanism. As argued earlier, inductive projection of properties is also governed by a taxonomic principle of generalization. Word learning might be interpreted by the child as just another instance of inductive projection and thus be governed by the taxonomic constraint. On this model, a more general constraint is simply applied to the specific case of word learning. The question of the origins of the constraint arise here too but now with respect to the taxonomic principle of generalization in inductive projection. There is surely a biological basis for this kind of generalization in animal and human learning. But this account would not require any specially evolved mechanism for word learning per se. It does require that children construe word learning as another case of inductive projection, however. Another possibility is that enough exposure to language is required to enable the system to trigger the taxonomic assumption. That is, once some words are learned, on the basis of a few examples of generalization that honor the taxonomic principle, it could then function as a general assumption about how words are extended.

Innate Versus Learned Reduced to Age of Onset.   Second, the innate-learned debate sometimes becomes treated as an argument only about age of onset. Although age of onset may serve as a rough guide as to what kind of experience is likely, it hardly resolves this issue. Innate abilities can be late emerging, and learned abilities can be acquired early. No one would seriously question the biological basis of puberty even though it does not occur early in life. Some constraints might appear later than others because some preconditions need to be met before they are relevant, rather than because they need to be learned. Mutual exclusivity might be one such case. Mutual exclusivity may be a simple way to begin to systematize a lexicon. As such, one could imagine a delay in the appearance of mutual exclusivity until enough of a lexicon has been acquired to warrant systematization. On this account, mutual exclusivity would not be expected to be used by babies acquiring their first few words. Such a delay in the onset, however, would not be evidence that mutual exclusivity is learned.

Assumption of Homogeneous Abilities.   A third way that the innate-learned dichotomy is problematic is that it seems to presuppose that a given constraint is a simple homogeneous ability. In contrast to this view, a given constraint might instead recruit components from a variety of sources. The resulting constraint in word learning would then reflect the convergence of several components each with its own developmental history. For example, consider the whole-object and taxonomic assumptions which operate at first in ostensive definition. Someone points to an object and labels it. The child takes the label to refer to the whole object and extends it to other objects of like kind. Ostensive definition has as one component ostension. Someone points to an object and the child's attention is drawn to that object. Ostension itself may be an important component of these constraints. Although it is well-documented that babies can follow the direction of pointing and eye gaze (Churcher & Scaife, 1982; Murphy & Messer, 1977; Scaife & Bruner, 1975), there are as yet no studies of exactly what the baby attends to or infers the adult is attending to. Perhaps the only information contained in pointing per se is information about direction. The baby would then attend to whatever interesting was found in that location—an event, interesting pattern, noise, or even the location itself. Or it could be that something like the whole-object assumption operates in ostension leading babies to search for an object per se as the referent of the point. If so, then to understand the origins of the whole-object assumption in word learning, we would need to understand its development in the context of nonlinguistic ostensive acts. Similarly, ostensive definition involves labeling at the time of pointing and labeling takes the form of some auditory stimulation. We know from studies of intersensory stimulation that babies' attention to what they are looking at is heightened if a moderate noise is heard at the same time (Mendelsohn & Haith, 1976; Paden, 1975; Self, 1975). Maybe some of the power of the whole-object assumption to direct and sustain babies' attention to objects comes from its being an instance of intersensory stimulation (see Baldwin & Markman, 1989). If so, then the origins of intersensory development would be relevant to the question of the origins of the whole-object assumption. Similarly, labeling phrases addressed to babies are carried by distinctive motherese intonation contours (see Fernald in press-a, for a review). At the start of language learning, babies may be interpreting these intonations per se rather than understanding any of the words. According to Fernald, the distinctive pattern that accompanies labeling serves to arouse babies and help sustain their attention. How human babies come to respond to differences in intonation would then be relevant to this question about the origins of the whole-object assumption as well. In sum, questions about the origins of word-learning constraints may require a subtle and complex analysis about their components. To formulate this question as a simple innate-learned dichotomy obscures rather than clarifies the issue.

Ethology of Learning

The oversimplification of the innate-learned dichotomy is further highlighted by investigators such as Rozin (1976), Rozin and Schull (1988), and Shettleworth (1972, 1983, 1984), who argue for an ethology of learning. This view treats learning itself as an adaptation, a product of evolution by natural selection. Learning allows for needed plasticity but also carries costs, such as periods of dependency to provide enough opportunity to learn and vulnerability and incompetence until learning has taken place (Rozin & Schull, 1988). Moreover, learning leaves open many more possibilities for errors than innate solutions: "Just as the vast majority of mutations are disadvantageous, many effects of experience on development would be maladaptive if not for adaptive constraints on plasticity" (Rozin & Schull, 1988, p. 525).

Learning as One of Many Possible Solutions. Ethologists view learning as one possible solution to a biological problem. It will be a successful biological adaptation in some circumstances but not others. One example used to illustrate this (Rozin & Schull, 1988) is to consider how animals come to recognize other members of their species—an ability essential for mating. Imprinting, a learning mechanism that solves this problem for some birds, would not work for cuckoos who deposit their eggs in the nests of other birds and so are reared by other species. Imprinting, or any other learning mechanism that depends on early exposure to one's own species, is impossible under these circumstances. Thus, species recognition in the cuckoo is largely innate.

Foraging provides many examples of the range of solutions available for solving the same biological function in different species. Animals need mechanisms for extracting information from the environment about the location and abundance of food. They need to know where and how to search for food, what and how much to eat. These answers often cannot be hard-wired—the location of food in the environment often changes, the availability of different foods fluctuates, and so forth. Different species have solved these problems using a wide range of mechanisms including simple reflexes where, for example, how much food is in the stomach of a mantid determines how near a fly has to be before the mantid will strike (Shettleworth, 1984), to sensitivity to operant reinforcement schedules, to elaborate communication systems such as the dance of the bees that specify the direction, distance, and kind of food (von Frisch, 1967). Abilities needed to forage range from simple memory or taste of what an animal has just eaten, to long-term memory of where food has been stored, from simple reflexes to strike at fixed perceptual patterns to complex spatial representations of a changing environment (Rozin & Schull, 1988; Shettleworth, 1984). In sum, there are a variety of mechanisms available to solve the same biological function of ensuring adequate nutrition. Learning may have evolved to ensure successful foraging for some animals and not others.

Redundancy of Mechanisms.   Another characteristic of biological solutions to important problems is that there tend to be multiple mechanisms for achieving the same end (Rozin, 1976; Rozin & Schull, 1988; Shettleworth, 1983). Equipping an animal with redundant means of achieving the same outcome offers a greater likelihood of success because any single mechanism has some probability of failing. Several mechanisms can work together to achieve a given end as when motivational, attentional, and learning abilities converge on a given solution. Alternatively, some mechanisms can serve as backup when dominant means fail. The example described earlier of how migratory birds navigate by magnetism only when the position of the sun is unavailable is one such example (Keeton 1974; Shettleworth, 1983).

Questions Raised by an Ethology of Learning.   An analysis of learning from an ethological perspective raises many issues not normally addressed by psychologists. In arguing that learning itself should be examined from an evolutionary perspective, Shettleworth suggested the following issues be considered:

Why learn in a specific case as opposed to relying on other solutions, including that of not making the adjustment at all?

What to learn? For example, when an individual must learn to recognize individual conspecifics or the approach of a predator, what cues does he use? Are they the optimal ones in the sense of being the most reliable predictors in the situation?

When to learn? Does learning begin immediately on first exposure to a situation? Does general learning about the environment occur during periods of "sampling" or play and get put to use when it is needed? . . .

How to learn? Trial and error, imprinting, observation, association: Is a particular process the only one that can solve the problem, or if several might serve the purpose, what determines which one a given species uses? How fast to learn and how long to remember? (Shettleworth, 1984, p. 429)

Ethological Principles Applied to Word Learning

The insights gained from biology can enrich our conceptions of learning without forcing psychologists to fabricate evolutionary models of psychological phenomena. Raising the issues, of "why to learn" or "how to learn" forces us to consider possible alternatives and thereby gain new perspective on psychological problems. The next section presents some examples of these issues applied to word learning.

Why Learn?   Following Shettleworth's suggestion, we should consider why words should be learned at all. Why not have an innately determined vocabulary? For such an evolutionary change to take place, there would have to be extraordinary stability and regularity in the environment in what kinds of things exist and are worth naming. Such things do exist: The sun and the moon, day and night, earth and sky, man, woman, boy, and girl, food and water, walking and running, laughing and crying are universal and certainly stable over long periods even in evolutionary time. Other natural kinds are possibilities although only when specified very generally: Plants, animals, and food are universal but the specific kinds of plants or animals found in a given location vary. So "plant" could be an innately determined word but not "tree" or "cactus." Thus, in principle, there are candidate words that could have been innately determined. Obviously, such a limited vocabulary would be drastically impoverished compared to the vocabulary of natural languages. One of the hallmarks of human languages is the fantastic range, richness, and diversity of the concepts that can be expressed. The vocabulary readily expands to include cultural artifacts and inventions, abstract concepts, and to distinguish between concepts with great subtlety and precision. As innovations occur, or ideas develop, they can be incorporated into the language. Another problem is that if languages were limited to forming propositions only about the absolutely universal concepts, such as sun and moon, walk, run, sleep, and so on, it would be a waste of the enormous expressive power of language. Given such limitations on the notions that could be expressed, there would seem to be little use for the complexity and richness of the grammars that characterize human languages. A number of much more limited signal systems might suffice if the range of concepts to be expressed were so limited. Further, to allow languages to contain even such basic words as "apple," "tiger," "cup," or "arrow" requires that words must be learned. If the majority of the vocabulary, or even some of it is learned then a learning mechanism must be available. A mixed system might be possible with some words innately determined and others learned. But if an effective learning mechanism existed, it would likely obviate a need to have any vocabulary innately specified. (See Pinker & Bloom, in press, for other ideas about why sound-meaning correspondences should be learned.)

How to Learn.   A second question one might speculate about is how to learn. Why would one kind of learning mechanism be preferred or more effective or selected over another? It is important to address this issue without falling into the trap of reasoning from how languages are as to how they must be. Facile ad hoc evolutionary speculations are easy to generate (see Fernald, in press-b; Rozin & Schull, 1988, for interesting discussions of this problem). Given what we know about language, we could speculate about how it could be learned, which is very different from arguing from basic principles about why one mechanism would be selected over another. The vocabulary of natural languages as we know them has two fundamental requirements that present conflicting goals: First, as mentioned earlier, one of the most distinctive characteristics of human language is the enormous range of ideas and concepts that can be expressed as well as the potential to expand to express as yet undiscovered or uninvented objects, events, and ideas. So, one goal of a learning mechanism would be to enable humans to acquire this variety of words. On the other hand, there is the problem that if the hypothesis space for what a given word might mean were unconstrained, word learning would not be possible—especially for 18-month-olds. There is tension then between the need for openness and flexibility in learning words and the need to solve the inductive problem. Certainly there are many ways, in principle, of resolving this tension. In other words, these goals do not dictate a single evolutionary solution. Treating constraints on word learning as default assumptions is one possible solution and fits with the existing evidence. Default assumptions provide some balance between constraining the hypotheses to simplify the task, especially at first, but still allowing flexibility.

Begin With What is Fundamental.   Another principle that might prove useful in considering which word-learning biases might be most useful, would be to build in a bias to begin with what is likely to be most fundamental. Objects are likely candidates for a variety of reasons. As I have already argued, because objects are so salient and basic to human perception and cognition, they are fundamental to any vocabulary and provide anchor points from which to elaborate the lexicon. Once object labels are known they along with mutual exclusivity provide a focus from which to expand to terms that refer to parts, substance, color, and so on. Another related point is that objects may be presupposed in many ways by other concepts. This can be seen in analyses of grammatical structure which incorporate a predicate-argument structure (Maratsos, 1991). Predicates contain terms that refer to properties and relations, whereas arguments consist of the things to which the properties and relations apply. Thus, predicates presuppose arguments: Properties and actions are most naturally conceived as properties or actions of something. One can think of a man without thinking of running but it is hard to think of running without a runner. On Maratsos' (1991) argument, "concrete object terms are natural argument head terms. Argument head terms are in turn a universal form class because they contain the concrete object terms, which give the class much of its resultant unity and distinctiveness." If learning mechanisms are established to begin with what is most fundamental, objects would make natural candidates as good first guesses about what words mean.

Redundancy of Mechanisms.   Some of the controversy surrounding the arguments and evidence for word-learning constraints involve claims either that such constraints are unnecessary because the input to the child could accomplish the same ends (Nelson, 1988) or that the constraints are better conceptualized as pragmatic (Clark, 1990; Gathercole, 1987) or social (Nelson 1988) than as lexical. For example, Gathercole (1987) has argued that the mutual exclusivity assumption falls out of pragmatic rather than lexical principles. On this view, children reject second labels for things based on assumptions about what speakers intend rather than because of a bias against second labels. A child who views a whisk and a ball as an adult says "Please hand me the whisk" would reason "If he meant the ball, he would have said 'ball', so he must mean the other thing." This would explain why children infer that a novel label refers to a novel rather than a familiar object. However, several investigators report children who deny that, for example, a poodle is a poodle insisting that it is a "dog," even when adults repeatedly clarify their communicative intent, stating, for example, "Yes it is a poodle." In such cases, the adults make their intent to refer quite plain but children nevertheless persist in rejecting the label. So a pragmatic constraint is not sufficient to account for the mutual exclusivity bias.

In concluding that there is a lexical constraint, however, I do not mean to preclude the possibility of a pragmatic constraint as well. Although I have argued that input or pragmatics is not sufficient to account for the evidence and that constraints on word meaning are needed, this is not to say that other sources of information are irrelevant or unnecessary. Pragmatic and lexical constraints should often converge on the same hypothesis providing redundant sources of information about the meaning of a term. First, the argument for word-learning constraints is an argument for how words are learned—not how they are hard-wired. Input is essential. Second, the lesson from the ecology of learning is that multiple mechanisms are to be expected for solving important problems. In the example just provided about mapping novel labels to novel objects there are at least three sources of information a child could use to arrive at the same conclusion: The mutual exclusivity assumption leads children to reject a second label for the familiar object; a bias to fill lexical gaps leads children to prefer a label for an object without a known label; and a pragmatic assumption leads children to infer that if the speaker had intended to refer to the familiar object he or she would have used the familiar label. A fourth converging source of information would be found in more naturalistic situations where the speaker's eye gaze or other ostensive cues indicate the appropriate referent.

In word learning, not only would we expect to find multiple mechanisms but also some degree of coordination among them. Children as listeners would be unlikely to depend heavily on input that speakers fail to provide. Learnability theorists emphasize one aspect of this problem in considering the problem of negative evidence in acquiring syntax. The claim is not that children are never corrected for ungrammatical sentences. The negative evidence argument is that a learning mechanism that relied heavily on feedback about ungrammatical sentences would fail to acquire grammar because such feedback is sporadic, undependable, and in some cases nonexistent.

When considering evolution of learning mechanisms for problems that involve social coordination or communication, there must be some degree of correspondence between the partners of the interaction. This is obvious in courtship displays: The ostentatious display of the peacock would not do much good if the hen wasn't impressed. Bird-song learning provides an example of the importance of coordinating the timing of receptivity to information with the timing of input (Shettleworth, 1984). The adult birds must be singing at the time the young bird is sensitive to the song. To take an example from human communication, consider how mothers use vocalizations to soothe a distressed infant. Fernald (in press-b) reviewed evidence documenting three types of acoustic signals that reduce crying: Low rather than high frequency sounds, continuous rather than intermittent signals, and white noise. Vocalizations mothers use to comfort an infant are typically continuous, low in pitch, and even provide white noise with "shhhh." Coordination is expected, then, between caregivers and offspring, between males and females in courtship rituals, between adults as providers of information and children as recipients of the information. Fernald (in press-b) presented a very thoughtful analysis of this problem in considering an evolutionary perspective in human maternal vocalizations, documenting the parallels between adult speech to human infants and what is known about the evolution of vocal communication systems in other species.

In the case of word learning, some degree of coordination between parental input to children and word-learning biases would be expected. Finding, for example, that parents tend to label objects for children does not in itself weaken the claim that children are predisposed to consider objects as the referents of novel labels. Such coordination between learning mechanisms and input is likely. Redundancy poses an experimental problem, however, in that alternative explanations for the same phenomena become possible. Experimental rigor requires that to document a given word-learning bias guides children's hypotheses one must rule out alternative explanations (including input) as possible contributing factors in a given experiment. But this should not be confused with a claim that in naturally occurring word learning these factors are irrelevant or should systematically conflict with the postulated word-learning assumptions. On the contrary, redundancy and coordination of word-learning biases and other sources of information should be common. Acquiring vocabulary is essential for language learning and any abilities children have to infer the communicative intent of the speaker, to retain information about past uses of words, to analyze the social situation in which a word is used will be exploited along with word-learning constraints to solve this problem.

ACKNOWLEDGMENTS

I thank Mark Lepper, Michael Maratsos, and Robert Siegler for their discussions of some of these issues and John Flavell, Paul Rozin, and Amanda Woodward for their helpful comments on this manuscript. This work was supported in part by NIH grant HD 20382 and by NFS grant BNS-9109236.

REFERENCES

Au, T. K., & Glusman, M. (1990). The principle of mutual exclusivity in word learning: To honor or not to honor? *Child Development, 61,* 1474–1490.

Backscheider, A., & Markman, E. M. (1990). *Young children's use of the taxonomic assumption to constrain word meanings.* Unpublished manuscript, Stanford University, Stanford, CA.

Baldwin, D. A. (1989a). *Infants' contribution to the achievement of joint reference.* Unpublished doctoral dissertation, Stanford University, Stanford, CA.

Baldwin, D. A. (1989b). Priorities in children's expectations about object label reference: Form over color. *Child Development, 60,* 1291–1306.

Baldwin, D. A., & Markman, E. M. (1989). Mapping out word-object relations: A first step. *Child Development, 60,* 381–398.

Banigan, R. L., & Mervis, C. B. (1988). Role of adult input in young children's category evolution: II an experimental study. *Child Language, 15,* 493–505.

Barrett, M. (1978). Lexical development and overextension in child language. *Journal of Child Language, 5,* 205–219.

Bloom, L., Lifter, K., & Broughton, J. (1985). The convergence of early cognition and language in the second year of life: Problems in conceptualization and measurement. In M. Barrett (Ed.), *Children's single-word speech* (pp. 149–180). New York: Wiley.

Bolinger, D. (1967). Adjectives in English: Attribution and predication. *Lingua, 18,* 1–34.

Bolinger, D. (1977). *Meaning and form.* London: Longman.

Bowerman, M. (1987). Commentary: Mechanisms of language acquisition. In B. MacWhinney (Ed.), *Mechanisms of language acquisition* (pp. 443–466). Hillsdale, NJ: Lawrence Erlbaum Associates.

Brown, A. L. (1990). Domain-specific principles affect learning and transfer in children. *Cognitive Science, 14,* 107–134.

Brown, R., & Hanlon C. (1970). Derivational complexity and order of acquisition in child speech. In J. R. Hayes (Ed.), *Cognition and the development of language* (pp. 11–53). New York: Wiley.

Carey, S. (1978). The child as word learner. In M. Halle, J. Bresnan, & A. Miller (Eds.), *Linguistic theory and psychological reality* (pp. 264–293). Cambridge, MA: MIT Press.

Carey, S. (1985). *Conceptual change in childhood.* Cambridge, MA: Bradford Books.

Churcher, J., & Scaife, M. (1982). How infants see the point. In G. Butterworth & P. Light (Eds.), *Social cognition.* Chicago: University of Chicago Press.

Clark, E. V. (1983). Meanings and concepts. In P. H. Mussen (Series Ed.) & J. H. Flavell & E. M. Markman (Vol. Eds.), *Handbook of child psychology: (Vol. 3). Cognitive development* (pp. 787–840). New York: Wiley

Clark, E. V. (1987). The principle of contrast: A constraint on language acquisition. In B. MacWhinney (Ed.), *The 20th Annual Carnegie Symposium on Cognition* (pp. 1–33). Hillsdale, NJ: Lawrence Erlbaum Associates.

Clark, E. V. (1990). On the pragmatics of contrast. *Journal of Child Language, 17,* 417–431.

Corrigan, R. (1983). The development of representational skills. In K. W. Fischer (Ed.), *Levels and transitions in children's development* (pp. 51–64). San Francisco: Jossey-Bass.

Dockrell, J., & Campbell, R. (1986). Lexical acquisition strategies in the preschool child. In S. Kuczaj & M. Barrett (Eds.). *The development of word meaning* (pp. 121–154). Berlin: Springer-Verlag.

Dromi, E. (1987). *Early lexical development.* New York: Cambridge University Press.

Fernald, A. (in press-a). Human maternal vocalizations to infants as biologically relevant signals: An evolutionary perspective. In J. H. Barkow, & L. Cosmides, & E. J. Tooby (Eds.), *The adapted mind: Evolutionary psychology and the generation of culture.* Oxford: Oxford University Press.

Fernald, A. (in press-b). Prosody in speech to children: Prelinguistic and linguistic functions. In R. Vasta (Ed.), *Annals of child development* (Vol. 8). London: Jessica Kingsley Publishers.

Flavell, J. H. (1988). The development of children's knowledge about the mind: From cognitive connections to mental representations. In J. W. Astington, P. L. Harris, & D. R. Olson (Eds.), *Developing theories of mind* (pp. 244–267). New York· Cambridge University Press.

Gallistel, C. R. (1990). *The organization of learning.* Cambridge, MA: MIT Press.

Gathercole, V. C. (1987). The contrastive hypothesis for the acquisition of word meaning: A reconsideration of the theory. *Journal of Child Language, 14,* 493–531.

Gathercole, V. C. (1989). Contrast: A semantic constraint? *Journal of Child Language, 16,* 685–702.

Gelman, R. (1990-a). First principles organize attention to and learning about relevant data: Number and the animate-inanimate distinction as examples. *Cognitive Science, 14,* 79–106.

Gelman, R. (1990-b). Structural constraints on cognitive development: Introduction to a special issue of *Cognitive Science. Cognitive Science 14,* 3–10.

Gelman, R., & Baillargeon, R. (1983). A review of some Piagetian concepts. In P. H. Mussen (Series Ed.) & J. H. Flavell & E. M. Markman (Vol. Eds.), *Handbook of child psychology: Vol. 3. Cognitive development* (pp. 167–230). New York: Wiley.

Gelman, S. A. (1988). The development of induction within natural kind and artifact categories. *Cognitive Psychology, 20,* 65–95.

Gelman, S. A., & Markman, E. M. (1986). Categories and induction in young children. *Cognition, 23,* 183–208.

Gentner, D. (1981). Some interesting differences between nouns and verbs. *Cognition and Brain Theory, 4,* 161–178.

Gentner, D. (1982). Why nouns are learned before verbs: Linguistic relativity versus natural portioning. In S. A. Kuczaj II (Ed.), *Language development: Syntax and semantics* (pp. 301–334). Hillsdale, NJ: Lawrence Erlbaum Associates.

Gentner, D., & Rattermann, M. J., (1991). Language and the career of similarity. In S. A. Gelman & J. P. Byrnes (Eds.), *Perspectives on language and thought: Interrelations in development* (pp. 225–277). Cambridge, MA: Cambridge University Press.

Gleitman, L. R. (1981). Maturational determinants of language growth. *Cognition, 10,* 103–114.

Goldfield, B.A., & Resnick, J. S. (1990). Early lexical acquisition: Rate, content, and the vocabulary spurt. *Journal of Child Language, 17,* 115–130.

Golinkoff, R. M., Hirsh-Pasek, K., Bailey, L. M., & Wenger, N. R. (in press). Young children and adults use lexical principles to learn new nouns. *Developmental Psychology.*

Goodman, N. (1955). *Fact, fiction, and forecast.* Cambridge, MA: Harvard University Press.

Gould, J. L. (1984). Natural history of honey bee learning. In P. Marler & H. S. Terrace (Eds.), *The biology of learning* (pp. 149–180). Berlin: Springer-Verlag.

Gould, J. L., & Marler, P. (1984). Ethology and the natural history of learning. In P. Marler & H. S. Terrace (Eds.), *The biology of learning* (pp. 47–74). Berlin: Springer-Verlag.

Greenberg, J. H. (1966). Some universals of grammar with particular reference to the order of meaningful elements. In J. H. Greenberg (Ed.), *Universals of language* (2nd ed., pp. 73–113). Cambridge MA: MIT Press.

Halliday, M. A. K. (1975). Learning how to mean. In E. H. Lenneberg & E. Lenneberg (Eds.), *Foundations of language development: A multidisciplinary approach* (Vol. I; pp. 239–265). New York: Academic Press.

Hutchinson, J. E. (1984). *Constraints on children's implicit hypotheses about word meanings.* Unpublished doctoral dissertation, Stanford University, Stanford, CA.

Hutchinson J. E. (1986, April). *Children's sensitivity to the contrastive use of object category terms.* Paper presented at Stanford 1986 Child Language Research Forum, Stanford University, Stanford, CA.

Huttenlocher, J., & Smiley, P. (1987). Early word meanings: The case for object names. *Cognitive Psychology, 19,* 63–89.

Immelmann, K. (1972). Sexual and other long-term aspects of imprinting in birds and other species. In D. Lehrman, R. Hinde, & E. Shaw (Eds.), *Advances in the study of behavior* (Vol. 4, pp. 147–174). New York: Academic Press.

Kanouse, D. E. (1971). Language, labeling, and attribution. In E. E. Jones, D. E. Kanouse, H. H. Kelley, R. E. Nisbett, E. S. Valins, & B. Weiner (Eds.), *Attribution: Perceiving the causes of behavior* (pp. 121–135). Morristown, NJ: General Learning Press.

Karmiloff-Smith, A. (1979). *Language as a formal problem–space for children.* Paper presented at the MPG/NIAS Conference on "Beyond description in child language."

Karmiloff-Smith, A., & Inhelder, B. (1975). If you want to get ahead, get a theory. *Cognition, 3,* 195–211.

Kassin, S. M., & Lepper, M. R. (1984). Oversufficient and insufficient justification effects: Cognitive and behavioral development. In J. Nicholls (Ed.), *Advances in motivation and achievement* (Vol. 3, pp. 73–106). Greenwich, CT: JAI.

Katz, J. J. (1964). Semantic theory and the meaning of good. *Journal of Philosophy, 61,* 739–766.

Keeton, W. T. (1974). The orientational and navigational basis of homing in birds. In D. Lehrman, J. Rosenblatt, R. Hinde, & E. Shaw (Eds.), *Advances in the study of behavior* (pp. 47–132). New York: Academic Press.

Kehoe, E. J. (1987). "Selective association" in compound stimulus conditioning with the rabbit. In I. Gormezano, W. F. Prokasy, & R. F. Thompson (Eds.), *Classical conditioning* (3rd ed., pp. 161–196). Hillsdale, NJ: Lawrence Erlbaum Associates.

Keil, F. C. (1979). *Semantic and conceptual development: An ontological perspective.* Cambridge, MA: Harvard University Press.

Keil, F. C. (1981). Constraints on knowledge and cognitive development. *Psychological Review, 88,* 197–227.

Keil, F. C. (1990). Constraints on constraints: Surveying the epigenetic landscape. *Cognitive Science, 14,* 135–168.

Kellman, P. J., & Spelke, E. S. (1983). Perception of partly occluded objects in infancy. *Cognitive Psychology, 15,* 586–593.

Kelly, H. H. (1973). The process of causal attribution. *American Psychologist, 28,* 107–128.

Kemler, D. (1983). Holistic and analytic modes in perceptual and cogitive development. In T. Tighe & B.E. Shepp (Eds.), *Perception, cognition, and development: Interactional analyses* (pp. 77–102). Hillsdale, NJ: Lawrence Erlbaum Associates.

Kemler-Nelson D. (1984). The effect of intention on what concepts are acquired. *Journal of Verbal Learning and Verbal Behavior, 23,* 734–759.

Landau, K. B., Smith, L. B., & Jones, S. S. (1988). The importance of shape in early lexical learning. *Cognitive Development, 3,* 299–321.

Lepper, M. R., Greene, D., & Nisbett, R. E. (1973). Undermining children's intrinsic interest with extrinsic rewards: A test of the "overjustification" hypothesis. *Journal of Personality and Social Psychology, 50,* 1207–1210.

Lepper, M. R., Sagotsky, G., Dafoe, J. L., & Greene, D. (1982). Consequences of superfluous social constraints: Effects on young children's social inferences and subsequent intrinsic interest. *Journal of Personality and Social Psychology, 42,* 51–65.

Liittschwager, J. C., & Markman, E. M. (1991, April). *Mutual exclusivity as a default assumption in second label learning.* Paper presented at the biennial meetings of the Society for Research in Child Development, Seattle, WA.

Macintosh, N. J. (1975). A theory of attention. *Psychological Review, 82,* 276–298.

Macnamara, J. (1982). *Names for things: A study of human learning.* Cambridge, MA: MIT Press.

MacWhinney, B. (1989). Making words make sense: Commentary on Merriman and Bowman. *Monographs of the Society for Research in Child Development, 54* (Serial No. 220, pp. 124–129).

Maratsos, M. (1991). How the acquisition of nouns may be different from that of verbs. In A. Krasnegor, D. M. Rumbaugh, R. L. Schiefelbusch, & M. Studdert-Kennedy (Eds.), *Biological and behavioral determinants of language development,* (pp. 67–88). Hillsdale, NJ: Lawrence Erlbaum Associates.

Markman, E. M. (1987). How children constrain the possible meanings of words. In U. Neisser (Ed.), *Concepts and conceptual development: Ecological and intellectual factors in categorization* (pp. 255–287). New York: Cambridge University Press.

Markman, E. M. (1989). *Categorization and naming in children: Problems of induction.* Cambridge, MA: MIT Press, Bradford Books.

Markman, E. M. (1990). Constraints children place on word meanings. *Cognitive Science, 14,* 57–78.

Markman, E. M. (1991). The whole object, taxonomic, and mutual exclusivity assumptions as initial constraints on word meanings. In J. P. Byrnes & S. A. Gelman (Eds.), *Perspectives on language and cognition: Interrelations in development* (pp. 72–106). Cambridge: Cambridge University Press.

Markman, E. M., & Callahan, M. A. (1983). An analysis of hierarchical classification. In R. Sternberg (Ed.), *Advances in the psychology of human intelligence* (Vol. 2, pp. 325–365). Hillsdale, NJ: Lawrence Erlbaum Associates.

Markman, E. M., & Hutchinson, J. E. (1984). Children's sensitivity to constraints on word meaning: Taxonomic versus thematic relations. *Cognitive Psychology, 16,* 1–27.

Markman, E. M., & Wachtel, G. F. (1988). Children's use of mutual exclusivity to constrain the meanings of words. *Cognitive Psychology, 20,* 121–157.

Markman, E. M., & Wasow, J. (in prep.). *Very young children's use of the mutual exclusivity principle to guide their interpretation of words.* Stanford University, Stanford, CA.

Marler, P., & Terrace, H. S. (Eds.). (1984). *The biology of learning.* Berlin: Springer-Verlag.

Matthews, G. (1953). Navigation in the Manx Shearwater. *Journal of Experimental Biology, 30,* 370–396.

McShane, J. (1979). The development of naming. *Linguistics, 17,* 879–905.

Mendelsohn, M. J., & Haith, M. M. (1976). The relation between audition and vision in the human newborn. *Monographs of the Society for Research in Child Development, 41*(4).

Merriman, W. E. (1987). *Lexical contrast in toddlers: A reanalysis of the diary evidence.* Presentation at the Biennial Meetings of the Society for Research in Child Development, Baltimore, MD.

Merriman, W. E., & Bowman, L. L. (1989). The mutual exclusivity bias in children's word learning. *Monographs of the Society for Research in Child Development, 54* (3–4, Serial No. 220).

Mervis, C. B. (1987). Child-basic object categories and early lexical development. In U. Neisser (Ed.,), *Concepts and conceptual development: Ecological and intellectual factors in categorization* (pp. 201–233). Cambridge: Cambridge University Press.

Mervis C. B. (1989). *Early lexical development: The role of operating principles.* Unpublished manuscript. Emory University, Atlanta, GA.

Murphy, C. M., & Messer, P. Mothers, infants and pointing: A study of a gesture. In H. Schaffer (Ed.), *Studies on mother-infant interaction.* London: Academic Press.

Nelson, K. (1973). Structure and strategy in learning to talk. *Monographs of the Society for Research in Child Development, 38* (1–2, Serial No. 149).

Nelson, K. (1974). Concept, word and sentence: Interrelations in acquisition and development. *Psychological Review, 81,* 267–285.

Nelson, K. (1988). Constraints on word learning? *Cognitive Development, 3,* 221–246.

Newport, E. L. (1984). Constraints on learning: Studies in the acquistion of American sign language. *Papers and Reports on Child Language Development, 23,* 1–22.

Newport, E. L. (in press). Maturational constraints on language learning. *Cognitive Science.*

Paden, L. (1975). The effects of variations of auditory stimulation (music) and interspersed stimulus procedures on visual attending behavior in infants. *Monographs of the Society for Research in Child Development, 39* (158), 29–41.

Pinker, S. (1984). *Language learnability and language development.* Cambridge, MA: Harvard University Press.

Pinker, S., & Bloom, B. (in press). Natural language and natural selection. *Brain and Behavioral Sciences.*

Premack, D. (1990). Words: What are they, and do animals have them? *Cognition, 37,* 197–212.

Quine, W. V. O. (1960). *Word and object.* Cambridge, MA: MIT Press.

Rozin, P. (1976). The evolution of intelligence and access to the cognitive unconscious. In J. A. Sprague & A. N. Epstein (Eds.), *Progress in psychobiology and physiological psychology,* (Vol. 6, pp. 245–280). New York: Academic Press.

Rozin, P., & Schull, J. (1988). The adaptive-evolutionary point of view in experimental psychology. In R. C. Atkinson, R. J. Herrnstein, G. Lindsey, & R. D. Luce (Eds.), *Perception and motivation* (Vol. 1, 2nd ed., pp. 503–546). New York: Wiley.

Scaife, M., & Bruner, J. (1975). The capacity for joint visual attention in the infant. *Nature, 253,* 265–266.

Self, P. A. (1975). Control of infants' visual attending by auditory and interspersed stimulation. *Monographs of the Society for Research in Child Development, 39* (158), 16–28.

Shettleworth, S. J. (1972). Constraints on learning. In D. Lehrman, R. Hinde, & E. Shaw (Eds.), *Advances in the study of behavior* (pp. 1-68). New York: Academic Press.

Shettleworth, S. J. (1983). Function and mechanism in learning. In M. D. Zeiler & P. Harzem (Eds.), *Advances in analysis of behaviour,* (Vol. 3, pp. 1–39). New York: Wiley.

Shettleworth, S. J. (1984). Natural history and evolution of learning in nonhuman mammals. In P. Marler & H. S. Terrace (Eds.), *The biology of learning,* (pp. 419–433). New York: Springer-Verlag.

Slobin, D. I. (1973). Cognitive prerequisites for the development of grammar. In C. A. Ferguson & D. I. Slobin (Eds.), *Studies of child language development,* (pp. 45–54). New York: Springer.

Slobin, D. I. (1977). Language change in childhood and in history. In J. Macnamara (Ed.), *Language learning and thought,* (pp. 185–214). New York: Academic Press.

Smith, C. L. (1979). Children's understanding of natural language hierarchies. *Journal of Experimental Child Psychology, 27,* 437–458.

Snyder, L. S., Bates, E., & Bretherton, I. (1981). Content and context in early lexical development. *Journal of Child Language, 8,* 565–582.

Soja, N. N., Carey, S., & Spelke, E. S. (1991). Ontological categories guide young children's inductions of word meaning: Object terms and substance terms. *Cognition, 38,* 179–211.

Spelke, E. S. (1988). Where perceiving ends and thinking begins: The apprehension of objects in infancy. In A. Yonas (Ed.), *Perceptual development in infancy. Minnesota Symposium on Child Psychology,* (pp. 197–234). Hillsdale, NJ: Lawrence Erlbaum Associates.

Spelke, E. S. (1990). Principles of object perception. *Cognitive Science, 14,* 29–56.

Taylor, M., & Gelman, S.A. (1989). Incorporating new words into the lexicon: Preliminary evidence for language hierarchies in two-year-old children. *Child Development, 59,* 411–419.

Tomasello, M., & Farrar, M. J. (1986). Object permanence and relational words: A lexical training study. *Journal of Child Language, 13,* 495–505.

Tomasello, M., Mannle, S., & Werdenschlag, L. (1988). The effect of previously learned words on the child's acquisition of words for similar referents. *Journal of Child Language, 15,* 505–515.

von Frisch, K. (1967). *The dance language and orientation of bees.* Cambridge, MA: Harvard University Press.

Waxman, S. R. (1990). Linguistic biases and the establishment of conceptual hierarchies: Evidence from preschool children. *Cognitive Development, 5,* 123–150.

Waxman, S.R. (1991). Convergences between semantic and conceptual organization in the preschool years. In J. P. Byrnes & S. A. Gelman (Eds.), *Perspectives on language and thought: Interrelations in development,* (pp.107–145). Cambridge: Cambridge University Press.

Waxman, S. R., & Gelman, R. (1986). Preschooler's use of superordinate relations in classification. *Cognitive Development, 1,* 139–156.

Waxman, S. R., & Kosowski, T. D. (1990). Nouns mark category relations: Toddlers' and preschoolers' word-learning biases. *Child Developement, 61,* 1461–1473.

Waxman, S. R., & Senghas, A. (1990, April). *Relations among word meanings in early lexical development.* Paper presented at the International Conference for Infancy Studies, Montreal, Canada.

Wexler, K., & Culicover, P. (1980). *Formal principles of language acquisition.* Cambridge, MA: MIT Press.

Woodward, A. L., & Markman, E. M. (1991). Constraints on learning as default assumptions: Comments on Merriman and Bowman's "The mutual exclusivity bias in children's word learning." *Developmental Review, 14,* 57–77.

4 The Origins of an Autonomous Biology

Frank C. Keil
Cornell University

In the heat of battle, nativists sometimes forget that your everyday empiricist would be perfectly happy with some modules and constraints on learning that are specific to certain kinds of inputs and that are innately predetermined. After all, no one doubts that the sense organs such as the eye and the ear have unique specializations for the kinds of inputs they receive nor that their structural properties exert constraints that bias how input information is initially picked up and how it is ultimately interpreted. Of course the remarkable demonstrations of perception across modules and the difficulties of decomposing perception into discrete stages of the sort so near and dear to traditional information-processing theories temper these observations somewhat, but they cannot do away with them altogether.

Much of the emerging interest in modules and constraints, and certainly most of the controversy, revolves not around their existence in any instance, and not only about domain specificity, but also about just how cognitive and belief-laden these constraints might be. Our everyday empiricist would not be nearly so complacent, for example, with claims that there is an innately predetermined module for constructing beliefs about the mechanics of physical objects or about the dynamics of a belief-desire psychology. He or she would want to keep any constraints and module-like notions as close to the periphery as possible. This peripheral/central issue may be why many empiricists and neo-empiricists found Fodor's (1983) book *The Modularity of Mind* to be much tamer than they feared. His proposed modules were quasi-perceptual in nature and not at all embodiments of the most belief-laden aspects of cognition.

Given Fodor's other claims that all concepts and the language of thought are innate (Fodor, 1975, 1981), these sorts of quasi-perceptual modules were relatively mild offenses. Of course, some were still horrified and attempted to show that even these modules were merely products of even more basic domain-general principles of automatization that yield Fodor-like modules through repeated experience. The point here, however, is to illustrate that a key aspect of this debate focuses on the level of cognitive "abstraction" of modules and constraints, how far "up-stream" they are from the sensory.

In this chapter I explore the feasibility of constraints and modularized knowledge acquisition devices (KADs) at the "highest" and most central levels of cognition; and I use the case of biological thought, for it is here that the most dramatic differences of opinion are still openly held.

Biological phenomena are among the most pervasive aspects of our daily lives. The ubiquity of biological forms and processes and the universality of principles governing them dominate the opening chapters of almost all introductory biology texts, chapters that are full of concrete examples in the world all around us. Although scientific biology certainly involves abstraction, much of it is also grounded in our phenomenal world (see Atran, 1990, for a full account of such a grounding and how scientific biology perches on top of the folk modes of construal). Yet, surprisingly, the predominant accounts of how we come to view and understand these phenomena suggest that we do not appreciate the domain as such until quite late in the course of cognitive development. Younger children are said not to appreciate biology for two interrelated reasons: First, because they simply have false beliefs about biological properties and the principles that govern them; and second because they fail to recognize the phenomena that make up an adult biology as forming a coherent domain. There are important reasons why these two reasons are interwoven and Carey (1985, 1989) has given us among the most forceful accounts of why emerging theoretical beliefs can radically redefine both the perceived domains of inquiry and the perceived relevance, or even existence, of properties and relations.

There are three main classes of views as to the sorts of constraints and KADs involved in the acquisition of biological knowledge. One class of views holds that biological thought emerges *de novo* from general associative or inductive mechanisms, views that have been held in several disciplines for some time (see e.g., Atran's, 1990, discussion of the anthropologist Gilmour and others). Patterns of explanation and discovery that eventually become associated with biology are said to have their origins in completely unbiased mechanisms of learning (or at least learning subject only to domain-general biases). In such accounts, early thought is structurally indistinguishable across domains, and by some accounts remains so for all but sophisticated scientists.

A different set of views holds that biological thought does not spring out of a net of associations or some other combination of unprincipled tabulations of and inductions over environmental regularities; instead it springs out of a wholly different mode of construal, a mode that nicely governs its own domain but wrongly engulfs biology as well until biology is able to emerge free and clear. Carey (1985), has presented this point of view most clearly and has shown how many of children's beliefs concerning biological kinds may be understandable on the assumption that, early on, they try to explain and predict the properties of such kinds in terms of the principles of a naive psychology. This account predicts two things early on: Gross misconstruals and distortions of biological things to make them fit the psychological, and an inability to make important distinctions between biological phenomena and psychological ones. A child understands eating only in terms of the beliefs and desires related to eating, not in terms of its physiological/nutritional role; similarly, the property of "has babies" is only understood in terms of the social roles in parenting not the reproductive sense. Carey has argued for this view by showing how, in some tasks, kindergartners and preschoolers say that animals eat to the extent that they are sufficiently psychologically similar to the prototypical intentional being, humans. Apparently, in these preschoolers' minds dogs eat and have babies, but worms do not. Carey (1988) quoted one child who said "worms don't have babies, they just have little worms," to illustrate how they construe having babies solely in psychological terms.

The final set of views holds that biological phenomena may be construed differently from the start, because in one way or another, we are predisposed to think about such phenomena in different ways from other things, even if they are superficially similar. We may be endowed with modes of construal that enable us to have extra insights into the nature of biological kinds and processes, and although they may become greatly elaborated and differentiated, certain core aspects of these modes of construal may remain invariant throughout the course of development. We may have specific cognitive affinities with recurrent regularities in the biological world. With respect to biology, this third view does not have much of a history in cognitive development; but there are increasing signs that it deserves a closer look. In addition, there remains the question of whether an early resonance between some mode(s) of construal and the biological world represents a domain-specific organization of knowledge specific to biology (hence one sense of an innate biology) or more general modes of construal that happen to fit nicely with biology but also fit with other phenomena.

DISTINGUISHING THE BIOLOGICAL WORLD

A useful prelude to experimental explorations examines whether there are reasonable grounds for biological phenomena to embody a distinct set of relations. Are some things especially true of the biological world? Some distinctions are clearly only known to sophisticated scientists but many others may be universal concepts among lay adults. I focus here on those that could be known to laypeople because they are most relevant to questions concerning how intuitive biology might emerge. None of the following seven distinctions are absolutes strictly true of all biological things and untrue of all else; instead they hold either more frequently or more strongly for biological things, or both:

1. Biological things reproduce, preserving the important properties of their kind both at the level of the species and the individual. Linked to reproduction are notions concerning inheritance of properties, both of what sorts of properties are inherited and how inheritance works.
2. Biological kinds have complex, heterogeneous internal structures. Except for broad axes of symmetry, if you chop them up into pieces, the pieces tend to be different from each other as well as not being simply smaller versions of the original. Gold and water clearly do not behave that way. Moreover, these heterogeneous units are often arranged in functional hierarchies.
3. Biological kinds grow and undergo canonical and usual irreversible patterns of change, patterns that strongly individuate biological kinds. Crystals may grow as well, but the change does not usually go through a distinctive patterned sequence (it is usually the same thing over and over again); nor are crystal changes so irreversible and unidirectional. Most artifacts do not grow in any normal sense of the word that sees growth as an endogenously governed process, although they can have characteristic patterns of deterioration, as in the particular way a specific brand of computer or car ages and/or fails. These patterns of growth are more kind specific than those general geometric and architectural principles proposed in D'Arcy Thompson's (1961) classic studies on growth and form, which generalized to both the living and nonliving world. Finally, the patterns of change move toward an ideal state for that kind, a state that is not usually the endstate (as elderly members of species illustrate).
4. Something intrinsic to biological kinds produces most of their phenomenal properties, not usually either external natural forces or human intentional ones. This is related to growth and endogenously

governed canonical patterns of change.

5. Typical phenomenal properties are usually diagnostic of underlying nonphenomenal ones. We assume not only a kind of essence, but also a rich set of causal links between that essence and the merely phenomenal, at the same time recognizing the potential of the phenomenal to mislead (fish-like mammals, lizard-like snakes, and so on).

6. Properties have purposes for biological kinds. There is a compelling, albeit sometimes mistaken (see Gould & Lewontin, 1978), sense that the properties of biological kinds are there for reasons, that they solve design problems for the kinds that possess them. This sense of teleological justification is much weaker for such nonbiological natural kinds such as gold, water, and icicles. Properties of artifacts also have purposes of course, but perhaps more subtle contrasts are relevant (such as that for artifacts, the purposes are usually seen as based on the goals of an external agent rather than for the artifact itself).

7. Biological kinds regulate resources so as to maintain various patterns of homeostasis. If Canon's (1912) book *The Wisdom of the Body* was as revolutionary as some claim, a full awareness of homeostatic mechanisms was not known to most laypeople or even most biologists prior to the early part of this century (the idea was first advanced by Bernard in 1856); but, in the simpler sense of knowing that parts work together to support each other, such a knowledge might have a much longer history across many cultures.

These seven distinctions are clearly not independent of each other and can be collapsed and expanded in ways such that, here at least, there is nothing magic about the seven (more on possible collapses later). For now, however, they illustrate not only the feasibility of having a different set of beliefs and different patterns of explanation for biological kinds, but also the likelihood that there are real-world contrasts for these belief systems to embrace.

Some especially salient distinctions are true of some, but not all, biological kinds and are not included in this list because of their narrower range of application. Most notable are the properties of being sentient and capable of self-produced motion, attributes that are easily observed in most animals and in no plants. These attributes may in fact be so salient to the young child that they could work against an early understanding of the category of living things by so highlighting the animal/other distinction. This possibility and its relations to behavioral modes of construal are discussed in later sections of this chapter.

Distinctiveness of beliefs about living kinds in adults, however, does not offer clear choices between the alternatives of how they become organized in development. One needs to directly explore how children construe biological kinds and processes and ask how those construals change with development. We start by evaluating the notion that biological thought coalesces out of atheoretical associations and inductions unencumbered by belief.

BIOLOGY OUT OF NOTHING: THE CASE OF CONCEPTS OF KINDS

There seems to be long-standing experimental support for the idea that biological knowledge comes out of raw induction over regularities in the world. Ever since people have looked at children's concepts either naturalistically or through more formal assessments (such as vocabulary tests), one common theme has been to argue that the younger child's concepts seem to be unprincipled tabulations of all salient information that correlates with instances (salience being only perceptually driven) and that these early concepts shift to more principled, tightly organized ones, or theory-driven ones. This sort of change has variously been referred to as holistic to analytic, concrete to abstract, accidental to essential, and so forth, and has been mentioned by such widely divergent figures as Vygotsky (1934/1986); Terman (1916); Werner (1948); Bruner, Oliver, Greenfield et al. (1966), and even Inhelder and Piaget (1964), almost all the major developmental theorists of the century. Moreover, it remains in somewhat more sophisticated forms in the current literature (e.g., in discussions of shifts from concepts organized on the basis of attribute similarity to those organized on the basis of higher order relational similarity; Gentner & Toupin, 1988). In addition, numerous philosophers have made similar claims. Quine (1977), for example, used biological kinds as his prime examples in his views of science and common sense being on a simple continuum along which the child moves through simple mechanisms of trial and error learning. "Science after all, differs from common sense only in degree of methodological sophistication. Our experiences from early infancy are bound to have overlaid our innate spacing of qualities by modifying our grouping habits little by little, inclining us more and more to an appreciation of theoretical kinds and similarities" (p. 167).

The early accounts tended to think of such changes in terms of global stages and thus children before, say age 5, had the same crippling associative representation for all concepts. Later work has more often favored the idea that the shifts occur on a domain-by-domain basis largely as a function of local expertise, expertise that could be acquired by domain-general learning procedures and thus be compatible with empiricist views (see e.g., Chi, Feltovich, & Glaser, 1981).

When I first started looking at how children come to understand biological kinds, such associationist origins seemed right on the mark. One experimental technique involved an operations paradigm where all the salient characteristic features of one kind are changed into those of another contrasting kind (Keil, 1986). Thus, a raccoon might be turned into a skunk by dying and shaving its fur, teaching it to act like a skunk and to hang around skunks, and by putting inside it a sack of something that smells to squirt out whenever it gets angry at other animals (or a tiger into a lion, a horse into a zebra, a pine tree into an oak tree). Artifacts are also changed in a control condition, because in contrast to natural kinds, most adults see this kind of operation creating a truly new sort of artifact.

These tasks change all those features that would normally be mentioned as most typically associated with one kind into those that are most typically associated with another kind. If these features are all there is to the concept then the sort of thing described should change kindhood as well; and, in these tasks, younger children (kindergarten and younger) do say the animal is changed into a new kind. It seems as if they are simply organizing their concepts solely in terms of tabulations of typical features with no appeal to deeper principles or biases.

There are very different developmental patterns for artifacts and biological kinds. At all ages the artifacts are normally judged to be changed by the operation, whereas only the younger children regard the biological kinds to be so changed. Resistance to biological kind change by older children appears to be caused by the emergence of biological beliefs that overrides the characteristic feature cluster, and others (e.g., Carey, 1985) have cited that work as evidence of the emergence for the first time in development of an autonomous biology.

TROUBLES WITH TYPICALITY

These developmental patterns seem to fit the empiricist account nicely in which domain-general procedures tabulate up the most typical features and use those typicality distributions to construct similarity metrics in which various kinds are embodied. There are, however, two dangers in rushing to embrace this account. First, it offers no explanation of how an interconnected set of explanatory beliefs, what many call an intuitive theory, could ever emerge. There are no satisfactory accounts of how a learner progresses from association or some other product of raw induction to domain-specific theory (see Keil, 1991, for more discussion of this problem). Second, all too often in developmental psychology it has been shown that prior researchers had underestimated young children's abilities to transcend the merely phenomenal; or as Wellman and Gelman (1988) said, to go beyond the obvious. Perhaps these children are not shifting from being spineless phenomenalists to biological theorists, but from being psychological theorists who try to explain biological things in psychological terms, to true biological theorists; or perhaps they are shifting from being crude biological theorists to better ones. If so, then we should be able to show how we can get that "empiricist look" without really having it. To do so, we need to view concepts themselves as alloys of association and belief.

As adults, even our most elaborate theories eventually "run dry" in their abilities to meaningfully distinguish one subkind from another and we have to then fall back on more associative means for clustering entities and storing information; but just as adults must have an atheoretical mode, perhaps even the youngest child may have some deeply held beliefs that can override the characteristic for them as well. There may be no purely associative construals except for completely artificial and meaningless concepts such as small blue triangles with fuzzy textures, unfortunately just the sorts of stimuli that dominated concept research for many years.

What develops in any domain therefore may not be the emergence of theory out of nothing, but instead the emergence of a new more powerful theory out of the old. (Those who feel uncomfortable with using the term *theory* with young children can substitute *explanatory belief system.*) Biological concepts would seem to shift in qualitative ways from no theory to theory, but perhaps only because they are reflecting the increasing ability of more and more powerful theories to explain what used to be representable only associatively. However, because we often presuppose common parts of the theory so strongly and completely with the young child, we may at first only see a shift from the associative residual to theory and thus be misled. If some parts of theories are so basic that we do not normally even consider them, we may at first only notice those parts that change, which more closely resemble an associative to theory shift.

If younger children's concepts are also partially structured by domain-specific principles, albeit less powerful ones, then they should be able to go beyond the phenomenal as well, if we just find properties that are closer to their central beliefs and pit those against the merely typical. Having made such demonstrations, we can then ask whether those beliefs are based on construing animals and plants in terms of an intuitive psychology or physics or whether they reflect principles that might resonate with biological phenomena from the start.

Over the last several years we have conducted a series of studies that converge to tell a common story (Keil, 1989): Young children will indeed override the phenomenal similarity spaces that we take to be the hallmarks of simple associative representations; and they do so in their judgments as to whether something is not only just an animal or a plant, but also as to what kind of animal or plant it is. Thus, if one changes the surface parts of an animal or plant so that it looks and even behaves like another animal or plant, preschoolers will maintain that the kind of animal hasn't changed if the particular way the change is achieved violates what they hold to be central principles governing membership in biological kinds. In one set of studies we manipulated transformations of animal properties by either changing, for example, a tiger into a lion by a skintight costume, or changing a tiger into a lion by changing surface parts or by having the change be made slowly by an internal cause (injection), given early in life (Keil, 1989).

Even preschoolers were able to see the animal as remaining the same with certain costume transformations, whereas half the fourth graders thought that an injection would in fact cause a change to a new kind of animal (most adults did not). With a sufficiently large array of different sorts of transformations one should therefore be able to recapitulate the apparent shift from phenomenal to theory-based judgments at virtually any point in development by adjusting the nature of transformation such that it gets at the heart of an age group's current beliefs and biological kinds. Preschoolers will overrule phenomenal similarity when we get to their most basic beliefs, whereas even fourth graders (and for that matter adults) will be indecisive when we change things most central to their beliefs.

These and other studies, such as those reviewed by Wellman and Gelman (1988), strongly argue against young children blindly following tabulations of feature frequencies and correlations in their construals of biological kinds. They do not prove that such domain-general tabulation procedures cannot work; but given no positive demonstrations of such procedures, they have shifted the burden of proof. Moreover, although aspects of these studies suggest that the psychological mode of construal may not be enough, they do not really discriminate between the idea that biological thought is emerging out of another belief system versus being distinctively construed from the start. More directed studies of beliefs about a wide range of biological phenomena are needed.

To fully explore biological thought, one needs to study not just concepts of species and kind, but also such things as growth, disease, physiology, reproduction, and inheritance. A related question asks if there are some unifying principles that guide beliefs across these subdomains of biology or whether each is fully distinct with the hazardous consequence of endless downward proliferation of domains and domain-specific thought. My colleagues and I are now looking at a wide range of biological phenomena, asking if, in general, biological entities and relations are part of a distinct, coherent domain for the child. In accord with the issues just raised, the strategy is to repeatedly use physical and psychological causes as foils to test the notion that biological ones might be truly distinct. One of the clearest illustrations of the strategy comes from our studies on beliefs about inheritance.

INHERITANCE

Offspring of all sorts inherit properties from their parents. Some notion of like begets like, both at the level of species and the individual, recurs throughout adults of almost all cultures (Jacob, 1982). Of course not all properties are equally heritable and all adults have intuitive estimates of the likelihood of inheritance of different properties. The question is how those adult intuitive probabilities contrast with those of children and what these differences might tell us more broadly about the emergence of biological thought.

In one set of studies, Ken Springer and I (Springer & Keil, 1989) told children that both parents had a somewhat atypical property (e.g., a white stomach, a pink heart, etc.) which then had values on each of the three dimensions: (a) being inborn versus experientially induced, (b) being important to the biological functioning (really more like physiological functioning) of an organism (either negatively or positively) versus being unimportant to their functioning, and (c) being a property that is internal versus external to the kind. For example, "born with a pink heart that helps them stay healthy" is inborn, internal, and biologically functional in a positive way, whereas "lost all their hair in an accident; now only their bare skin shows" is experientially induced, external, and nonfunctional.

A developmental shift was found with respect to which properties are judged heritable. Early on, biological/physiological functioning seems to be the main predictor of whether a property will be inherited, not whether it is inborn or whether it is internal, or whether the functional effects are positive versus negative, as seen in Fig. 4.1, which shows how each of the three contrasts differentially influenced judgments at the three ages.

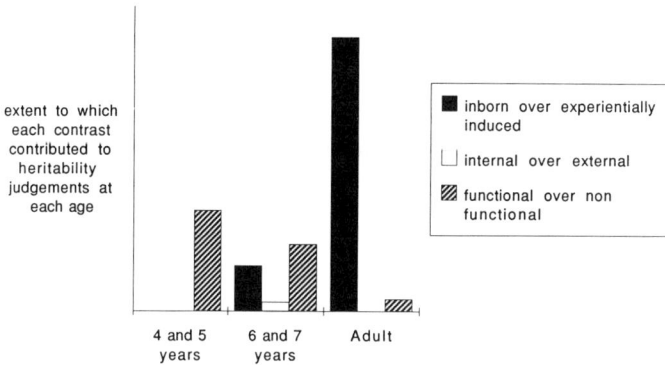

FIG. 4.1. Judgments of the degree to which different property types were transferred from parents to offspring (based on data in Springer & Keil, 1989).

A second inheritance study showed that not just any function could elicit a judgment of heritability. The function had to have biological/physiological kinds of effects as opposed to social ones. Thus, if the parents lose all their hair and it results in their getting cold and sick in the winter (a biological/physiological effect), it is inherited; but if the same hair loss instead results in their being "bare so that everyone can see their skin" (a social effect), it is not inherited. Properties with either adverse or beneficial social/functional outcomes are considered much less likely to be heritable than the same properties with biological/functional outcomes.

Finally, in a noninheritance task where children are asked to guess how well animals will "get along" or be able to cope socially, the social functions are much more potent in influencing judgments than the biological ones, demonstrating that the social functions chosen were not just generally weak and ineffective; rather they were weak for making inferences about the likelihood of something being inherited (i.e., a biological problem), but strong for inferences about a social problem. Useful analogies to known inherited properties were not available here either, given how different these properties are from familiar inherited ones.

In short, younger children seem to think that properties with important consequences for the physiological functioning of an animal are so central and basic that they must be inherited. Perhaps they assume that if one changes properties linked to physiological functioning, one has changed something so fundamental that it is transmitted to the child. Properties with biological functions therefore seem to be close to an animal's essence, or at least to those parts that get passed on to offspring, much more so to the young child than whether those properties are inborn in the parents. A clear shift then starts to occur between kindergarten and Grade 2 as the inborn/experiential dimension comes to increasingly dominate judgments of heritability, and ends up being the sole factor for most adults.

These beliefs about inheritance may be linked to beliefs about the mechanism of transmission from parent to offspring. In a second series of studies, Springer and I (Springer & Keil, 1991) described and pictorially depicted an offspring inside its "parent," which is initially colorless but gradually acquires the color of its "parent" by the time of birth. Children are asked to chose among three classes of mechanisms for how the offspring comes to have the external color of the parent: (a) an internal natural class of mechanisms (something inside the "mother" gets passed on to the child), (b) an external natural class of mechanisms—wherein some external natural force contributed the color and, (c) mechanisms involving intentional human agents that contributed the color. All three mechanisms were presented for dogs, flowers, and a machine that made small reproductions.

Even 3- and 4-year-olds clearly thought that something intrinsic to the biological kind was critical to inheritance. Thus, for the dog, the color was almost invariably transmitted by internal natural causes. For plants, internal and external natural causes were roughly evenly split. By contrast, for the machine, most 3- and 4-year-olds picked the human agent, five times more often than for dogs, and even more overwhelmingly in comparison to plants. Biological kinds, especially animals, are much more likely to be seen as transferring properties through the transmission of something that is intrinsic to the mother. There was still plenty of room for the children's responses to differ from those of adults, however. Follow-ups showed that they strongly prefer an account in which little brown pieces are passed from mother to fetus rather than a set of instructions or "recipe" for making the "skin" brown.

More recently, Springer has looked at links between beliefs about inheritance and those about kinship, an area where both biological and social modes of construal are important and must be kept distinct in all cultures (Springer, 1990). In a series of four studies, he showed preschoolers displays of three animals in which one was visually highly similar to Animal A but unrelated, whereas the other was related by kinship but visually much less similar. Children were asked whether either of the two animals, or both, had certain nonperceivable biological properties (e.g., has tiny bones inside it) or, in some cases, nonbiological properties (e.g., is very dirty from playing in the mud) possessed by A. Across several studies, preschoolers (roughly 4 1/2 years old) were shown to be more likely to attribute biological properties to dissimilar related animals than to similar unrelated ones. When the property was nonbiological, it was attributed more often to the similar animal than the dissimilar, even when kinship relations clearly held between the dissimilar animal and Animal A. This pattern of results may seem surprising given that children this young usually define such kinship terms as mother and uncle purely in social terms. Here, however, embedding the use of such terms in tasks that contrast social and biological relations was apparently enough to elicit biological construals of those terms. Figure 4.2 summarizes the different response patterns made by preschoolers across two of Springer's studies when asked to make inductions about biological versus nonbiological properties. It clearly illustrates a reversal in the pattern of attribution as a function of the type of property.

In these studies, intuitions about plausible mechanisms for previously never considered biological phenomena reveal what seem to be a theory about that phenomenon; but one cannot really have a specific theory about something one has never contemplated. Something at a more abstract level is constraining theory choice. These preschoolers have fundamentally different preferences for inheritance mechanisms for animals versus machines. Moreover, while treating animals and plants somewhat differently, these two are treated similarly in contrast to machines, even though of course the machine and the animal are both animate. These children seem to have strong intuitions about biological function as being more central to a species identity than social function. There is also the notion of intrinsicness, that is, the expectation that something inside biological kinds determines the nature of their offspring. Perhaps similar notions will surface again in reasoning about other biological phenomena.

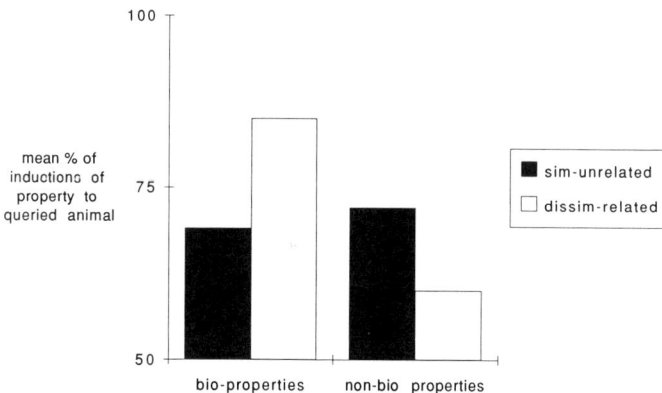

FIG. 4.2. Judgments of the degree to which different property types are shared between a target animal and similar but unrelated animals versus dissimilar but related ones (based on data from Studies 1 and 3 in Springer, 1990).

GROWTH—PATHS OF ORIGIN AND KINDHOOD

As adults we expect that flowers of a particular kind will go through a standard progression from seed through initial sprout, to bud, to final full flower, with further typical progressions until the flower's demise. Within the class of flowers, superficially similar flowers might go through quite different progressions. For example, if shown a plant that looked like a rose, we might judge it to be one until we learn that its pattern of growth was dramatically different from that of all other roses and very much like that of begonias (it starts from a tuber, etc.; indeed such "rose-form" begonias do exist). How a thing comes to have its final form matters a great deal for animals and plants, but normally not so much for artifacts. Thus, if one encounters an object that looks and functions like a chair, but then learns that it was not made in the way most chairs were made (say the maker started with the back, then added the seat and finally the legs as opposed to the opposite order) such information is unlikely to influence one's judgment that it is a chair. As long as its maker intended it to be a chair, the causal path taken to bring it into being is less important. There are interesting exceptions with artifacts where origins matter more, and biological things where they may matter less, but in general the difference is a strong one between the two sorts of things; and with nonbiological kinds, such as gold and water, paths of origins either are not a relevant concept or do not seem to matter much.

An understanding of the importance of canonical patterns of change to the individuation of biological kinds would seem to be linked to an understanding of how unseen causes can regulate enduring, species-specific properties. This may represent a linking of a general essentialist bias to more detailed beliefs about mechanisms of growth and inheritance. One can be an essentialist of sorts without such an understanding, but it would seem that one way of making essentialist assumptions more concrete is by suggesting the causal potency of the essence. A study was therefore conducted on how an appreciation of patterns of change develops.

Although canonical patterns of change may be primarily associated with species, they may also be relevant to other sorts of biological kinds, such as disease. As adults, we consider diseases to be biological phenomena and at least part of our understanding is based on an assumption that how things become sick is as important as the final set of symptoms. If two individuals come down with very similar symptoms but we learn that the causal routes to these symptoms, as well as the early stages of the disease, were very different, we would probably consider them to be different diseases caused by different agents. Thus, stomach flu and food poisoning can have extremely similar end symptoms, but one is inclined to see them as being very different diseases if the paths of origin are known for both. To explore whether some common insight emerges for a broad range of biological phenomena, it was therefore decided to include both disease and species concepts in the study.

Children were shown sequences of three to five pictures depicting the origins of either an artifact, a plant, or a disease. In one study, they were then shown a different sequence with an identical endstate, but different causal path and asked if the entity depicted at the end was the same. In a second study, children were shown a similar initial sequence and were then shown two other sequences, one of which was very different but ended up with an identical endstate, the other of which was an identical sequence but ended up with a somewhat different final state. The children were then asked which was of the same kind as that in the first sequence. As examples of the first study, consider the pairs of animal and artifact sequences shown in Fig. 4.3.

A summary of the results for all biological kinds in contrast to artifacts is shown in Fig. 4.4.

The important finding is that there is a clear developmental pattern in which children learn with increasing age that paths of origin are much more important for biological kinds than for artifacts. At first they seem irrelevant in all cases, but then come to play a major role, as seen by the separation of the curves in Fig. 4.4. Equally important is the finding that, when the biological curves are broken down into diseases, plants, and animals, the differences between these are relatively modest, suggesting that the child comes to see all of them as biological kinds in similar ways. (Indeed, diseases are seen as essentially identical to animals.) Thus, increasing general knowledge about biological sorts of things should have a direct relevance to helping the child's more specific knowledge of disease.

Kindergartners did not attach much importance to origins for individuating kinds at the level of species, even though this seems so basic to adult concepts in biology. We are still trying to come up with other tasks that show such an appreciation at earlier ages, but have not yet been able to demonstrate that 5-year-olds realize that path of origin is an important distinguishing property for individuating biological kinds. (Other studies do show they realize origins are important for general distinctions between biological kinds and artifacts.) If an appreciation continues to elude younger children, we will want to ask how this shift is more broadly related to other changes in the development of biological thought. Note, for example, that the shift parallels the shift found for an understanding of the importance of inborn properties in parents for predicting their transmission to offspring. Therefore, there may be a broader development occurring involving an understanding of

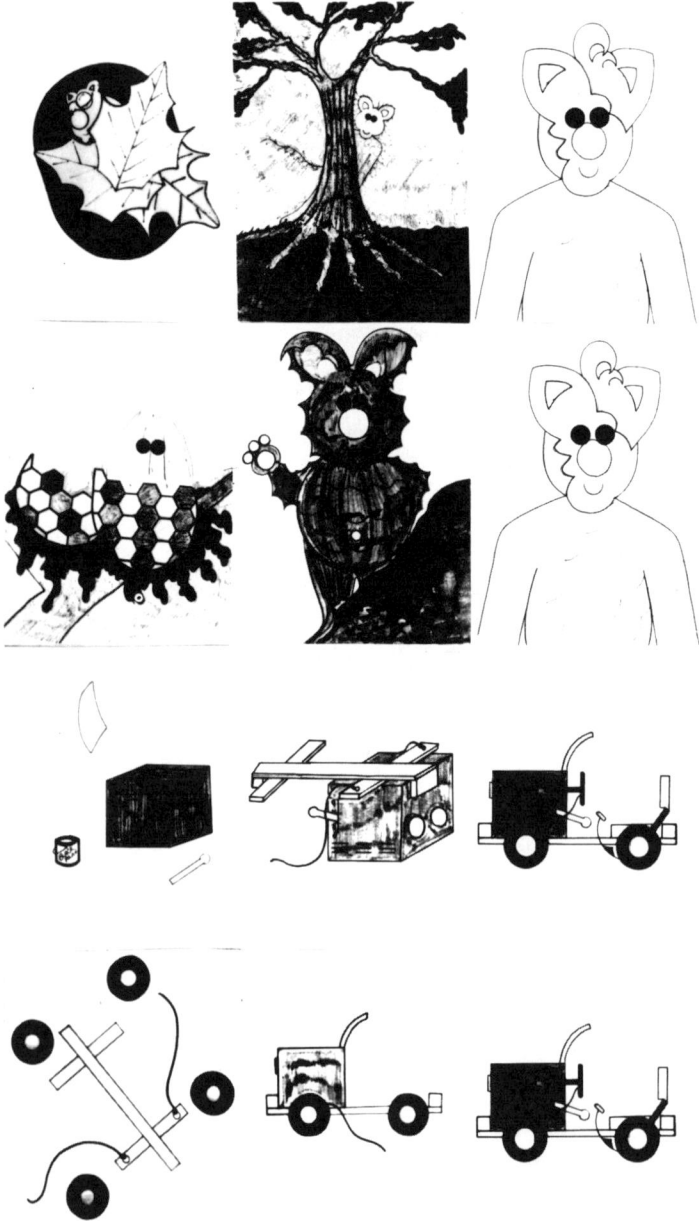

FIG. 4.3. Two examples of the sequence pairs used in the first study on causal paths of origins. In this study, the paths are different but the endstates are the same.

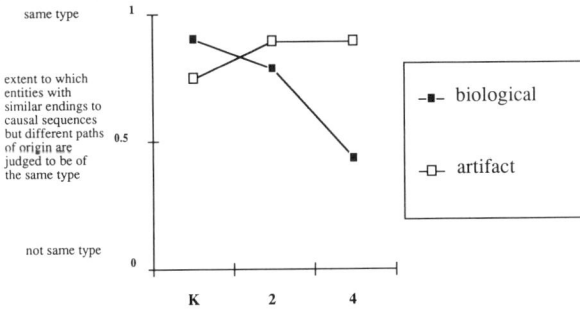

FIG. 4.4. Responses form the first study on causal paths of origins, showing that children in Grades 2 and 4 come to clearly recognize the greater relevance of such paths for the proper individuation of biological kinds as opposed to artifacts.

predetermined patterns in organizing and structuring biological kinds, and understanding those patterns may form the basis for a more sophisticated notion of essence.

This study clearly illustrates that major developmental changes in the nature of biological thought do occur in the elementary school years; kindergartners do not simply have the adult theories with a few missing details. It would be a mistake, however, to interpret such differences as signs that the younger children are simply raw phenomenalists whose thinking about biological kind is solely driven by the immediately salient. The broader pattern of studies described so far, as well as several to follow, suggest that biological thought may emerge in a systematic and coherent way that has continuous threads reaching far back into the preschool years.

DISEASE—PATTERNS OF CONTAGION

One of the most salient phenomena associated with some diseases is their contagiousness. The mechanisms of contagion for living things are highly distinctive, but they can have imposters in other domains, such as social relations. One way to explore the special nature of biological contagion is to examine what sorts of symptoms are considered contagious. Any set of beliefs about biological contagion must regard only some afflictions as communicable, in general only those that have major physiological components. If all possible human afflictions were viewed as contagious we would be neurotic wrecks in a world rampant with infectious individuals.

Jackie Raia, Rebecca Lutomske, and I have asked what sorts of symptoms are ones that can be "caught." Three dimensions were likely candidates for organizing subjects' intuitions: sudden onset versus congenital; good versus bad; and behavioral versus physiological. As adults, we would put strong emphasis on the behavioral/physiological and sudden onset/congenital contrasts and would have weaker intuitions whether good versus bad symptoms were relevant. This design therefore presented "symptoms" that deviated from normal states on various combinations of these dimensions. Some examples are given in Fig. 4.5. The symptoms were all intended to be sufficiently dissimilar from familiar diseases that simple analogies to them would not be helpful. In addition, some of the behavioral afflictions were deliberately constructed to have clear physiological side effects, to assess if younger children would differentiate similar endstates on the basis of different underlying mechanisms. Consider, for example, the obsessive hand washing case in Fig. 4.5 where there is a clear physical consequence (bleeding hands as depicted in the accompanying illustration) but the real cause is mental. Similarly, consider the converse case where there are no overt biological symptoms and abnormal behavioral ones, but nonetheless a physiological cause (the "victim" who never eats vegetables because they make him sick).

The procedure involved presenting a pictorial representation of a child visiting another child for the weekend and having the two be in close proximity for much of the time. One of the children was depicted as having the symptoms, either directly in the case of perceivable symptoms, or indirectly through situational and contextual information for nonperceivable symptoms. Having described the close proximity relationship and the symptoms of the "diseased" child, the subject was asked if the other child was likely to "catch" those symptoms.

Not only kindergartners but also 4-year-olds adamantly maintained that abnormal behaviors are not contagious. The behavioral/physiological contrast is far and away the strongest dimension driving their judgments (see Fig. 4.6). The good–bad distinction, which might afford the simplest comparison to known diseases, not only had a smaller overall effect, it also appeared to have less of an effect on judgments in the younger children, who judge many "good" physiological symptoms as contagious, whereas older children appeared to have more difficulty thinking of something good being contagious, probably because of no known exemplars (the condition by age interaction approached but did not reach significance, however). Finally, the congenital–sudden onset dimension had no influence whatsoever in preschool and kindergarten groups, but a dramatic one starting at Grade 2, again reinforcing the finding of the emergence of awareness of the central role of that dimension after age 5.

The rejection of behavioral afflictions including such things as involuntary mumbling, obsessiveness, uncontrollable laughter, and having hallucinations, is a powerful conviction for these children. This is

Marianne was feeling OK, but then one day, suddenly she started washing her hands all the time. She washes them so much that they bleed and are all sore, but she can't stop washing them even though they are not dirty at all. She doesn't know why she does it; she just can't help it. Do you think if her friend X came to visit her and hang around with her for a while that she could not catch washing her hands so much from Marianne or could catch the washing her hands so much from Marianne?

This is Danny and he has something different in his stomach so he can't eat vegetables, and he's been like this ever since he was born. The Doctor said that he couldn't eat vegetables, so he just takes a little vitamin pill in the morning. Well, Danny thinks that this is the greatest thing in the world, and he is very happy because he hates vegetables. When his friend X came to visit and stay for a while, do you think that X could catch not being able to eat vegetables from Danny or couldn't catch that from Danny?

This is Patty and one day for no reason she started giggling really hard at rocking chairs, and she hasn't been able to stop since then. She giggles like crazy whenever she sees a rocking chair; she just can't help it. Do you think if her friend X came to visit and stay with Patty, do you think that X could catch the giggles from Patty and giggle when she sees rocking chairs, even when there's no one else around, or do you think that she could not catch those giggles from Patty?

FIG. 4.5. Examples of descriptions used in the first study on beliefs about patterns of contagion for different symptom types. The first description is negative symptoms, behavioral, and sudden onset. The second is positive symptoms, physiological, and inborn. The third is positive symptoms, behavioral, and sudden onset.

especially impressive considering how often we colloquially talk about the contagiousness of behaviors, such as laughter. Even some kindergartners explicitly pointed out the contrast, as with one who said of the uncontrollable laughter "you might have to giggle with them, but you couldn't really catch it." These children had absolutely no doubt that psychological and biological causes could mix. They were wholly separate.

The major developmental change of an increasing understanding that congenital things are less likely to be contagious, again illustrates that the younger children can and do differ quite dramatically in some ways from adults. Sharing certain biases with adults therefore in no way ensures that younger children will possess the same theories of disease. It only ensures that common modes of construal at much broader levels will prevail. Finally, a second age-related change involves increasing conservatism in

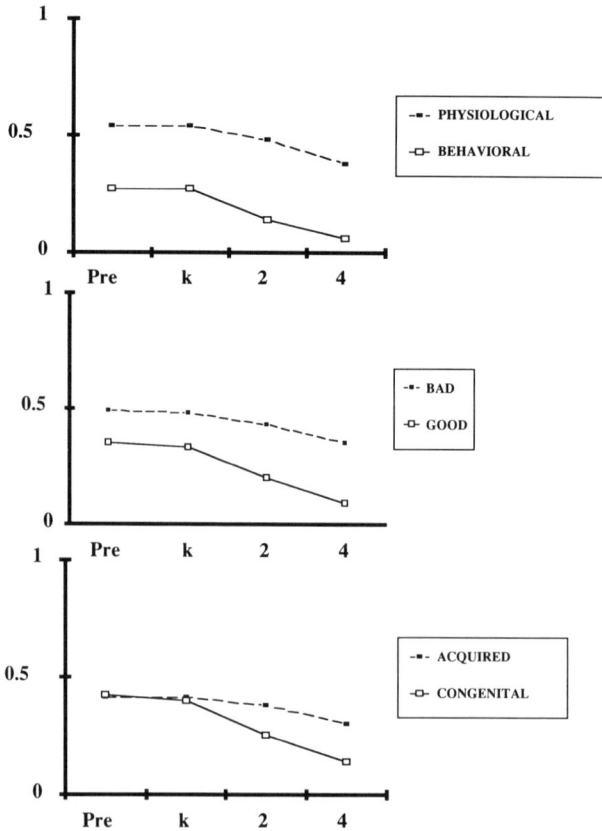

FIG. 4.6.   Response patterns from the first study on beliefs about patterns of contagion for different symptom types. The physiological behavioral contrast was the strongest factor influencing intuitions at all ages.

estimates that any symptoms will be contagious. Protocols suggested this was simply a consequence of increased experience and an ability to think up detailed accounts of how a potentially contagious affliction might not really be caught in every instance of exposure.

It must be remembered that a clear distinction between the behavioral and the physiological in conceptions of disease does not mean that beliefs about mental causation of physiological states might not also be held. Such beliefs certainly seem to be evident in several cultures (Atran, 1990). It does suggest, however, that the two sorts of afflictions are not considered the same nor medicated and caused in the same manner and that all cultures may make such a distinction, a point to be pursued in further studies.

DISEASE—TYPES OF POSSIBLE AGENTS

A different line of work explores beliefs about disease agents, which offer several attractive features for research: First, because the causal agents for most diseases have never been seen by most children, guesses about their properties are more likely to rely on appeals to abstract biological principles than to known exemplars. Second, there are, for adults at least, two very clearly different causes of diseases: biological agents such as germs and viruses, and nonbiological ones such as poisons and toxins. This contrast allows one to ask if the child sees identical symptoms as possibly having very different ways of being caused and cured. Does simply knowing that something is biological lead to different patterns of inferences about how it would produce a set of surface outcomes also generated by a nonbiological agent?

In one set of studies on agents, children were shown various amorphous microscopic objects (we carefully explained what "microscopic" means) and sometimes had the agents described as poison pellets or powders and other times as germs or viruses. All the children had heard of germs before and, as we see here, assumed that they were biological sorts of things. Most parents do tell children that germs are contagious and little else. The contagion study suggested, however, that knowing that germs are contagious might well be enough to promote many other inferences about them being biological sorts of things. In contrast to germs, pilot work showed that most kindergartners claim to have never heard of viruses. Consequently, in addition to calling them viruses, the following phrase was used: "a virus is something that has to get inside people's bodies and use parts of their bodies, or it won't last long." Note that this description carefully avoids using any predicates here that clearly identify it as a living kind, it simply refers to the virus as a whole as having a purpose related to its existence. Whether that purpose is interpreted in intentional/psychological terms or biological ones is addressed shortly.

These agents all cause identical symptoms in a human victim (again counterbalanced), symptoms that do not resemble any well-known disease. Children were asked a series of questions about how the disease is manifested and gotten rid of (the victim does always get better): Is it contagious? If you chop it up into tiny pieces will it still make you sick? Does it think? Does it move on its own? Is it alive? Does it change size inside you? The purpose of all these questions is to determine if the causal and functional properties of biological versus nonbiological agents are seen as importantly different even though most of these children have no prior information about any of these details. Therefore, the study asks whether children will show different patterns of guesses because of different expectations and beliefs about the fundamental natures of biological versus nonbiological agents.

Children at all ages see different mechanisms for the nonbiological and biological agents, as shown in in Fig. 4.7. Thus, children at all ages see the biological agents as more likely to be alive, contagious, move, and change in size inside the body. Interestingly, they are judged equally likely to make you sick when chopped up, an issue addressed in a follow-up study. In addition, both types are judged to not think, a point returned to later. Thus, four of the six questions showed clear contrasts among biological and nonbiological agents in children as young as 5 years old, even though the agents are relatively unfamiliar and are invisible. A preliminary study with preschoolers suggests that they too may distinguish such agents on the basis of such properties.

Even when most children had no idea what the virus term meant, the simple description of its functional role was enough to trigger for them a set of biologically constrained inferences about how it causes the symptoms and how it is eradicated, inferences that made it basically indistinguishable from a germ. Something about the functional description used suggested a biological agent so strongly that it was construed in the same manner as a "known" biological agent.

The virus, functional role, finding suggested a follow-up study more systematically assessing what such a functional description was triggering. In the follow-up, the agent was simply called a "thing" to ensure that any connotations from a familiar term could not have an influence. In addition, four different sorts of descriptions were made concerning the "thing" to see how they might differentially guide inferences about mechanisms: a functional or teleological description with phrasing similar to the virus case described earlier, a simple mechanical description in which the "thing" rubs around inside your body causing abrasion, an

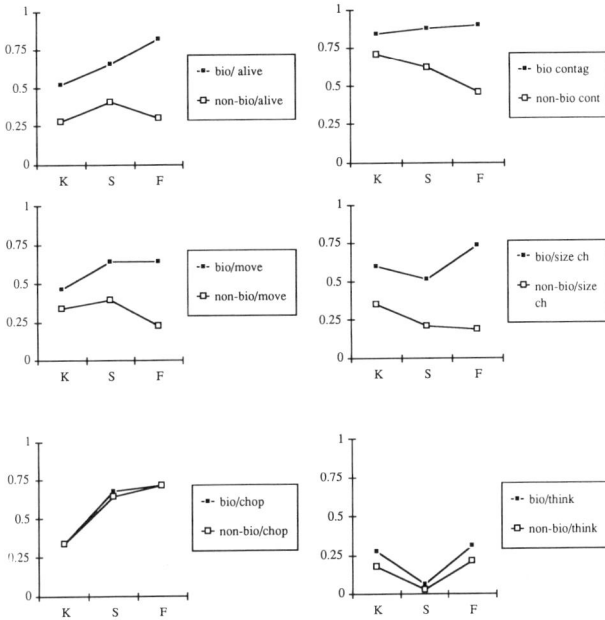

FIG. 4.7. Response patterns from first study on beliefs about causal mechanisms underlying disease agents that produce identical symptoms. Children at all ages clearly contrasted biological and nonbiological agents on the basis of being alive, contagious, moving, and changing size, while at the same time thinking that neither was capable of thought, thus arguing against a simple behavioral construal of biological kinds by the younger children.

intention description that directly attributes goals and desires to the "thing" (this is an important contrast case with the teleological description), a description of the "thing" as designed by a human, and no description at all. For adults, the teleological description provides a kind of minimal information that a biological thing is involved. The goals and desires description implies not only a biological thing, but also a psychological one, the mechanism description suggests a nonliving thing, and the human designed description, an artifact. Children at Grades K, 2, and 4 each received all descriptions.

The results are straightforward: Describing a "thing" as using parts of the body resulted in its being seen at all ages as just as alive, just as able to move on its own, just as able to reproduce as an intentional "thing" described as "wanting to get inside you and make you sick," and just as likely to have heterogeneous internal structure (inside parts that were "different from each other, not all the same") all in strong contrast to the abrasion case. Thus, the functional and intention/desire entities were, on the average, more than twice as likely to have the traits of reproduction, motion, heterogeneous structure, and being alive. On the other hand, children at all ages thought that the teleological "thing" did not know what it was doing any more than a simple mechanical one and in strong contrast to the intentional one, attributing knowledge roughly three times as much to the intention/desire entity. This pattern demonstrates that even the youngest are not simply equating these disease agents to prototypical animals or people exemplars, which do know what they are doing. They are apparently not taking the teleological description as simply making the "thing" an intentional agent with mental goals. A "thing" for these children can apparently be biological without being sentient. They are not modeling biology via mental states such as goals and desires or via other nonphysical internal states as far as we can tell. They do think that sentient beings must also be biological kinds but not the reverse, a finding also suggested in earlier work on the differentiation of ontological knowledge (Keil, 1979, 1983).

Describing something as having a functional role leads to a conviction that it is a biological kind with heterogeneous internal structure unless you specifically flag it as an artifact. In the artifact condition, the children thought it much less likely that the "thing" was alive, or able to reproduce.

With respect to cutting up things like germs, a follow-up study suggests that cutting up does make the "thing" become not alive, that the cut up parts are heterogeneous, that it can no longer move on its own after being cut up, but that it can still make you sick. Apparently, and the transcripts support this, the younger children do think germ-like things are biological kinds with complex internal structure that is important for movement and life, but they do not see this biological machinery as being used to cause the disease. Several kindergartners reported that simply having the germ or its parts inside you made you sick, just because they are foreign bodies, not because their specific biological apparatus makes you sick. As in the case of inheritance, having a notion that something is a biological phenomena hardly guarantees that one will have precisely the right theory. Considerable theory development is also going on here as well, again illustrating that these early principles are just that, guidelines and not a completed theory.

In general, these studies on intuitions about invisible disease agents illustrate that young children do not reason about biological things simply by making analogies to the most familiar biological beings with intentions. A more abstract set of beliefs about biological things is guiding their assumptions, beliefs that suggest some intertwining of notions of heterogeneous structure, functional rules, and growth into a connected system.

A Teleological Stance

Across these studies I have repeatedly suggested that young children are sensitive to the advantages of teleological–functional modes of construal for all biological kinds and tend to associate them more strongly with these kinds than with other sorts of things. I have also suggested that they seem to construe biological things as if they have richer more causally potent essences. These modes of construal may be the most important constant constraints on emerging biological thought and may be what give coherence to that thought across other developmental changes in beliefs about living things. More direct support for these ideas can be advanced on both conceptual and empirical grounds.

Perhaps our ways of thought about biology are as basic to the human species as those about objects and persons. Following Dennett (1987), we can wonder if in addition to the intentional and physical stances, there might not also be a "design" stance—a stance that looks at things as if they had functions, or as I have put it, as if their properties were designed for purposes. This stance confers on its user the ability to understand relations and make inductions and construals that might well be opaque to a purely mechanistic stance. Looking at systems in terms of their functions or in terms of the design problems they solve can often be a much more valuable level of analysis than asking about mechanical interactions of their physical constituents. There are many inductions, predictions, and explanations that can be made at the design level that would be hopeless if reduced to a mechanical level and far too metaphorical if described at the intentional level.

There is ample support for the design stance in the history of biological thought. Richard Dawkins (1986), for example, in his popular book *The Blind Watchmaker*, noted that, prior to Darwin and Wallace, one was almost crazy not to be religious, for the view of biological kinds as designed for purposes was so inescapable and cognitively compelling that, without the insight of natural selection, one would not help but conclude that they were artifacts of God. The argument from design repeatedly occurs throughout history in culture after culture as a motivation for a god or gods. Even after Darwin and Wallace, some maintain that we overzealously use teleological explanations in evolutionary biology (e.g., Gould & Lewontin, 1978).

Dawkins made other points that are relevant here, such as that biological kinds have heterogeneous structure in contrast to other natural kinds and that they tend to have hierarchical structure with organized subsystems. We have seen evidence for an early awareness of these properties as well.

The design stance may therefore be a compelling mode of thought, so compelling that we apply it to biological kinds overzealously by sometimes inferring a designer, or a God; but these conjectures could use more direct experimental grounding. It should be possible to directly show that the "design" stance is the preferred mode of explanation for aspects of biological kinds. We have been wrestling with this problem for well over a year and have found it far more subtle and complicated to explore than anticipated. It is useful, however, to briefly describe the progression of exploratory studies as that progression may hint at how a mode of construal expands and becomes more powerful and informative.

Our jumping off point was the simple intuition that adults do not generally ask certain kinds of questions about nonbiological natural kinds. We can ask why water is transparent, but not in the why sense that asks "What does being transparent do for water? What good is it? Why wouldn't water be just as good if it was opaque?" But all of these sorts of questions sound just fine when asking why a jellyfish, for example, is transparent. Similarly, one can ask what a pointy sharp exterior does for a cactus, but not for stegnite (a pointy sharp mineral). As adults at least, we see these kinds of explanations as being appropriate for most biological kinds and not for most other sorts of natural kinds. They are of course also fine for many artifacts, but we have seen that there are other ways in which artifacts differ.

Many philosophers and biologists have talked about the kinds of phrasing that seem to go with these sorts of teleological or functional or design-stance explanations. For a Property P, because phrases that end like the following are common: Because "it needs to be P," "P makes it a good one," "P helps it be a better one," "it would be bad for it without P," "P is very important for it," "having P is just right for it," "it really makes sense to have P," "P works well for it," "it wouldn't last long without P," "there wouldn't be very many without P," "without P something else that does what P does would have to be there," "P solves a problem for them," "P makes all the difference for it," and so on through many other related versions.

Obviously all of these explanations appeal to the functional utility of a property or the functional crisis that ensues if it is not present. They also carry various senses of optimization and adaptation and design. Vigorous controversies have existed in the philosophy of science concerning the real values of such forms of explanation (Nagel, 1961; Wright, 1976, etc.), but a fair summary of recent work is that the older criticisms of teleological thought as reversing causality, or anthropomorphizing and intentionalizing things into ones with goals are not widely regarded as legitimate objections to more careful teleological formulations all the way back to Aristotle (see Mayr, 1988; Salmon, 1989; Woodfield, 1976; Wright, 1976). This legitimacy of teleological explanations in science is important to interpreting what is happening when children see a meshing between these modes of construal and biological things, because it licenses the conclusion that they do not do so because they have anthropomorphized plants or because they are reversing causality. More important for this context is the recognition that, in the natural world, this mode of construal for most adults, in most cultures, works best for biological things. Apparently there are real things about biological phenomena that resonate strongly with this level of explanation.

Our first experimental attempt involved presenting just the teleological mode of description with no other decipherable content for the average child. Thus, the child might be told that "Fangdaps are insouciant because being insouciant is very important for them." They would then be shown three jars, one with pictures of animals and plants, one with pictures of artifacts, and one with pictures of nonbiological natural kinds like rocks, crystals, and gold nuggets. When asked where the named thing should be put, virtually all kindergartners looked at us with complete bewilderment, as did many second graders. The task was simply too difficult. We tried simplifying it in several ways: We ascribed a real property, such as redness, to the nonsense word, or we ascribed an unfamiliar property to a familiar thing, or we left the identity of the thing completely vague (e.g., Mary showed John something and said that it was red because...). In all of these versions, there was somewhat more connecting of the teleological with the biological among second graders, but kindergartners still appeared lost. Incidentally, in all these cases, we also included in a balanced fashion, other modes of explanation, such as simple reductionist explanations (it's red because little tiny parts of it mix together to give it a red color), external agent explanations (it's red because someone carefully painted/dyed it), natural environment causes (it is always found in places with lots of red dust that gets all over it and won't come off). A different version tried minimal syntactic changes and forced choices as in "one of these is green because it blends in with other green things and is hard to see" versus "one of these is green and because it is green, it blends in with other green things and is hard to see ... which is which?" These nuances of phrasing were not usually appreciated by the younger children.

Certain tantalizing teasers continued to motivate more studies. Even the youngest children would occasionally make spontaneous remarks suggesting that they did prefer the teleological with the biological. Moreover, some informal observations of my own children at much earlier ages convinced me that some version of this mode of construal was organizing concepts at a much earlier age. For example, my son Dylan, when 2 1/2, one day came across a novel insect with unusual pincers and pointed to them and asked "What are those things for?" None of our children has asked a similar question about a natural protuberance on a rock.

Unfortunately, spontaneous utterances of this sort are the worst way to collect adequate data, so we tried yet another experimental approach. Two possible explanations were given for why something had a property and the child was asked to pick which sounded better. Thus, we might say "Two people are talking about why plants are green. This person says it is because it is better for the plants to be green and it helps there be more plants. This person says it is because there are little tiny parts in plants that when mixed together give them a green color. Which reason is a better one?" The same choice was given for why emeralds were green. Note that both explanations are adequate for plants, but only the reductionist one works for the emeralds.

In this version, second graders strongly preferred teleological explanations with the biological kinds and kindergartners showed appropriate tendencies. Thus, for biological kinds, teleological explanations were favored for roughly 2.5 times as many items as were the reductionist explanations. Reductionist explanations were preferred for nonbiological natural kinds like emeralds for roughly five times as many items as the teleological. A final study now underway simplifies things even further: A child is presented with two pictures, one of say a prickly plant and one of a prickly kind of mineral; indeed, in some cases, the drawings are nearly identical except for the labels. They are told that both are prickly but only one is prickly because being prickly is good for it and are asked to pick which one. This method appears to be yielding clear preferences among kindergartners for teleological explanations with biological kinds. We are still looking for clear evidence of such preferences among preschoolers.

I have reported the entire sequence of exploratory studies rather than just the last two full-fledged ones because the overall pattern may be giving some hints as to how a principle becomes more manifest with development. With appropriate simplifications and reductions of the verbal demands, it may be possible to show that young preschoolers seek different sorts of explanations for biological kinds, just as my son did; but such a demonstration does not mean that they have the same degree of appreciation as older children. Surely in come cases, such as with our most arcane constructions, failure is simply caused by general difficulties with nonsense items and syntactic complexities. Other cases, however, may reveal an increasingly conscious awareness of an implicit principle. We have already seen several studies that, in more implicit terms, suggest an early linking of functional relations to biological kinds, but explicit recognition of the role of these sorts of explanations may take considerably more time to develop. Using such a bias to guide spontaneous exploration and questioning about novel objects may be a good deal more basic than using linguistic constructions with teleological phrasings to infer biological kinds. This may be a very general pattern across many different domains of how intuitive knowledge and biases broadens their scope.

ESSENTIALISM AGAIN

As has been pointed out several times, teleology also works for artifacts, and although we might simply accept Dawkin's (1986) move and call them "honorary biological kinds," perhaps a more appropriate move is to see if other important differences are meaningful to young children. The first place to turn is the notion that biological kinds have more clear-cut essences and causally more potent ones. I have alluded to hints of this in several of the studies described so far, but there are few studies that directly explore this issue. We have some underway, but the best hints so far come from studies conducted by S. Gelman and her colleagues and by Atran's (1990) cross-cultural analysis of biological belief systems.

Incidentally, historical support for an essentialist bias in construing biological kinds is quite compelling. A common explanation of why no one ever came up with an evolutionary theory until Darwin and Wallace is irrational essentialism. Ernst Mayr (1988) and many others have argued that the assumption of biological kinds having fixed essences worked directly against the Darwinian notion of species as more of a probabilistic construct. Indeed, one philosopher (Hull, 1965) published a paper on the topic with the somewhat dramatic title "The Effect of Essentialism on Taxonomy: 2,000 Years of Stasis." This title misses something important, however. Essentialism can be a very useful heuristic that compels us to go beyond the merely typical and look for underlying causes. Like teleological thinking, however, essentialist biases may emerge first in more spontaneous forms and only later become linked up with things like inheritance and canonical patterns of change.

CONCLUSIONS

The list of empirical studies just summarized now needs to be put into a broader perspective of how biological thought might emerge and become a distinct domain. First, a summary of the empirical findings:

1. Although many developmental phenomena might suggest a shift from preschoolers being domain-general associative type learners to later being domain-specific theorists, a closer look at many apparently associative-like phenomena reveals that their concepts have cores of explanatory beliefs (or what we have called theories), usually less

powerful cores that give way sooner to associative nets, but beliefs nonetheless. Children might conceivably still be domain-general tabulators at even earlier ages; but the studies do reveal how several apparent cases are not. Moreover, there are no clear positive demonstrations of completely unbiased concepts in even the youngest of children; thus, the burden has shifted. I am not at all sure that one could ever get explanatory beliefs out of simple association, but that is another issue for another paper.

2. There is no pattern in all the studies reported here that supports a gradual emergence of biological theory out of the folk psychology. As we look at younger and younger children, we do not see their judgments becoming more and more psychologically driven. So, although we cannot be sure where biology does come from, it does not seem to come from a psychology and probably not from a mechanics either.

3. It is not going to be right to say that young children have conscious theories of all aspects of biology. They clearly have never thought about many of the things we ask and yet they still have strong biases to prefer some classes of mechanisms over others, biases that do not seem to spring out of a naive physics or psychology. Thus, they may have a set of principles, highly abstract ones that are generative or productive such that they can account for intuitions about an indefinitely large set of novel biological phenomena. Such a generative framework would seem to be the most realistic and natural way of explaining how explanatory beliefs develop, especially about novel phenomena.

What might these biases be in more detail? Returning to the seven contrasts outlined at the beginning of this chapter, much of their import may be distilled to ramifications of the teleological and essentialist biases and their interactions. We have seen how functional roles of properties play a key role in early beliefs about inheritance and that beliefs about heterogeneous structure may also be linked to notions that feature functions interconnect. Essence may become closely related to other views about mechanisms of inheritance and to the importance of canonical patterns of change, and to reproduction itself. Similarly, essence relates the asssumption of causal links between the phenomenal and underlying structure. Homeostasis may not be captured except perhaps in the vague sense of interdependencies among functional subunits.

Domain-specific knowledge can emerge either because something like an innate theory (or more cautiously, mode of construal) is particularly tailored for that domain, or because one or more modes of construal find a particular affinity with a set of phenomena in the world but never really embody a theory in themselves prior to encountering the world. They just lead to common sets of theories through a combination of shared biases and resonances with real-world structure. In addition, one bias may not always serve to single out a particular domain, but various combinations, such as teleology and essentialism, may serve to neatly demarcate a domain. There is a related issue of whether essentialism and the teleological/design mode of construal are really equivalent sorts of things. The teleological/design mode of construal is normally described as a form, or level, of explanation perhaps with its own distinctive patterns of causation and sense of "cause." Essentialism seems to be more of an assumption about the way things are structured. To the extent that these are interestingly different sorts of biases, they will probably play different sorts of roles in how they guide the growth of biological thought.

There may be intriguing relations between the teleological/design stance and the intentional one. For example, it might be that the intentional stance is more basic and that some notion of goal seeking in the intentional sense becomes generalized into teleological terms. I doubt this, because there are other indications that very young children can have functional awareness of inanimate artifacts, even at ages when there is still debate about their level of competence as folk psychologists (e.g., Zelazo & Kearsley, 1980, on functions and objects in 1 year olds). There are interesting relations between the two stances concerning notions such as goals and purpose, but I am skeptical about the intentional stance being the original source of both.

A different model might hold that teleological modes of construal are first used for animals and animate artifacts and only later for plants and nonanimate artifacts. Perhaps self-produced motion immediately suggests functional relations in ways more salient than in plants. Some of R. Gelman's (1990) suggestions about young children's inferences about the motions of animate and inanimate objects might be used to support such a claim. In such an account, early "biological" thought would exclude plants, but not because animals are being construed in intentional terms that do not work for plants, but rather because there is an increased difficulty in using a teleological stance with plants. This needs to be explored further, but if an awareness of the functional properties of nonanimate artifacts is also seen very early on, as some suggest, it probably exists for some plants as well. In contrast to most of the inanimate natural world, most artifacts and most biological kinds (not only animals but also plants) have perceivably different parts that do different things and serve different purposes. This may be the simplest way in which the teleological stance first connects with biological things. In perceiving those different parts, perhaps we are drawn immediately to making inferences about different functions. Talk about immediate perception of functions starts to sound more like the Gibsonian notion of affordance as well and raises the possibility that perception–conception contrasts here may be misleading (Gibson, 1979).

All this talk of constant principles cannot overlook that a great deal of conceptual change does occur with respect to biological thought from, say 3–10 years; and many of the studies described here illustrate dramatic changes: the rise of an awareness of the special status of inborn properties seen clearly in the inheritance studies and the contagion study. The importance of canonical patterns of change to type of kind seemed to also develop considerably during the elementary school years and both it and an appreciation of inborn properties may be linked to an increasingly complex version of essentialism and an understanding of how essence might causally individuate kinds. Moreover, a host of smaller misconceptions were evident in every study. A critical question is how well most known patterns of conceptual change can be accommodated within a system where some versions of essentialist and teleological biases are always present. In suggesting that we may think somewhat differently about biological things from the start, I do not mean to rule out all conceptual change. I do mean to wonder if that change has to be seen as occurring within a larger and relatively stable framework that helps orient us cognitively toward biological sorts of things.

Most generally we may want to distinguish between broad modes of construal and detailed sets of beliefs in our accounts of how knowledge becomes organized into domains and changes over time. We may be endowed with relatively few modes of construal (or stances, if you prefer) such as the mechanical, the teleological, and the intentional (and perhaps a half dozen more); but we may be able to use these as footholds into acquiring much more elaborated belief systems in an extraordinary number of specialized domains.

A final issue asks whether, even if the mechanical, intentional, and teleological stances precede and guide the differentiation of more local belief systems, those three stances themselves might not be initially learned through more general learning procedures. I am increasingly persuaded by infancy research that this is unlikely for the mechanical and the intentional, but there is much less evidence concerning the earliest origins of a functional mode of construal. I am struck, however, by the extraordinary ease with which all of us do learn about functional objects such as tools relative to other species that exhibit sophisticated learning in so many other areas. If there is indeed a strong species specificity for a functional/design stance, it can serve as evidence for its domain specificity as well.

Getting back to the issues that began this chapter and that organized this symposium as a whole, the emergence of biological thought would seem to support a view of constraints working at the most belief-laden aspects of condition, constraints moreover that are not equally felicitous with all classes of phenomena. It is now clear that there are really four potential ways in which biological thought could emerge: First, it could arise out of completely domain-general learning procedures such as association, typicality tabulation, and induction. Second, it could arise out of another predetermined domain or mode of construal such as an intuitive psychology or mechanics. Third, it could arise out of a fortunate match of one or more modes of construal that, although limited in scope of application, are not exclusively tailored for biology. Finally, it could arise out of a predetermined mode of construal or combination of modes that is specifically tailored for biological phenomena. I have argued on both principled and empirical grounds that neither of the first two accounts have any support. It is still an open question, however, as to whether the modes of construal have evolved just because of a need to better understand biological things or whether they have more general purposes that just happen, especially in some combinations, to work particularly well with living things. Distinguishing between these two alternatives may be an exceedingly subtle problem, and may require a highly specific characterization of the biases at all points in development. Only then can we fully characterize the level of abstraction and domain specificity of such biases and the true manner in which biological thought emerges in the child.

ACKNOWLEDGMENTS

Many thanks to Mike Maratsos for his comprehensive comments on an earlier version of this chapter. Much of the research reported on herein was supported by NIH grant R01–HD23922

REFERENCES

Atran, S. (1990). *Cognitive foundations of natural history: Towards an anthropology of science.* Cambridge: Cambridge University Press.
Bruner, J. S., Oliver, R. R., & Greenfield, P. M., et al. (1966). *Studies in cognitive growth.* New York: Wiley.
Canon W. B. (1912). *The wisdom of the body.* New York: Norton.
Carey, S. (1985). *Conceptual change in childhood.* Cambridge, MA: MIT Press.
Carey, S. (1988). Conceptual differences between children and aduls. *Mind and Language, 3,* 167–181.
Chi, M. T. H., Feltovich, P. J., & Glaser, R. ((1981). Categorization and representations of physics problems by experts and novices. *Cognitive Science, 5,* 121–152.
Dawkins, R. (1986). *The blind watchmaker.* New York: Norton.
Dennett, D. C. (1987). *The intentional stance.* Cambridge, MA: MIT Press.
Fodor, J. A. (1975). *The language of thought.* New York: Crowell.
Fodor, J. A. (1981). *Representations: Philosophical essays on the foundations of cognitive*

science. Cambridge, MA: MIT Press.

Gelman, R. (1990). First principles organize attention to and learning about relevant data: Number and the animate-inanimate distinction as examples. *Cognitive Science, 14,* 79–106.

Gelman, S. A. (1988). Development of induction within natural kind and artifact categories. *Cognitive Psychology, 20,* 63–95.

Gelman, S. A., & Coley, J. D. (1991). Language and categorization: The acquisition of natural kind terms. In S. A. Gelman & J. P. Byrnes (Ed.), *Perspectives on language and thought: Interrelations in development* (pp. 146–196). Cambridge: Cambridge University Press.

Gentner, D., & Toupin, C. (1988). Systematicity and surface similarity in the development of analogy. *Cognitive Science, 10,* 277–300.

Gibson, J. J. (1979). *The ecological approach to visual perception.* Boston: Houghton-Mifflin.

Gould, S. J., & Lewontin, R. C. (1978). The spandrels of San Marco and the Panglossian paradigm. *Proceedings of the Royal Society, London, 205,* 581–598.

Hull, D. (1965). The effect of essentialism on taxonomy: 2,000 years of stasis. *British Journal for the Philosophy of Science, 15, 16,* 314-326, 1–18.

Inhelder, B., & Piaget, J. (1964). *The early growth of logic in the child.* New York: Norton.

Jacob, F. (1982). *The logic of life: A history of heredity.:* New York: Pantheon.

Keil, F. C. (1979). *Semantic and conceptual development: An ontological perspective.* Cambridge, MA: Harvard University Press.

Keil, F. C. (1983). On the emergence of semantic and conceptual distinctions. *Journal of Experimental Psychology: General, 112,* 357–385.

Keil, F. C. (1986). The acquisition of natural kind and artifact terms. In W. Demopoulos & A. Marras (Eds.), *Language learning and concept acquisition.* Norwood, NJ: Ablex.

Keil, F. C. (1989). *Concepts, kinds and cognitive development.* Manuscript submitted for review.

Keil, F. C. (1991). The emergence of theoretical beliefs as constraints on concepts. In S. Carey & R. Gelman (Eds.), *The epigenesis of mind: Essays on biology and cognition* (pp. 237–256). Hillsdale, NJ: Lawrence Erlbaum Associates.

Mayr, E. (1988). *Toward a new philosophy of biology: Observations of an evolutionist.* Cambridge, MA: Harvard University Press.

Nagel, E. (1961). *The structure of science.* Indianapolis: Hackett.

Quine, W. V. O. (1977). Natural kinds. In S. P. Schwartz (Ed.), *Naming, necessity, and natural kinds.* Ithaca, NY: Cornell University Press.

Salmon, W. C. (1989). *Four decades of scientific explanation.* Minneapolis: University of Minnesota Press.

Springer, K. (1990). *Children's awareness of the biological implications of kinship.* Unpublished doctoral dissertation, Cornell University, Ithaca, NY.

Springer, K., & Keil, F. C. (1989). On the development of biologically specific beliefs: The case of inheritance. *Child development, 60,* 637–648.

Springer, K., & Keil, F. C. (1991). Early differentiation of causal mechanisms appropriate to biological and nonbiological kinds. *Child Development.*

Terman, L. M. (1916). *The measurement of intelligence.* Boston: Houghton Mifflin.

Thompson, D. W. (1961). *On growth and form* (abridged ed.). (J. T. Bonner, Ed.). Cambridge: University Press.

Vygotsky, L. S. (1986). *Thought and language.* Cambridge, MA: MIT Press. (Original work published 1934).

Wellman, H., & Gelman, S. (1988). Children's understanding of the nonobvious. In R. J. Sternberg (Ed.), *Advances in the psychology of human intelligence* (pp. 99–135). Hillsdale, NJ: Lawrence Erlbaum Associates.

Werner, H. (1948). *Comparative psychology of mental development* (2nd ed.). New York:

International Universities Press.

Woodfield, A. (1976). *Teleology.* Cambridge: Cambridge University Press.

Wright, L. (1976). *Teleological explanations: An etiological analysis of goals and functions.* Berkeley: University of California Press.

Zelazo, P. R., & Kearsley, R. (1980). The emergence of functional play in infants: Evidence for a major cognitive transition. *Journal of Applied Developmental Psychology, 1,* 95–117.

5

Language, Affect, and Social Order

Carol Malatesta-Magai
Bruce Dorval
Long Island University

This chapter addresses the question of modularity in human communication systems from the perspective of affect theory and sociolinguistics. Two communication systems—the nonverbal, which has been traditionally linked with the affect system, and the linguistic, which is generally not linked with the affective—are considered. We argue that the kind of heuristic that guides contemporary theorizing about brain modularity is not sufficiently social to speak to the reality that both kinds of language are socially constitutive (Bruner, 1983). This is true of Chomsky's theory of language in particular, because it emphasizes individual minds rather than communicating individuals.

Here we consider how reembedding language within the social context and relational system sheds light on how language and emotion subsystems operate in modular but essentially cooperative ways and what that cooperation looks like. We first present a brief exposition of Chomsky's position, contrast this with the sociolinguistic perspective, and then relate it to affect theory and nonverbal communication. Finally, we illustrate the points we wish to make with an affective and sociolinguistic analysis of communication, in this particular case using a portion of a videotaped conversation of three members of a family. We apply the more social view of language and affect to describe the conversation and to arrive at an integrated account of the cooperation of those systems of communication in that context.

CHOMSKY'S VIEW OF LANGUAGE

Chomsky's theory of transformational grammar revolutionized language studies. In place of the descriptive approaches that predominated in the mid-20th century, he proposed a model of grammar that directed attention to the means by which speakers produce utterances that are grammatically acceptable and use knowledge of grammar to interpret utterances. He posited a language faculty to account for such competencies and continues to refine hypotheses about the nature of that faculty. This is not the place for a detailed discussion of either Chomsky's current model of the language faculty or the changes that the model has undergone over the past 30 years. Suffice to say that the theory of transformational grammar has had a tremendous impact on the science of linguistics; moreover, Chomsky's efforts have provided a model for other research on cognitive processes and even a conception of the overall functioning of the mind as the interaction of subsystems of various kinds both within and between domains of mental activity. The prospects for such efforts are substantial. However, the utility of this approach for understanding communication processes seems to be more limited.

In our view, the primary limitation of Chomsky's approach for the study of communication is that despite revisions in his theory over the past 30 years, it remains firmly centered on individual mental processes. Chomsky (1986) posed the question: "How is that knowledge put to use in speech?" and then answered it by dividing it into two related questions, "the perception problem" and "the production problem" (p. 4). Thus, he framed the problem of communication in terms of individual abilities. Although individual mental processes are undoubtedly heavily implicated in communication, conceptualization of the specifically interpersonal is completely lacking. Elsewhere, Chomsky acknowledged that his theory entails an idealized homogeneous language community, one without social and linguistic differences (Chomsky, 1986, pp. 16–17). Without conceptualization of the interpersonal aspect of communication, questions of communication are reduced to questions of individual performance; and even these questions are treated in a distinctly secondary way in Chomsky's theorizing.

The limitation noted earlier is evident both in Chomsky's rather restricted definition of language use and in his inability to integrate his political convictions with his theory of language. Chomsky was an active anti-war advocate during the Vietnam War. Since then, he has consistently espoused the view that American society is dominated by corporate interests. He was a supporter of the Sandinista revolution in Nicaragua and traveled there to give lectures on language theory as well as on his political views. Those lectures were distinct enough from each other that they were published separately with very little cross-referencing. In another context, Chomsky made strenuous efforts to relate his passions for language theory and politics: "Plato's problem, then, is to explain how we know so much, given that the evidence available to us is so sparse. Orwell's problem is to explain why we know and understand so little, even though the evidence available to us is so rich" (Chomsky, 1981, p. xxvii).

Plato's problem is the wider framing Chomsky has given to his investigations of language, specifically the puzzling questions raised in formulating the biological basis of universal grammar. Orwell's problem refers to the pervasive and largely unconscious control over thought exercised by the modern state. Chomsky relegated discussion of Orwell's problem to the last chapter of an extended treatment of his language theory, and that discussion is not tied to his political theory. Thus, Chomsky has been unable to incorporate his keen interest in problems of social control into his theory of language.

Sociolinguists, in contrast, provides an approach to language study that encompasses Orwell's problem. Although a variety of approaches are covered by the term *sociolinguistics*, they share theoretical premises and associated methods that sharply distinguish them from those of Chomsky. The fundamental theoretical tenet of sociolinguistics is to focus on communication rather than on individuals. Instead of viewing communication as a product of individual communicative competencies, individual competencies are viewed as the product of preexisting communication patterns, patterns that vary socioculturally and entail issues of social difference and relatedness, such as status, dominance, and affiliation. As a result, sociolinguists investigate the structural properties of communication events rather than examining utterances in isolation.

In this chapter we take the more sociolinguistic orientation toward interpretation of language and communication. Our perspective is also deeply informed by affect theory, especially that version that is developmentally and interpersonally oriented (Izard, 1971, 1977; Malatesta & Izard, 1984; Tomkins, 1962, 1963, 1991).

AFFECT THEORY

Affect theory embraces a modular conceptualization of mental faculties in specifying semi-autonomous subsystems of personality including the cognitive, affective, and motor (Izard & Malatesta, 1987; Malatesta & Izard, 1984; Tomkins, 1962, 1963, 1991). It also emphasizes the essential cooperation between separate subsystems that is achieved in the context of information processing and in responding to adaptational demands.

Although language and affect are not often thought of in conjunction with one another, we argue here that they stand in essential relation to one another, indeed that they operate in "co-assembly" (Tomkins, 1962) whenever the social world is engaged.

Most emotions theorists refer to a set of basic or fundamental emotions as being part of our biological heritage. Darwin (1872) wrote eloquently on this topic some 120 years ago, and since that time much cross-cultural and developmental work has come to sustain the thesis (Ekman, Sorenson, & Friesen, 1969; Izard, 1971; Izard & Malatesta, 1987; Malatesta, Culver, Tesman, & Shepard, 1989; Scherer, 1988).

The neurophysiological basis of emotion is limbic (Le Doux, 1990; MacLean, 1973), the limbic brain being a phylogenetically early core of the cerebral hemispheres that arose with the order, *Mammalia*. Among the specializations that set mammals apart from other animals is the tendency to form social organizations and to invest extraordinary energy in the care of the young. The elaboration of emotional experience and response systems can be considered critical to the formation and maintenance of social bonds.

To the extent that language is also fundamentally social, permitting communication between social interactants, one expects, and indeed recent neuroanatomical and neurophysiological studies confirm (Newman, 1988), physical connectivity between the limbic and language modules. As such, language and emotion, although not typically considered in conjunction with one another, must be regarded as intimately related and cooperating mental organs, both neuro-anatomically, and, as we hope to illustrate, functionally.

Their cooperation is joined in the social sphere. Indeed, a careful analysis of human speech discloses the fact that language is saturated with affect—the linguistic communicational system that in many ways is totally and artfully interwoven with the nonverbal communication system. When we speak, we not only reveal our thoughts, but also our momentary feelings as well as our affective biases (Malatesta, 1990). We also reveal basic dimensions of relatedness such as status, dominance, and affiliation. As such, Chomsky's inability to relate the political and the linguistic may be particularly idiosyncratic. Our analysis of the conversation as presented in this chapter illustrates that the "political" is indissociable from the social, and the social from the affective and linguistic.

In summary, we have argued that affect and language, as socially constitutive activities, are not only modular subsystems of com-munication, but that they function essentially in a complementary and cooperative manner. If our premise is correct, an analysis of affect and language in the context of the overall structure of communication should reveal both parallel linguistic and affective processes, as well as sharp differences between them that are organized at a higher level. Both should be identifiable in the same communicative event; moreover, we expect that either analysis—linguistic or affective—should yield comparable images of the larger system in which the subsystems are engaged—in this case, the family system, and that it should reveal systemic properties. We turn now to an examination of the material. We use this to demonstrate modularity and co-assembly of affect and language. However, more importantly for theory construction, we illustrate how affect and linguistic systems are conditioned on one another as a social product.

THE COMMUNICATIVE INTERCHANGES OF ONE FAMILY

The Family

The family for our study was selected from a larger collection of families who had participated in a project by Dorval designed to explore the development of conversational styles. The original study population included 42 families and their 12-year-old children. The children were videotaped in two interaction contexts—with their mother and/or father, and with a "best friend." The instructions for both sessions were simply to talk with each other and to "feel free to talk about whatever you like." The family chosen for the present study was selected at random. The family is suburban and upper-middle class; the father is a lawyer, the mother works at home, and their 12-year-old son, whom we call "Joseph," attends a private school nearby. In this chapter we report only on the first 24 minutes of the family interaction session.

In the following, we perform an analysis of emotion as encoded in the ongoing narrative exchange among the family members (attention is paid to face/body/voice and verbalizations that have affective content); we then examine the talk activity itself and analyze it from a sociolinguistic perspective.

Affective Analysis

The following treatment describes where and how affect is encoded in the communicative interchanges of the family. This analysis discloses that language is saturated with affect; indeed it is hard to parse one from the other. It also reveals the affective biases of the individual members of the family as well as illustrates how individual biases are overridden by dyadic control parameters. As we see in the following case, the mother's prevailing affective bias is one that is organized around shame; this shame also permeates the nature of her interactions with her husband and son. In contrast, the husband's and son's individual emotional profiles are not identical to their dyadic patterns of interaction, but are particularized, depending on conversational partner and the type of affective messages communicated. In fact, the father and son are revealed to consist of a communication subsystem within the family; consequently their affective communications have to be understood within that context.

The affective analysis also provides information on which to base inferences about the "family system"—its dynamics, its mode of relating, and the topics and modes of communication. The sociolinguistic analysis that follows the affective analysis also yields a picture of the family as a communication system as a whole. At times the picture derived from the two analyses are consistent, at times divergent. Only when we consider the analyses from a larger organizational framework do we find a deeper coherence that explains it. For example, as indicated earlier, the affective analysis indicates that the mother is shame-dominant. From this information one might conclude that her role in the family is a passive one. However, from a sociolinguistic perspective, she is the prime mover in the speech event. These two aspects of her persona seem at first to be difficult to reconcile and even seem contradictory. However, when the family's communication system is evaluated as a whole—using both the affective and sociolinguistic levels of analysis—these two aspects of her communication repertoire are revealed to be codetermined. We turn now to the affect analysis. However, before proceeding to an examination of the data we briefly describe the conceptual framework and the analytic strategies chosen to examine this family's affective interchanges.

Conceptual Framework.   In Tomkins' scheme, there is a limited number of primary or fundamental emotions, each with distinctive neurophysiological, physiognomic, and motivational properties. Among the 8–10 primary emotions that Tomkins, Izard, and other researchers have identified, we chose to focus on the emotions that tend to be most salient in the intimate social system of families. Based on the literature, the emotions most relevant to close interpersonal bonds or their disharmony are the emotions that communicate rejection (i.e., *contempt* and *disgust*), and the emotions that are subsumable under the rubric of *affiliation* (i.e., all of those actions that communicate positive affect and liking—mutual smiling and laughter, touching, etc.). A third crucial affect, that of *shame*, is intimately related to both contempt/disgust and affiliation. Shame is the dynamic reciprocal of these emotions in that it is naturally evoked by the experience of rejection and lack of affiliation. Although anger is also considered a rejecting or potentially rejecting emotion, one rarely sees its overt expression in ordinary interchanges, certainly not in the context of observational studies of average families who are asked to appear before a videocamera. Consequently, we chose to focus on the three emotional domains indicated here, and developed a coding system commensurate with the task of coding the relevant expressions, as based on theory. (Details concerning the coding system and its use are found in the appendix.)

Data Analytic Considerations.   Contempt, shame, and affiliation were the three prevailing types of affective communication encountered in this family; we coded all instances of these affects as they occurred during the session whether they occurred verbally or nonverbally. It is important to point out here that distinguishing the degree to which an affect was encoded in the face versus voice versus body proved to be unnecessary because the vast majority of messages was communicated redundantly and multimodally.

Each of the three affective expressions were coded independently of one another, of the context in which they were expressed, and of the family member who expressed or was targeted by them. That is, separate runs were made for each individual and for each affect; the criteria for coding an affective expression were focused solely on the individual being coded and did not depend on the prior communication or on other contextual features. Intercoder reliabilities ranged from a low of 55% up to perfect agreement; the average reliabilities were in the 70s and 80s. Because of our concern about the lower reliabilities, both coders coded the entire interaction session and all discrepancies were resolved by consensus. Examination of the pool of disagreements and the direction of their eventual resolution indicated that neither coder dominated the decisions.

In the next step, instances of expression were categorized and multiply classified as follows: (a) kind of affect (contempt, shame, affiliation), (b) family member expressing the affect (mother, father, son), and (c) family member to whom the message was directed (e.g., for mother-expressed affects: to father, son, both, or other; the "other" category consisted of utterances directed at persons outside the family, such as a teacher or pet).

Because each unit of analysis—the affective expression—meets the criterion of independence as coded, and because we wished to explore several dimensions of interaction as well as higher order interaction effects, log-linear analyses (which produce chi-square statistics) seemed both the most appropriate and promising means of examining our data (Feinberg, 1980). In the current project we performed a series of log-linear analyses to examine the relations among the multiple-classification criteria described earlier. Our purpose was to determine the degree of empirical independence that actually obtains among the classification criteria (see Bakeman & Dorval, 1989, for a discussion of this point).

Overall Affective Climate of the Family.   Table 5.1 presents the overall frequency of contempt, shame, and affiliative communications expressed by each family member. In a very general sense one may regard the patterns as representing familial and individual affective biases. Later we see that the biases are distributed differentially depending on the particular target of the communication.

The first thing that is striking about the data in Table 5.1 is the sheer density of discrete affective communications. Although on first viewing of this videotape the family does not appear to be unusually emotional, one subsequently finds that there is an enormous amount of affective interchange woven into the fabric of conversation. Much of it is subtle, but it is readily codeable. In the course of the 24 minutes of

TABLE 5.1
Frequency and Percent of Types of Emotional Expression
by Each Family Member

| Family Member | Emotional Expression | | | Total Marginals | % |
	Contempt	Shame	Affiliation		
Father	42	47	18	107	21.9
Mother	33	76	19	128	26.2
Son	102	97	54	253	51.8
Marginals	177	220	91	488	
	36.0	45.1	18.6		

Column Marginals: $X^2 (2) = 155.1$, $p < .01$; Father v. Mother: $X^2 (1) = 2.1$, n.s.;
Father v. Son: $X^2 (1) = 59.18$, $p < .01$; Mother v. Son: $X^2 (1) = 41.8$, $p < .01$.
Row Marginals : $X^2 (2) = 70.2$, $p < .01$; Contempt v. Shame: $X^2 (1) = 4.7$, $p < .05$; Contempt v. Affiliation: $X^2 (1) = 27.6$, $p < .01$; Shame v. Affiliation: $X^2 (1) = 53.5$, $p < .01$.
Family Member x Emotional Expression: $X^2 (4) = 15.8$, $p < .01$
Orthogonal contrasts
Father plus Son v. Mother: $X^2 (2) = 14.5$, $p < .01$
Father v. Son: $X^2 (2) = 1.4$, n.s.
Each Family Member's Emotional Expressions (Father and Son combined as a result of orthogonal contrasts)
Father plus Son: $X^2 (2) = 28.8$, $p < .01$; Contempt v. Affiliation: $X^2 (1) = 3.8$, n.s.; Shame v. Affiliation: $X^2 (10 = 34.2$, $p < .01$; Contempt v. Shame: $X^2 (1) = 17.0$, $p < .01$.
Mother: $X^2 (2) = 41.4$, $p < .01$; Contempt v. Affiliation: $X^2 (1) = 3.8$. n.s.; Shame v. Affiliation: $X^2 (1) = 34.2$, $p < .01$; Contempt v. Shame: $X^2 (1) = 17.0$, $p < .01$.

interaction, there were 488 discrete affective signals, amounting to 20 per minute.

When we look at the relative distribution of affective communications (see column marginals, Table 5.1), it is clear that some expressions are more preponderant than others. Shame is the predominant affective expression (220 instances or 9.2 per minute, constituting 45.1% of the affective interchanges) in this family although the density of contempt is also high (177 instances of 7.4 per minute and amounting to 36% of the affective interchanges). Of the three emotions coded, affiliation has the lowest frequency, with only 91 instances or 3.8 per minute, thus constituting only 18.6% of the interchanges. Chi-square analyses indicate that shame is expressed significantly more frequently than contempt and affiliation and contempt is expressed significantly more frequently than affiliation. In summary, this is a family that is high on shame and low on affiliation. Subsequent analyses indicate that there is a dynamic and reciprocal relation between these two affects. Our next analysis was directed at determining the affect-specific profiles of individual family members.

Individual Profiles: Relative Rate of Affect Expression.   First we examine the relative density of affective communications among family members. The low marginals and chi-square tests (Table 5.1) indicate that the son is more affectively expressive than either parent. He shows the greatest density of affective expressions (253 or 10.5 per minute); the mother's rate is about half her son's (128 or 5 per minute), and the father's rate is also lower than the son's (107 or 4.5 per minute). This relative distribution of affectivity across family members is consistent with notions about children being more emotionally expressive than adults (Izard, 1971).

Relationship Among Family Members and Types of Emotion Expressed. In this analysis we examined whether profiles of emotion expression were similar or different across family members. An interaction effect between the two dimensions of family members and types of emotion was obtained (see Table 5.1); subsequent analysis indicated that father and son had similar affective profiles, and both differed from the profile exhibited by the other. In terms of relative frequency, contempt and shame are dominant emotions for both the father and son, whereas affiliation is low. In contrast, the mother's dominant emotion is shame and she is low on both contempt and affiliation.

Who Sends What Emotional Communications to Whom?   Our next level of analysis was directed at determining whether there was any bias in the kinds of emotional communications different family members directed at one another. Recall that a speaker could direct an emotional communication to either of the two other parties in the three-way interaction, to both parties, or to a person outside of the immediate conversation. The "both" category was dropped from subsequent analyses because instances were relatively rare (23 out of 488). Expressions to someone not present in the interaction were somewhat more frequent (80 out of the remaining 465), but because we were primarily interested in communications among family members, this category was also dropped from subsequent analysis.

Table 5.2 displays the frequency of each affect expressed by each person to each other person. Log-linear analysis revealed a three-way

TABLE 5.2
Frequency of Types of Emotional Expression that Each
Family Member Expressed Toward the Others

Expressor	Target	Emotional Expressions			Marginals
		Contempt	Shame	Affiliation	
Father	Mother	19	22	5	46
	Son	14	11	13	38
	Marginals	33	33	18	84
Mother	Father	20	9	12	41
	Son	9	43	8	60
	Marginals	29	52	20	101
Son	Mother	63	56	13	132
	Father	18	10	40	68
	Marginals	81	66	53	200

Overall Analysis
Emotional Expression x Expressor x Target; $X^2 (2) = 7.8, p < .05$ (using structural
    zeros for Father to Father, etc.)
Analysis of three-way interaction in terms of three 2–way analyses
    For Father: Target x Expressions: $X^2 (2) = 7.5, p < .05$
    For Mother: Target x Expressions: $X^2 (2) = 14.8, p < .01$
    For Son: Target x Expressions: $X^2 (2) = 70.4, p < .01$
Pairwise comparisons for each Emotional Expression comparing the two Targets
    Father: Contempt: $X^2 (1) = 0.8$, n.s.; Shame: $X^2 (1) = 3,7, p < .10$; Affiliation: $X^2 (1)$
        $= 3.6, p < .10$
    Mother: Contempt: $X^2 (1) = 4.2, p < .05$; Shame: $X^2 (1) = 22.2, p < .01$; Affiliation: $X^2 (1) = 0.8$, n.s.
    Son: Contempt: $X^2 (1) = 25.0, p < .01$; Shame; $X^2 (1) = 32.1, p < .01$; Affiliation: $X^2 (1) = 13.8, p < .01$

interaction among those dimensions. Subsequent analyses indicated that the son was most differentiated in his communications to the two other members of the family. He expressed more contempt and shame to his mother than to his father and more affiliation to his father than to his mother. The mother's pattern of expression was somewhat differentiated in that she expressed more contempt to the father than to the son and more shame to the son than to the father. Finally, the father's responding was least differentiated. He expressed marginally more shame to the mother than to the son and marginally more affiliation to the son than to the mother.

Thus far, we have described the affective profile of the family, the affective profile of individual members of the family, and their degree of differentiation with respect to the kinds of emotional communications they tend to send to one another. Although this has given us a feel for the personality organizations of the individual members as well as a sense of the family's emotional climate, it fails to inform as to the dynamic and reciprocal patterns of communication—that is, the actual ebb and flow of the process and how and why the patterns may develop and be maintained over time. We now turn to the more dynamic analysis. Here we examine sequential patterns of interaction.

Sequential Patterns.   Before proceeding to sequential analysis we looked at the distribution of affective communications by expressor, respondent, affect expressed, and affective response. In order to understand affective sequences between dyads, several factors must be taken into consideration. Ideally, we should perform a four-way log-linear analysis with expressor, respondent, affect expressed, and affective response as the four dimensions. However, we do not have sufficient frequencies to carry out that kind of analysis. The next best procedure would involve performing all possible three-way log-linear analyses using the four dimensions; this approach would yield results identical with the four-way analysis with the exception that the four-way interaction itself is not tested. The next best procedure was applied.

Table 5.3 (lower portion) displays the results of these analyses. As indicated, only the respondent x affect expressed x affective response interaction was significant. Orthogonal contrasts revealed that the father and son's performance as respondents were similar and that they both differed in their patterns of responding from the mother. Thus, the father and son's data is collapsed in subsequent analysis. Table 5.3 (upper portion) displays the frequency and type of family member's response to each of three types of prior communication.

In order to look at patterns of contingency between types of emotional communication, we applied lag-sequential analysis (Sackett, 1987), using

Allison and Liker's (1982) formula for computing z scores for Lag 1 transitions. The frequencies in Table 5.3 were transformed into z scores to determine which transitions were more likely than chance to occur and which ones less likely to occur. The data indicated that the mother's pattern of responding is not influenced by the affect to which she is responding. In contrast, there are a number of noteworthy contingencies in the pattern of the father and son. First, we note that the probability of a shame response is significantly elevated following a prior shame response and affiliation is elevated following an affiliation communication. This pattern indicates that there are runs of shame and affiliation and that in effect there is something about these two emotions when enacted interpersonally that recruits more of the same, at least in the case of the father and son. We suspect that shame is particularly contagious and, moreover, that affiliative bids have an implicit and inherent reciprocal demand aspect, as suggested by Cornelius (1984). Contempt is apparently less contagious; it is equally likely to be followed by shame, contempt, and affiliation.

Two negative z scores in the father–son data indicate that there is a significant inhibition of affiliation following shame and in inhibition of shame following affiliation. This finding is consistent with the notion that shame is an emotion that is particularly relevant to affiliative bonds or exclusion from affiliative bonds (Kaufman, 1989; Lewis, 1971; Tomkins,

TABLE 5.3
Sequencing of Emotional Expressions

A: Frequency with which each emotional expression is followed
by each of the Others, Broken down into mother's response
pattern and father and son's response pattern.

Mother's Data			Father & Son's Data		
Prior: Shame	Contempt	Affiliation	Shame	Contempt	Affiliation
Subsequent response of Mother:			Subsequent response of Father and Son:		
Shame	33	29	14	79	48	17
Contempt	18	9	6	64	58	21
Affiliation	10	7	2	16	26	30

B: Z–scores for the transitional relationships in Panel A

Shame	-1.16	0.86	0.45	3.30**	-1.10	-2.82**
Contempt	0.97	-1.10	0.18	-0.41	1.33	-1.67
Affiliation	0.47	0.17	-0.83	-4.22**	-0.13	5.50**

Performed all four possible three-way log-linear analyses among expressor, respondent, affect expressed, and affective response. Only respondent x affect expressed x affective response was significant: $X^2 (8) = 20.97. p < .01$.
Orthogonal contrasts of significant interaction revealed a difference between father and son mother: $X^2 (4) = 14.6, p, .01$, but none between father and son: $X^2 (4) = 6.0$, n.s.

1963). The experience of affiliation is emotionally rewarding and thus unlikely to elicit interpersonal shame. On the other hand, shame is a natural precipitant of severed or interrupted emotional bonds.

As noted earlier, the mother's data do not conform to the pattern shown by the father and son. The mother is, in effect, "shame saturated," so much so that she does not differentiate her responses to different communications. Her pervasive and nondiscriminating shame organization is interpretable from within the context of the family dynamic. As revealed in earlier analyses, there is greater affiliative exchange between father and son, and they appear to have an affective alliance that excludes the mother. Given the dynamic relationship between shame and affiliation, we interpret her shame as at least partially a function of her relative exclusion from the father–son alliance.

Given the high degree of negative affectivity in this family (high contempt and shame, low affiliation), somewhat offset in the case of the father and son by the occasional affectionate play in which they engage, this family looks unhappy to the outside observer. Assumedly it is difficult to maintain a warm interpersonal relationship in the face of high rates of critical, derogatory communications especially when unameliorated by significant levels of positive communication. One suspects that the family members are more alienated from one another than they are intimate. To test this, we generated an intimacy–alienation index for each pair of interactants. This was done by creating ratios of the amount of expressed affiliative communications divided by the amount of expressed contempt/disgust and shame communications. Figure 5.1 diagrams the positive–negative flow of communication with the study family based on these ratios. In an affectionate (vs. alienated) relationship, one would expect positive affective communications to prevail; the ratios should be greater than 1. In relationships where negative affective communications predominate, the ratios will be less than 1. As indicated in Fig. 5.1, only one ratio—representing the pattern of communication from the son to the father—is greater than 1. The smallest ratios occur in the context of husband's and son's communications to the mother; in both cases, positive communications are rare relative to negative communications. Thus, the family, for the most part, appears to be at risk for alienation, with the mother most at risk.

Summary.   To summarize, the pattern that emerges from the affect analysis, we could say that this is a family in which rejecting communications prevail over affiliative communications. Affiliation is low and contempt and shame high. The son directs a good deal of contempt toward the mother and the mother toward the father. The father and son also express a good deal of shame in the presence of the mother, although

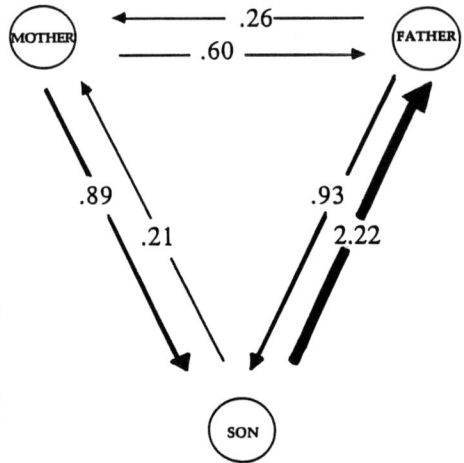

FIG. 5.1. Relative index of intimacy–alienation between pairs of interactants based on ratio of positive (affiliative) to negative (contempt–shame) communications between the two.

the nature of their reactivity appears to be different. We hypothesize that the husband is reacting to the wife's contempt communications, whereas the son is reacting to her shame; as a 12-year-old, he is less socially skilled in affect modulation and, thus, will have less well-developed ability to isolate the contagious effects of the mother's surfeit of shame. Alternatively, or perhaps additionally, the husband and son may experience her behavior to be over-regulatory or overly directive as she schedules the family's activities. Indeed, as we see in the sociolinguistic analysis, discussion of the family's work and social schedule for the coming week was the primary topic of conversation.

The preceding analyses provide one window on the affective and communicative patterns of the individual members of this family and on relationships within the family and between family members. It also provided support for several formulations concerning affect dynamics, as formulated by Tomkins (1962, 1963) and Izard (1971, 1977). Another window on the family's communication patterns can be had from a sociolinguistic analysis of their talk activity. We turn to this analysis next. As we see, such an analysis provides additional and complementary data on the family's communication patterns—data that are instrumental in verifying and clarifying the account from the affective analysis.

Sociolinguistic Analysis

In this section we present a description of the organization of the family's communication event, including an analysis of the modes of domination and resistance associated with its establishment and maintenance. Then the relation between such speech-event organization and the affective analysis presented earlier is assessed by examining the distribution of shame, contempt, and affiliation within the speech event as well as the role of these affects in the structuring of the speech event itself. This results in a description of the relational/affective culture of the family.

The sociolinguistic analysis provides important data concerning the family's dynamics and further substantiates the claim that the linguistic and affective components of communication are coordinated in actual use. In brief, the analyses reveal that the mother is very active in the organization of the speech event and that she persists despite blatant resistance and frequent subterfuge on the part of her husband and son. Such resistance reinforces her shame and creates a communication system that marginalizes her as enacted in communications that are contemptuous and distancing although moderated by intervals of cooperation. The husband occasionally displays alignment with his wife, but with some degree of conflict, which places him in a contempt–shame bind. The son's contempt–shame bind is more a direct product of his interaction with his mother. He is contemptuous of her and also shamed by her.

Another crucial aspect of the interaction that is revealed in this analysis is how dominance and hierarchy operate in the family. Initially, the mother pursues her agendas and attempts to hold the father and son accountable to these agendas. This demand for accountability sets up hierarchical relations and establishes grounds for linguistic–affective struggle. According to Tomkins (1963), any nonegalitarian, hierarchical posture sets the stage for contempt–shame dynamics. The dominating partner signals contempt, which releases shame in the partner, and, in many instances, consequent countercontempt. Here, as the mother struggles for her position in the family system by forwarding her agendas, she simultaneously creates the conditions for rebellion. The sociolinguistic analysis is presented momentarily. Before this, we present a description of the conceptual framework and notation concerning methodology.

Conceptual Framework. In undertaking this analysis we assume that a fundamental use of language is to produce a speech event that is mutually recognizable to the members. We also assume that the consequence of this joint effort is to privilege certain family matters, ways of talking about them, and alignments among family members. As a result, we expect that the family's joint effort will not result in just any kind of speech event but rather one that displays crucial features of the family's culture.

The family's communication event was first segmented into a series of talk activities using criteria derived from Hymes (1972) and operationalized by Dumesil and Dorval (1989). Hymes distinguished three levels of organization for any communication event: (a) the speech situation (e.g., a group-therapy session), (b) the speech events composing the speech situation (e.g., pretherapy talk among members as they gather, the therapy session itself, posttherapy talk to arrange the next meeting and perform leave-taking), and (c) the speech acts that compose each speech event (e.g., greetings in pretherapy talk, narratives of troubles in the session itself, etc.) (Hymes, 1972, p. 56). Dumesil and Dorval also distinguished the series of talk activities composing each speech event (e.g., discussion of one member's troubles with a spouse, discussion of another member's difficulties with being in the group, etc.) and the sequences of talk composing each talk activity (e.g., narrative of troubles with a spouse followed by narrative about related troubles with a boss and finally questioning about the personal limitations that predispose to such difficulties).

In the present study, the speech situation consisted of an experimenter's visit to the family's home for the purpose of videotaping a conversation among father, mother, and son. The speech events consisted of (a) the experimenter's directive to provide a sample of how they talk together by discussing whatever they liked for half an hour, (b) the resulting family discussion, and (c) a postdiscussion chat with the experimenter. In this study, we examine the first two speech events beginning with the second.

The first step in the analysis was to segment the speech event into the series of talk activities and each of the talk activities into its series of consequences. We used the criteria developed by Dumesil and Dorval (1989) for the talk-activity segmentation and a simplified version of their definition of episodes. Episodes in informal talk are marked by a noticeable shift in the focus of talk that may include a change in the formatting of talk and the person or persons who are focal. In this study, we counted episode shifts where either the format of talk changed or the person forwarding talk changed, or both. Thus, what we are defining here as a segment was composed of one or more episodes where both the format of talk and the person responsible for forwarding talk do not change.

Two coders independently divided the family's speech event into talk activities and segmented each of them. Intercoder reliability was 88%— the coders agreed on 15 out of the 17 breaks; the two differences were resolved by a third coder. The coders agreed completely on the description of each talk activity and the segments within them. The results are displayed in Table 5.4.

The results of the talk-activity analysis reveal that the family's talk was relatively focused. Discussion of the family's agenda forwarded by the mother (Talk Activity 2) consumed more than half of the 24-minute speech event (13'43"). Agenda matters include plans for family outings, arranging a babysitter for Joseph when the parents go to a cocktail party, and organizing Joseph's studying for an upcoming school project. Related

TABLE 5.4
The Sequence of Talk Activities in the Family Interaction

				Affect Frequencies			
TA. Seq.	Time	Initiator	Format/ Uptake	Subject	Sh.	Ct.	Aff.
1.1	0'55"	Joseph	Narr./ Failed	Ribs father	0	1	1
2.1	1' 3"	Mother	Q-A/ Uptake	Family agenda	115	98	36
3.1	12'43"	Joseph	Q-A/ Uptake	LSU game, stocks	4	7	5
4.1	14' 9"	Joseph	Play/ Uptake	Thumb play	3	2	13
4.1	14'58"	Mother	Q-A/ Uptake	Track practice	3	2	0
4.2	15'12"	Father	Q-A/ Uptake	Track practice	14	10	5
4.3	17'44"	Joseph	Narr./ Uptake	Track practice	42	12	8
4.4	21'37"	Mother	Q-A/ Uptake	Track practice	9	2	0
2.2	22' 5"	Father	Q-A/ Uptake	Agenda making	2	2	1
5.1	22'15"	Joseph	Q-A/ Uptake	Neck cracking	2	0	1
6.1	22'29"	Mother	Q-A/ Uptake	Dentist	3	6	3
6.2	22'50"	Joseph	Narr./ Uptake	Hygenist	3	8	6
6.3	23'20"	Mother	Q-A/ Uptake	Dentist	10	6	2
7.1	23'52'	Joseph	Narr./ Failed	Criticizes painting	3	9	6

discussion of Joseph's track practice (Talk Activity 4) and dental needs (Talk Activity 6) also forwarded primarily by mother and father consumed another third (8'31"). Finally, there were relatively few segments in these longer talk activities. Thus, the family's speech event was overwhelmingly a discussion of family agendas that were forwarded primarily by the mother.

The mother played a more active role in organizing discussion than the father. She initiated the two sustained talk activities that are composed of such talk. The father's initiations were either in support of a prior initiation by the mother or reinstated talk activities that she had previously initiated. The mother initiated the talk activity about Joseph's track practice and also organized its closing segment (Segments 4.1 and 4.4), whereas the father forwarded talk about the technicalities of his performance (Segments 4.2). The mother instituted sustained talk about family agendas (Segment 2.1), whereas the father reinstated such talk later (Segments 2.2, 2.3, and 2.4). The father performed these reinstatements by backreferencing matters that were previously raised in the segment that the mother forwarded, for example, the cocktail party and Joseph's school performance. Thus, the father's role in the organization of the speech event was subordinate to the mother's role.

Joseph's participation in the organization of the speech event is distinct from that of his parents who act in concert. The only sustained talk activity that he instituted pertains to a football game, a question about the stock market, and thumbwrestling, none of which bear on agenda making. Furthermore, all of the talk activities that were not sustained were initiated by him. These either do not bear on agenda making (Talk Activities 1, 5, 7, and 8) or seek to disrupt it. For example, in the midst of an agenda-making discussion, Joseph serves a volley of disparaging remarks about the artwork in the home.

> Mom, why'd you get this stupid thing? Ma, why do you buy these? How much was this? I could make you one of those. Why do you buy these stupid things? Dad, you actually like it?

Finally, the formatting of the talk that Joseph forwards is different from that of his parents; they exclusively forward questions–answer formats, whereas he more frequently forwards narrative or play formats [Chi square: Joseph, Parents X Q–A or other formats: x^2 (1) = 8.8, < .01]. Thus, Joseph's role in organizing the speech event is distinct from that of his parents, both in terms of what he wishes to talk about and the way he pursues talk.

We next performed a microanalysis of the opening of the second speech event. Like others (e.g., Cuff & Sharrock, 1985; Pittenger, Hockett, & Danehy, 1960; Scheff, 1990; Turner, 1972), we believe that crucial social dynamics are displayed in the process of establishing a speech event. This is the case because the structure and affective quality of a speech event are co-constructed by the members at the outset. When people engage each other in talk, they must achieve co-orientation for talk to proceed. Such co-orientation occurs spontaneously and largely unconsciously in the first few turns at talk. Linguistic and affective co-orientation occur simultaneously. They may be thought of as distinct aspects of speech-event organization; but, in actuality they are interwoven both in the production of an individual's speech and in the social organization of speaking. Thus, microanalysis of the opening of a speech event is a search for the fundamental social dynamics that underlie the entire speech event. What follows is the opening 35 seconds of the second speech event, the family's conversation:

001 Joseph: Dad, the whole time you're um, um (head nodding that
002   mocks Father's compliant stance toward experimenter
003   during prior speech event when she gave instructions)
004 Father: (Looks at Joseph, keeps forced smile from prior talk)
005 Mother: Joseph, let's review the plans for this weekend and what
006   we're going to be doing–(serious tone)
007 Father: (Looks at Mother as she begins to speak, then away with
008   shame face at "this weekend")
009 Joseph: (Laughs, smiling broadly, looking at Mother)
010 Mother: Tonight. (Louder with insistent tone)
011 Joseph: (More laughter, smiling broadly, head tilted up)
012 Mother: No, come on, son. This is what we'd normally be talking
013   about. (Insistent and pleading tone) Tonight you're
014   going to be home by yourself.
015 Joseph: Yeah. (Smiling)
016 Mother: O.K. (Staccato tone, touches nose [shame marker],
017 Joseph: Wait, You're going– (serious face and tone)
018 Mother: We're going to a party = (declarative tone)
019 Joseph: =Ooooh= (disappointed tone, throws head back onto
020   couch)
021 Mother: =late. (Firmly stated)
022 Joseph: Uh, can I ask you something (Softly, sits up again)
023 Father: Just watch TV, babe, you'll be alright. (Soothing and
024   pleading tone, looks toward TV, shame face)
025 Joseph: Fred has to be here. H-he can come over tonight but he
026   has to, um, be gone—he has like this=
027 Father: He can't spend the night?
028 Joseph: He can—Can you wake him like at 8:00?=
029
030 Father: =Sure= (Soothing)
031 Mother: =Why? (Firm tone, motions with hand to hurry up)
032 Father: (Touches nose [shame marker])
033 Joseph: 'Cause he, he has to go to . . . He's playing at Clearview at 9:30.

As indicated, the speech event opens with Joseph's commentary on his father's stance toward the experimenter in the first speech event when she sat with them and gave instructions (Lines 001–002). His mother moves

quickly to head off further discussion of this matter by instituting talk
about family agendas (Lines 005—006). Joseph persists in expressing his
mocking stance toward his father by laughing and smiling broadly (Line
009). The mother becomes firmer in tone (Line 010), but the son persists
in his efforts by producing extended laughter (Line 011). Mother then
produces a sustained attempt to shift his orientation. She censures, pleads,
argues that the talk activity she is forwarding is appropriate for the
situation, and then announces that Joseph will be at home alone that
night (Lines 012-014). Joseph then uptakes her talk activity with the
token "Yeah" as he is still registering this fact (Line (015), and mother
ratifies their co-orientation with a firm "O.K." (Line 016). Thus, mother
attempts to coerce Joseph's participation in the talk activity about agenda
making that she is forwarding.

Participation in the agenda-making talk activity entails a substantial
shift in Joseph's affective stance. It appears that the implications of being
left at home are unpleasant to him and that this turn of events is "news"
to him. In fact, the mother's flat delivery of this datum suggests that she
assumes that Joseph will have such a reaction and may also anticipate the
subsequent argument over whether he still needs a babysitter. Thus,
mother's presentation of this piece of agenda making at this particular
point appears to be nonrandom. It serves to jolt Joseph into participation
in her talk activity.

Joseph shifts affective stance as soon as he realizes he will be alone that
night (Line 017). Mother asserts that she and father are going to a party
(Line 018). Joseph displays pronounced disappointment (Line 019–020),
and mother counteracts that display with a firmly stated "late" (Line 021).
Mother's assertion succeeds in coercing compliance from Joseph, who
attempts in a whispered and markedly dysfluent utterance to get his
parents to let him have a friend over instead of a sitter and to wake him in
the morning at 8:00 (Lines 025—029). In reply to his mother's demand for
explanation (Line 031), he explains that Fred has other activities early in
the morning.

This discussion of the opening of the speech event reveals it to be a
struggle between Joseph and his mother over who will establish the first
talk activity. The struggle is overt and somewhat protracted. It is also
consequential for Joseph's affective stance. He shifts from boisterous and
mocking to disappointed and ultimately defeated. By deploying resources
associated with agenda making, the mother establishes dominance over
him.

Mother also establishes dominance over father at the same time. He is
curiously silent during the opening of the speech event. However, he
displays a telltale shame reaction when mother brings up plans of the
weekend (shame face, Line 007), a reaction that persists and constitutes

his background affect during much of the talk about agenda making. His reaction is conditioned by his desire to avoid being implicated in his wife's agenda making. Shortly after the opening he declines to participate in Saturday's activities and later he declines to participate in Sunday's activities. Mother reacts contemptuously in both instances and he displays shame although she is unable to make him comply with her desires. Finally, late in the speech event, he reopens talk about the cocktail party that he had apparently agreed to attend and attempts to exclude himself with the plea "Do we have to do it if we're tired?" Thus, there is ample evidence that father struggles to extricate himself from mother's agenda making and that he pays a price in eliciting her contempt and in his own experience of shame. These facts give meaning to father's shame reaction at the very mention of making weekend plans.

It might be argued that the facts reveal that the mother is not able to establish dominance over the father. He does extricate himself from weekend plans—for the present at least. Perhaps he is more dominated by his son who feels free to unmask his false sociability with the experimenter. In order to make a more convincing case, further definition of what we mean by the mother's domination is necessary as well as some additional information about the context of the second speech event.

It is important to point out that *domination* is a social achievement. It is contingent on events, partial in its scope, and invariably accompanied by the deference and/or resistance of those dominated. The affects that are dynamically associated with dominance, deference, and resistance, are, respectively, contempt, shame, and anger (Scheff, 1988). In the context of this particular interaction sequence, discussion of family agendas is a vehicle of domination that is employed almost exclusively by the mother. She consistently struggles with the father and son to make them accountable to various family agendas, and they conform under this pressure as often as not. However, they challenge the legitimacy of her efforts or seek to turn them against her; both son and father resist, express contempt from time to time, and exchange collusive looks. As well, nearly all of the agenda-making talk is contentious. Part of the father–son resistance takes the form of attempting to circumvent the mother's demands indirectly by hiding things from her—such as the father's concealing his plans for the weekend, that Joseph already knows of. Alternatively, they use mockery. For example, at one point the mother tells Joseph that his father's teeth are straight now because he had braces as a child; father mocks her for producing such a fabrication, with Joseph joining in the ridicule. Thus, the mother's domination is contingent upon the establishment of agenda-making talk activities, at which she was largely successful. Although her domination was not complete, it was often locally effective as the opening illustrates.

Finally, the resistance that she encounters is typical of the behavior of people who are oppressed; son and father suffer shame in their deference, and counteract it with contempt (mockery) and subversive activity (evasion, collusion).

Some additional information is necessary to explain the context of Joseph's actions at the beginning of the second speech event, an explanation that will shed light on his relationship to his father. At the outset of the first speech event recorded, the experimenter turned on the videotaping equipment as the family assembled to be taped. As recording commenced and she was walking over to sit with them and give instructions, the following exchange occurred:

001 Father:	Get the picture a little better and move it 6 inches
002	over (smiling mischievously at Mother)
003 Experimenter:	(Nervous, high-pitched laughter)
004 Joseph:	Dad. (Smiling, humored and complaining tone)
005 Mother:	(Looking at Father, somber expression)
006 Father:	What do you think? (Parodic tone)
007 Mother:	(Remains impassive with head tilted down)
008 Father:	No?
009	Is that O.K.? No? (Parodic tone and facial expression.)
010 Joseph:	Dad.
011	(Elbows Father). Dad, you're looking . . .
012	(Smiling, humored and disciplinary tone)
013 Mother:	(Extended noserubbing)
014 Father:	I'm not looking. (Matter-of-fact tone, looking at
015	Joseph)
016 Joseph:	Why'd you—why'd you—I put it up and we [can't
017	watch it]
018 Experimenter:	O.K. (Highly modulated tone of voice)
019 Father:	O.K. (Similar modulation, puts arm around Joseph)

At the opening of this exchange, the father is referring to moving the television set so that he can watch it (Lines 001-002). He is needling his wife who is not humored (Lines 005, 007). The experimenter produces an extended laughing as she finishes adjusting the equipment (Line 003), which is high pitched, conveying tension. Father continues his jest in spite of his wife's reaction (Lines 006, 008-009).

Joseph is humored and also disciplinary toward his father. He interrupts a few times to get his attention (Lines 004, 010), and then says that his father was watching the television (Lines 011-012,) since he has moved it out of the way before and now it was back where it could be watched

(Lines 016-017). Father denies the allegation (Lines 014-015) as mother produces an extended noserubbing (Line 013). Thus, Joseph has unmasked his father's jest as something more than a jest, and mother produces a shame marker indicating that she shares in the shame of his exposure.

At this point, the experimenter utters "O.K." in a high pitch (Line 018) indicating that she is ready to begin giving instructions. The father replies with a similarly intoned "O.K." (Line 019), and the experimenter sits with them and begins giving instructions. The false politeness between father and experimenter, which is marked by the high pitch as well as other markers, is maintained throughout the minute or so of instruction.

Description of the beginning of the instruction-giving speech event provides a context within which to understand Joseph's behavior at the beginning of the succeeding speech event. His father's strained politeness during instruction is in marked contrast to his humored and mocking stance just prior to that. Thus, it is noteworthy.

Additional information that Joseph offers in the course of the second speech event highlights the inconsistency of father's stance during instruction. First, a football game is to begin during the time of the taping; and, during the second talk activity father indicates a strong interest in seeing it. In the first talk activity, Joseph notices that his father had moved the television back to where he could view it and infers that he was watching just before the videotaping. Later he infers that he was watching the pregame show. Second, also during the second talk activity, Joseph reenvoices a contemptuous comment that his father made about the study—"Hey, I thought we were going to be done with this study!"—that was apparently uttered when he was asked to find time for this videotaping session. Thus, father has given ample evidence of his resistance to the project.

This discussion creates the basis for arguing that Joseph is not merely "acting up" at the beginning of the second speech event when he mocks his father. He is unmasking his father's forced sociability with the experimenter; he has ample evidence that that stance does not represent his father's true feelings about participating in the study, that his demeanor is strikingly forced. Furthermore, Joseph is persisting in the same stance of mock-serious unmasking that he had adopted toward his father just before the experimenter gave instructions.

Joseph's alignment to his mother shifts from the first to the second talk activity. The father adopts a mocking stance toward the other, teasing her about watching television during the videotaping. Mother is displeased and does not play along. Father and mother are in conflict, and Joseph quickly enters the fray, siding with mother by unmasking father's jest as reflecting his actual desires. Father interprets Joseph's utterances as such

as reflected in his seriously intoned denial (Lines 014-015). At the same
time, Joseph aligns with his father in using the term *Dad* with an
affectionate tone and smile. Thus, he engages in the unmasking as a kind
of play between them.

In the opening of the second speech event, Joseph maintains the same
mocking but affectionate alignment with his father. However, in
maintaining that alignment, his alignment toward his mother shifts. On
the first occasion he has aligned with his mother's displeased reaction to
father's jest. Both are well aware of his prior protest and his desire to
watch the game instead of participating. On the second occasion, Joseph
undermines his father's compliance rather than his resistance; and, in so
doing, he becomes misaligned with his mother who has sought the father's
compliance.

This suggests that Joseph's primary alignment is with his father, an
alignment that entails playful unmasking. If this is the case, Joseph's
alignment with his mother should be a function of this alignment with his
father which is, in turn, a function of father's alignment with mother. The
foregoing account is consistent with this hypothesis, but more description
of the father's alignment with mother is necessary to complete the
description of the family's relationship dynamic.

At various points throughout the communication event, the father
attempts to evade the mother's agenda making.

M: What time? What are the times [you will be away]?
F: I don't know.
M: I want details.
F: I don't know.
M: What are your plans tomorrow?
F: Tomorrow I do have to go down to the dock.
M: From when to when to when to when?

On other occasions he produces contemptuous outbursts against it, makes
plans without her knowledge, and mocks her efforts. Thus, he adopts a
childlike position toward her authority. Yet he also conforms. The very
fact of his involvement in the study reflects on the mother's power to
enlist his compliance. Moreover, he does end up agreeing to go to the
cocktail party. In addition, as we see in the opening to the second speech
event, he participates in her agenda-making talk activity, attempting to
soothe Joseph's disappointment at being left at home when they go to the
cocktail party. Furthermore, he is in a subordinate position during such
talk, displaying deference and tolerating shame. Consistent with this
stance, he internalizes mother's agenda-making constraints even as he

struggles against them. Later he reintroduces agenda-making talk that was unresolved and uses resources deployed in agenda making to discipline Joseph. In addition, on occasion he addresses his wife with an affectionate term such as *honey*, indicating an affective bond with her.

Thus, the father's alignment with the mother is ambivalent and ridden with resistance; he is capable of contemptuous defiance as well as overcompliance, and they do not establish mutual coordination through metacommunication about how talk is going. Nevertheless, both periodically express affiliation toward one another, which buffers their continuous conflict. For this reason, Joseph's alignment with his father causes him to be buffeted about as his father's alignment to his wife shifts back and forth.

As a final analysis, we examine the distribution of affects within talk activities. The results are displayed in the three righthand columns of Table 5.4 (see p. 155). There are several points worth noting.

Sustained talk activities (2.1, 3.1, 4.1, 4.2, 6) contain high rates of shame and contempt and low rates of affiliation. This is symptomatic of shame–contempt binds, as described by Tomkins (1963), Kaufman (1989), and Scheff (1987). Mother periodically derides both son and father in order to elicit compliance during her pursuit of agenda making, but because they often repay her in kind, with countercontempt or subversion, she suffers a price in shame for her efforts. Son protests contemptuously, is disciplined by his parents, and thus is shamed. Father expresses shame during agenda making and periodically rebels contemptuously.

The microanalysis demonstrates that these shame–contempt binds are more within-individual phenomena than between–individual phenomena. There is, in general, no prevailing close-order contingency between the shame of one member and the contempt of another, although there are critical moments of such contingency from time to time. However, it is clear that each member oscillates between these two affects during agenda making; and these talk activities reflect the structuring imposed by these affects.

There is a contingency with respect to shame, especially in the case of father and son. Both father and son express shame at the beginning of agenda making. Another instance of affective alignment between them is symbolized by their thumbwrestling activity and the commentary that accompanies it (Talk Activity 3.2). They achieve a sustained exchange of positive affect and affiliation during this activity. It is also important to note that the bulk of sustained affiliation activity occurs in this single episode.

Although much more could be said about the result of the sociolinguistic analysis, the foregoing is sufficient to provide a description of this family's culture, one that is consistent with the portrait gleaned from the affective analysis. This rendition of communication is far from the kind of description of language that Chomsky offered. In the account we provide, members' utterances co-construct a speech event and are, at the same time, constrained by that co-construction. In such a view of language use, the social world plays a structuring role rather than being merely a consequence of individual's intentions as in Chomsky's formulations. In order for the social world to play that role, it must be structured itself as well as exercising a structuring influence on the members. The foregoing sociolinguistic analyses demonstrate both aspects of the social world.

Integration of Affect and Language Analyses

In this concluding section we pursue the line of argument that affect and language are integrally related in the construction of this family's encounter. We examine individual profiles of affect and language use and illustrate how they are mutually constructed and co-assembled.

We also consider the systemic functions of these two domains. Family systems theory (Hill, 1971; Ramsey, 1989) has emphasized that the family is a crucial unit for both creating and perpetuating intra- and interindividual dynamics. In addition, the developmental literature has stressed that the family is the primary locus of children's emotion socialization. As such, the family must be viewed as a crucible for the intergenerational transmission of linguistic and affective patterns. The results of our analyses support these formulations, as we show here. We also consider the implications of our analyses of the family's communication for Joseph's socialization—both in his style of affect management and his use of language for interpersonal goals.

Consistencies Within Individuals in the Deployment of Affect and Language

Father. The father's contempt–shame bind is readily apparent in the manner in which he participates in talk as well as reflected in his emotion profile. The shame component of the bind is evident in his generally withdrawn behavior, his somewhat slumped posture, the softness of his voice and the tendency to trail off from time to time, and in his off-again, on-again pattern of deference and compliance on agenda making. The contempt component is displayed in the derogatory intonational pattern the father often uses when he addresses his wife, when he contests assertions of the wife or son, and in various facial and postural gestures. He is also emotionally and verbally withholding, relative to the other two, having the lowest level of affective communications and verbalizations.

At the level of discourse analysis, we find that the father is predominantly reactive rather than proactive. The bulk of talk activity is between mother and son, with the father being a relatively infrequent, although at times pivotal, participant. The father rarely initiates talk activities or commandeers the lead; instead, for the most part, he is passive in the face of the mother's agenda making. He is, in fact, trapped in her agenda making, resenting it but having no mature language resources with which to renegotiate it. Instead the husband constantly challenges and resists openly as well as in more subtle ways.

One can interpret the father's relative withdrawnness as indexing an immobilization generated by shame. He appears to experience his wife's agenda-making activities as infringing on his independence, as being overregulating, and even controlling. Shame is said to be a consequence of any non-egalitarian, dominating relationship (Tomkins, 1963) and contempt and subversion have been hypothesized to be the expectable interpersonal consequences. The person in a state of shame wants nothing more than to escape and hide; alternatively, he or she may elect a counteractive strategy and shame the other person in turn. This appears to be the husband's preferred mode of coping. His shame alternates with contempt on a fairly regular basis.

Finally, as we stand back and evaluate the entire content and texture of the full 24-minute transaction, taking into account data from both the talk activity and affect analyses, we are led to formulate the possibility that the father's true level of contempt is being suppressed on this occasion. First, we know that the father regards the experimental task with disdain, as evident, for example, in the son's mocking and embarrassing reinvoicement of the father's off camera disparagement of the upcoming task. Second, the father's relative lack of participation—the poverty of contribution to the speech event and his less-than-enthusiastic affectivity when he does participate—and his conflicted style of engagement, suggests overly controlled emotionality on this occasion. Third, we know from previous analysis that many of his conversational responses to the mother's agenda making take the form of subtle and not-so-subtle resistance; at times he is subversive and even openly anarchaic.

This suppressed contempt is consistent with a compliance–noncompliance bind that also entails a shame component. He resents her dominance in the present activity and this is reflected by his periodic rebellion or withdrawal, but he also continuously displays shame. Lewis (1971) and Scheff (1987) described the shame–rage spiral as both an intra- and interpersonal affect dynamic. The father's alternation between shame and contempt illustrates this theoretical formulation. Although he refrains from ventilating overt anger, contempt and scorn adequately communicate a repressed but smoldering anger. The father's shame–contempt bind both constricts his affective and linguistic communications at the same time as it perpetuates the social basis that motivates his constricted performance. The strictures of the bind make it difficult for him to participate in a constructive manner—he either underparticipates, or participates in a disruptive manner—being alternatively withdrawn, then engaged, and then resisting. His resistance results in his getting shamed; at the same time it triggers the anger component of the shame–rage spiral, resulting in contemptuous and contentious eruptions. We surmise that these patterns of family interaction have been repeatedly enacted and internalized over time and that they form the nucleus of the father's shame–contempt organization as well as his disengaged style of family participation.

The father's behavior with respect to the son at first blush appears to have more of an affiliative component than is seen in the case of the wife, as noted in the distribution of emotional communications taken from the affect analysis. However, inspection of the distribution of affects *within talk activity* segments shows that the bulk of father–son exchanges occur in a protracted burst within a single segment (Talk Activity 3.2), that is, during the thumbwrestling engagement. Although some instances of affiliation occur during agenda making, they are typically isolated gestures that moderate contempt or brief collusive exchanges between father and son. Thus, the father's affiliation with the son is revealed to be immature in character.

Mother.   As noted from our affect analysis, the mother is shame-dominant. Although there are eruptions of contempt, and a few affiliative gestures, the bulk of her communications are marked by shame; moreover, her responses to others' communications are not contingent on the affective character of the prior communication. She is repeatedly shamed by the relative lack of compliance by the husband and son; typically, they do not cooperate with her agenda making. She is continually attempting to make them accountable to family agendas, but her tone of voice is more typically plaintive and distressed, rather than authoritative.

The mother copes with this pall of shame largely by disattending to it and single-mindedly pursuing her agendas. This kind of response has been characterized as bypassed shame by Lewis (1971). Scheff suggested that it is a crucial feature of Type A behavior pattern. Type A individuals are characterized by a sense of "time urgency," impatience, fast propulsive speech, lack of trust in others, and a tendency to be critical and to use sarcasm. Joseph's parents both displayed aspects of the Type A profile. In addition to the high rate of contemptuous and sarcastic communications, the rate of speech interruptions (characteristic of impatience as well as disrespect) was found to be frequent (about 75 instances in the space of 24 minutes). To substantiate our impressions of

Type A personality, the family was recontacted and asked to complete a questionnaire. The questionnaire was one of the more widely used devices used to classify individuals as to Type A versus Type B personality—the Jenkins Activity Scale. As it were, the mother's score was found to fall in the 85th percentile for Type A behavior and the father's in the 95th percentile, thus confirming our subjective impressions. The finding that the father falls in the highest decile of the Type A scale provides further support for the argument that the father's more characteristic level of contempt was being masked in the present situation.

The Type A pattern serves both the intrapsychic motive of avoiding awareness of shame but also the interpersonal goal of family control and conflict avoidance. The mother was clearly shamed by the father and son's collusive subversion of her agenda-making goals, by their disrespect and mockery, and by their isolation of her; nevertheless, she forges ahead. This does not mean that she escapes from the shame, as we note from the surfeit of shame markers in the non-verbal behavior. It simply means that she temporarily keeps it at bay and out of consciousness. This facility is locally effective in keeping the family to the agreed-upon task so that the mother's promise to the experimenter is fulfilled. More importantly, it insulates the family members from connecting with their alienation from one another at the present moment and thus more overt and embarrassing conflict is avoided. Although this is clearly a coping mechanism, rather skillfully managed in this instance, it is not completely functional because it perpetuates the mother's shame dynamic.

Given the mother's exposure to her son's heavy-handed contempt, the husband's withholding stance, and her exclusion from the occasional bouts of affiliation enjoyed by the father and son, we can surmise that she may experience a great deal of distress and frustration. Her Type A behavior and bypassed shame provide the mechanisms to cope with her distress, but the price the mother pays is insensitivity and the reinforcement of alienation. The Type A behavior pattern is an emotionally distant style of relating because the compulsive and perpetually high activity level it entails makes the person less available for affiliative contacts and robs the person of whatever affiliative support may be available in the system.

The mother's role in the avoidance of conflict is pivotal and consistent with another of her roles, that is, her position as the family's link with the wider community. The family lives in an upper-class, largely professional neighborhood, where public face and sociability are essential requirements of being a good citizen. There is every expectation that members of this community will socialize frequently, engage in community events, and partake of the city's various cultural offerings. As observed earlier, the father's sociability appears to be limited. Thus, the role of social arbiter is left to the mother. However, she is in a precarious position because the family is not organized to show positive face to the community; thus, the mother must organize their activities and superintend their behavior to camouflage their socially alienating disdain and mockery. Thus, the mother's shame appears to be multiply determined. On the one hand, she is overly deferential to the community's ideals of active socializing; she also appears to be overly compliant with the feminine ideal of acquiescence to the requests of others. It is the mother who agreed to be in this experiment and corralled the family into participation in the study. She draws the outside social world into the family as a bridge to the social world but also as a mechanism to control the family. It is clearly the principle source of power open to her and she uses it with a vengeance. Every day of the week appears to be scheduled with one kind of activity or another—cocktail parties, benefits, classes, and so forth.

Although the father may be a prisoner of a contempt–shame bind, the mother is trapped by a shame–shame bind. Shame is her dominant affect, although she is capable of the strategic use of contempt to coerce compliance. However, these instances of contempt are reactive, rather than an expression of her affective biases. In contrast, in the father one has the sense that contempt is primary and shame reactive. The mother is particularly sensitive to shame, absorbing it like the proverbial sponge. She is the protagonist in the family's talk, and thus exposed to shame when others do not cooperate in her efforts. She accepts responsibility not only for her own shame, but also takes responsibility for absorbing some of the shame that more rightfully belongs to the other family members. For example, it is she who apologizes to the camera for the content of the family's conversation ("This is what we normally talk about"). She also covers for them in embarrassing moments, such as when the son rebels, or talks about forbidden topics, such as his classmates' smoking marijuana on the ballfield. Filled with the painful affect of shame, the only way to remain intact is to bypass as much of it as possible, and to deflect it with her own contempt when the shaming becomes too flagrant and unbearable.

Son. The son's expression of contempt and the language in which it is embedded are co-extensive. His rate of contempt is higher than any other family member; it is primarily directed at the mother, but the father is not immune from his barbs. He is also high on shame, and manifests a contempt–shame bind like his father.

Part of the son's contempt that is directed at the mother is a result of the fact that he experiences her day-to-day control and regulation of his behavior, and part of it is owing to the fact that he is a preadolescent and, thus, has not yet learned all of the various strategies for modulating affect. The mother exercises more overt coercion of Joseph, but his behavior also requires more active management because he has an underlying tendency to resist compliance. Moreover, his expressions of noncompliance and disrespect are more flagrant and unmodulated ("Ma, where'd you get that stupid picture!?"). In fact, there is every reason to believe that he has modeled himself after his father and that his noncompliance and mockery is an exaggerated, unrestrained version of his father's contemptuousness. However, although the father can isolate the contempt temporarily, the child has not yet learned the skills of displacing, deferring, and minimizing affective displays to any great extent. His contempt is overt, unmodulated, and untamed.

Although the affect analysis indicates a relatively balanced distribution of shame and contempt in the son, our conclusion is that contempt is primary, shame only secondary and reactive. The evidence for this is multiple. The talk activity analysis indicates that he tends to initiate talk activities with open contempt ("[Tsk] We can *talk* about TV, *Mom*"). Moreover, the language by which the son participates in the family conversation is marked by contentiousness and rebellion. Further support is found in his narratives about activities outside the family. Joseph constructs others in a contemptuous manner, highlighting them as laughable figures (mocking a dental assistant's obsession with teeth, ridiculing the behavior of some of his classmates) constructing narratives with a contemptuous background. The out-of-family narratives are a good diagnostic indicator. Here, Joseph is not being coerced, so there is less interactional constraint. Yet contempt is his dominant posture.

Joseph, himself, is exposed to volleys of contempt on occasion, from both the mother and father. His overt rebelliousness also calls forth more active management from his mother, and occasionally his father, and he is shamed by their domination. These experiences are occasions for shame and help explain why shame is so frequently displayed, in addition to the contempt.

Systemic Properties of the Family's Communication Pattern. Our analyses reveal that this family does not have pronounced systemic properties in addition to the individual's interactive tendencies. The system operates as a collection of individuals that have dyad-specific and interlocking patterns of affectivity and talk: mother with son (regulatory control, shame, and rebellion), husband with wife (withholding , passivity, contempt), father with son (subterfuge against the mother, affiliation), mother with father (struggle for respect, experience of resistance, and reactions of shame).

One of the reasons for the lack of more cohesive and system-wide character is owing to the fact that there is a poverty of system-wide affiliative exchange. The only sustained affiliation is localized in one play activity between father and son. Lacking a system-wide buffer of affiliation, the family members seem to ricochet back and forth from contempt to shame and back to contempt in a cyclical, counteractive fashion. That is, this family does not participate in any jointly shared, mutually gratifying activities in their talk—there is no family narrative style where they can tells stories together and entertain and enjoy one another. As a result, the individual contempt–shame binds and shame–shame binds are sufficient for describing the family system.

Further Ramifications for Joseph's Socialization.   Joseph is well on his way to developing a shame–contempt bind as a structuralized feature of his personality. Both affects are well represented in his repertoire and are unmitigated by mature affiliation. His nonverbal behavior is laced with shame markers, and his talk activity style is crudely rebellious and contentious. The high rates of contempt and shame emitted by the son appear to be related to the culture of contempt and shame in his family and the shaming practices the parents use in disciplining him. Tomkins (1963) has suggested that children acquire personal styles of learning to deal with parental shaming. The child may submit, render deference (and reexperience shame), and/or fight back by turning contempt against the parent(s). In Joseph's case, he seems to have absorbed the family's shame as well as learned the defense of countercontempt. In our analysis, it appears that the son derives the shame component of his personality primarily from his mother and the contempt component from his father.

Contribution of the Mother.   Because the mother has taken over or has been relegated the responsibility for scheduling the family's activities, as well as being the disciplinarian in terms of quelling Joseph's rebelliousness, she galvanizes the son's shame. Her socialization strategies are largely ones of control and power assertion (which are inherently shaming), rather than of induction and reasoning. She also provides the occasion for further amplification of the son's shame experience by modeling a pervasive shame bias of her own. Although the father may be insulated from the contagion of her shame through strategies he has learned in his own socialization history, the son is more vulnerable because of his immaturity and lack of modulatory control.

Contributions From the Father.   The father is well-versed in modulated expressions of contempt; he is also mature enough to have developed strategies of masking and even deferring its expression when it is strategically advantageous to do so. However, he is not affectively competent when it comes to the socially constructive or "*verbindine Affeckte*" (binding emotions), a term coined by Adler (1923) to connote those emotions and behaviors that temper negative emotions and promote positive affectivity between interactants. He is also not very skilled with respect to the discourse skills of mutuality and respectful participation. Thus, the father presents, on the one hand, a well-developed model for contempt affect and, on the other, a poorly developed model for interpersonally skilled interactions.

Joseph's Development.   We can perhaps expect the son to follow suit, as he shows every inclination of doing. His exposure to the monopolistic affect-bias profiles (Tomkins, 1963) of his parents—shame dominant on the part of the mother and contempt dominant on the part of the father— provides both the catalyst for the son's own monopolistic styles of emoting, relating, and conversing, as well as precludes the learning of a more varied and flexible repertoire, at last within the confines of the family. Because he is exposed to two sources of differential influence, he will not be an exact replica of either of his parents. Instead, as would be predicted from Tomkins (1963) of his parents—shame dominant on the part of the mother and contempt dominant on the part of the father— provides both the catalyst for the son's own monopolistic styles of emoting, relating, and conversing, as well as precludes the learning of a more varied and flexible repertoire, at least within the confines of the family. Because he is exposed to two sources of differential influence, he will not be an exact replica of either of his parents. Instead, as would be predicted from Tomkins (1963), he will display the countercontempt styles of shame management, moreover, his countercontempt will be fairly blatant because he does not have access to other socioemotional or conversational strategies for social engagement other than compliance or resistance. He will not learn proactive strategies of social negotiation and, in fact, will tend to alienate social partners because of his raw and poorly modulated contempt. Indeed, the contempt will be exaggerated and amplified, given the fact that he has aligned himself with his father and the father communicates implicit support for his contempt and rebelliousness. The son will also have little experience with family-oriented affiliative engagement because the parents are more estranged than intimate.

Summary and Concluding Comments

In the foregoing we attempted to make a case for the proposition that affect and language are modular systems whose individual activities are engaged cooperatively in the service of socially constitutive goals.

Subsystems of personality, like individual members within a larger social network, have unique properties and characteristics, but become coordinated to achieve adaptation to the demands of the social world. Affect and linguistic systems are coordinated in the production of social events and are at the same time constrained by such social productions. We argued that, to the extent that affect and language are primordially social activities, one should be able to document their co-assembly during social interaction by directly examining the construction of social events. In this study, we provided support for this contention by analyzing the conversation of a family on an occasion that was notable for its very ordinariness. There were no particular stressors involved in the task, the conversation took place in the comfort of the family's own home, and they were given total freedom to talk about whatever they liked.

Even under such benign, relatively stress-free, and neutral conditions, this family produced a speech event that was linguistically well-structured and also remarkable for the sheer density of affective communication. The affect analysis revealed that individual members of the family had their own personal emotional biases and each dyad within the larger unit had differential interpersonal dynamics. We found, also, that the family's talk and affective postures are mutually constructed and co-extensive, which illustrates our claim that affect and language are primordial social activities and, thus, are coordinated to achieve superordinate principles of social organization.

In the current study we did not undertake examination of the grammaticality of the individual family members' speech. However productive that approach might have been, it would have obscured the essentially social nature of communication and we would not have had the opportunity to examine and come to some understanding of the socially driven co-assembly of language and affect, nor of this particular family's culture and dynamic. This is not to devalue the important work that is being done in the Chomskian tradition, but to suggest that a more social conception of language is necessary to understand the coordination of language and affect as communication systems.

APPENDIX

Coding Procedures

1. Locating displays. This coding scheme is designed to locate display of shame, contempt, and affiliation in ongoing conversation. Because they are conceived as discrete behaviors, it is appropriate that the coder locate the onset of each display. In attempting to determine whether doubtful cases should be coded, look for concurrent signs

of the same affect and use the directly prior interaction as interpretive context.

2. Tracking each affect separately for each participant. Because affect displays are often subtle, the coder should code only one at a time and do so for each participant separately. Furthermore, it is best to code the videotape in 2- or 3-minute blocks because of the degree of focus required, to watch the segment a few times before coding, and to check the coding on a subsequent day for lapses of attention.

3. Judging onset and offset of a display. In most cases, an affect display has a discrete onset and offset and brief duration. However, a few displays such as posture or speaking may have a longer duration. This necessitates a technical definition of onsets and offsets so that the coder can determine when such longer duration displays should be coded more than once. The general rule is to code a display only once if it is *continuously produced* and *functionally homogeneous*. However, if there is an offset of 1 second or more in a display, the next segment should be coded separately. As well, if there is a noticeable shift in its communication function or the manner/locus of display (e.g., face different from ear) each distinct segment should be coded separately.

4. Judging the directedness of a display. Each affective display is coded according to whether it is directed toward one of the other interactants *in partiucular,* "both," or "other," which includes a primary someone or something other than those present.

5. Multiple coding of the same display. In the large majority of instances, we expect a display to receive only one code. However, multiple codes are possible because each affect is coded separately. This does not constitute a problem; it represents a finding, determining *how* affect displays occur. Nor do double codings necessarily create analysis problems. However, the first step in sequential analysis will be to treat these cases. Depending on the researcher's interests they will be treated differently. They can be treated as instances of co-occurrence when a time-interval definition of co-occurrence is employed (e.g., plus or minus 1 second). In lag-sequential analysis, co-occurrences are the Lag 0 outcomes, and their frequency of occurrence can be assessed much like that of any other lag.

Shame Displays

1. Facial displays of shame and embarassment

    1.1 blushing
    1.2 abashed or ashamed look
  2. Hiding behaviors
    2.1 covering face
    2.2 averting face or body, includes prominet gaze aversion
   *2.3 lowered head or eyes
   *2.4 slumped or lowered posture
  3. Self-grooming/touching
    3.1 touching face, head, hair, or neck
   *3.2 touching hands, jewelry, clothes, includes self-inspection
  4. Verbal and vocal displays of shame
    4.1 statements of shame, self-contempt, or defensiveness
    4.2 tone of shame or plaintiveness in any statement
    4.3 statements of submission, especially in response to domineering statement
    4.4 embarassed or self-conscious laughter, laughter accepting another's contempt or dominance
   *4.5 low or lowered voice, trailing off
   *4.6 marked disfluency, stuttering, false starts, particles (e.g., "um," "wha")
   *4.7 marked inhale or exhale, gasping, whining

*code only in conjunction with other shame displays if it is not *unequivocally shameful.*

Contempt Displays

  1. Facial displays of contempt
    1.1 curled lip of disgust, retracted upper lip
    1.2 disgust face: nose flattening with flared nostrils and mouth set
    1.3 William F. Buckley face: head tilted back, looking down nose or nose in the air, haughty
    1.4 smile of derision, contempt, or superiority
    1.5 eye roll of dismissal, mocking, or sarcastic face
  2. Postural displays of contempt
    2.1 pulling away, either whole body or just upper body or head or twisting body away or to present shoulder
    2.2 shoulders back, chest out in display of superiority
   *2.3 raising up, becoming erect in posture or more erect
  3. Verbal and vocal displays of contempt
    3.1 contemptuous, derrogatory or domineering statements (e.g., put downs, sarcasm, criticism, mocking, dismissing, also "Virginia Woolf" use of terms of endearment)

3.2 contemptuous, derrogatory or domineering tone in any statement, "tsk" of contempt

*3.3 disciplinary statements offered as such, disciplinary tone

3.4 derisive snorts, "hrumphs" or laughter

3.5 Sharp inhale, exhale or other displays of a "huff"

3.6 collusion against someone on the basis of contempt

*3.7 interrupting or coopting another's talk, especially if inconsiderately performed

*3.8 yawning or other signs of disengagement, especially if not hidden or performed apologetically

*code only in conjunction with other contempt displays if it is not *unequivocally contemptuous.*

Affiliation Displays

1. Facial displays of affiliation
   1.1 face-to face rapport seeking whether or not successful
   1.2 exchange of smiles or other gestures of rapport (e.g., eyebrow raises, eyebrow and eye flashes)
   1.3 collusion with another either in itself (e.g., secrets, humor), or against a third person
2. Postural displays of affiliation
   2.1 touching, grooming or caressing another unless accidental
   *2.2 leaning into, postural alignment with
3. Verbal and vocal displays of affiliation
   3.1 helping, reassuring, praising, or encouraging statements
   3.2 markedly warm, helpful, enthusiastic, or otherwise supportive tone in any statements
   3.3 agreement that implies statements categorizable as 3.1
   3.4 joking with another or to align with another's predicament
   3.5 names and terms of endearment (honey, son, babe), offered in an endearing, plaintive or neutral tone
   *3.6 language or intonation that indicates familiarity

*code only in conjunction with other affiliation displays if it is not *unequivocally affiliative.*

ACKNOWLEDGMENTS

We wish to acknowledge the assistance of Christopher Malatesta in preparing the transcript of the family interaction and in doing the scoring as the second coder on the talk activity analysis. He was particularly helpful in giving us an adolescent's point of view on the parents and their preadolescent son.

REFERENCES

Adler, A. (1923). *The practice and theory of individual psychology* (P. Radin, Trans.). London: Routledge & Kegan Paul.

Allison, P. D., & Liker, J. K. (1982). Analyzing sequential categorical data: A comment on Gottman. *Psychological Bulletin, 91,* 393-403.

Bakeman, R., & Dorval, B. (1989). The distinction between theoretical independence and empirical independence in sequential analysis. *Behavioral Assessment, 11,* 31-37.

Bruner, J. (1983). *Child's talk: Learning to use language.* New York: Norton.

Chomsky, N. (1981). *Knowledge of language.* New York: Praeger.

Chomsky, N. (1986). *The Managua lectures.* Cambridge, MA: MIT Press.

Cornelius, R. R. (1984). A role model of adult emotional expression. In C. Z. Malatesta & C. E. Izard (Eds.), *Emotion in adult development* (pp. 213-233). Beverly Hills: Sage.

Cuff, E. C., & Sharrock, W.W. (1985). Meetings In T. Van Dijk (Ed.), *Handbook of discourse analysis* (Vol. 3, pp. 149-160). London: Academic Press.

Darwin, C. (1872). *The expression of emotions in man and animals.* London: John Murray

Dumesnil, J., & Dorval, B. (1989). The development of talk-activity frames that foster perspective-focused talk among peers. *Discourse Processes, 12,* 193-225.

Ekman, P., Sorenson, E. R., & Friesen, W.V. (1969). Pan-cultural elements in facial displays of emotion. *Science, 164,* 86-88.

Feinberg, S. E. (1980). *The analysis of cross-classified categorical data.* Cambridge, MA: MIT Press.

Hill, R. (1971). Modern systems theory and the family: A confrontation. *Social Science Information,* October 7-26.

Hymes, D. (1972). *Foundations of sociolinguistics.* Philadelphia: University of Pennsylvania Press.

Izard, C. E. (1971). *The face of emotion.* New York: Appelton-Century-Crofts.

Izard, C. E. (1977). *Human emotions.* New York: Plenum.

Izard, C. E., & Malatesta, C.Z. (1987). Perspectives on emotional development I: Differential emotions theory of early emotional development. In J. D. Osofsky (Ed.), *Handbook of infant development* (pp. 494-554). New York: Wiley.

Kaufman, G. (1989). *The psychology of shame.* New York: Springer.

LeDoux, J. E. (1990). Cognitive-emotional interactions in the brain. *Cognition and Emotion, 3,* 267-290.

Lewis, H. B. (1971). *Shame and guilt in neurosis.* New York: International Universities Press.

MacLean, P. D. (1973). A triune concept of the brain and behavior. In T. Boag & D. Campbell (Eds.), *The Hincks memorial lectures* (pp. 1-53). Toronto: University of Toronto Press.

Malatesta, C. Z. (1990). The role of emotions in the development and organization of personality. In R. A. Dienstbler (Series Ed.) & R. A. Thompson (Vol. Ed.),

Socioemotional development: Nebraska Symposium on Motivation (Vol. 36, pp. 1-56). Lincoln: University of Nebraska Press.

Malatesta, C. Z., Culver, C., Tesman, J., & Shepard, B. (1989). The development of emotion expression during the first two years of life. *Monographs of the Society for Research in Child Development, 54*(1-2, Serial No. 219), 1-104.

Malatesta, C. Z., & Izard, C. E. (1984). The ontogenesis of human social signals: From biological imperative to symbol utilization. In N.A. Fox & R. J. Davidson (Eds.), *The psychobiology of affective development* (pp. 161-206). Hillsdale, NJ: Lawrence Erlbaum Associates.

Newman, J. D. (Ed.). (1988). *The physiological control of mammalian vocalization.* New York: Plenum.

Pittenger, R., Hockett, C., & Danehy, J. (1960). *The first five minutes.* Ithaca, NY: Paul Martineau.

Ramsey, C. N. (Ed.). (1989). *Family systems in medicine.* New York: Guilford.

Sackett, G. P. (1987). Analysis of sequential social interaction data: Some issues, recent developments, and a causal inference model. In J. Osofsky (Ed.), *Handbook of infant development* (2nd ed., pp. 855-878). New York: Wiley.

Scheff, T. J. (1988). Shame and conformity: The deference-emotion system. *American Sociologicalk Review, 53*, 395-406.

Scheff, T. J. (1987). The shame-rage spiral: A case study of an interminable quarrel. In H. B. Lewis (Ed.), *The role of shame in symptom formation* (pp. 109-149). Hillsdale, NJ: Lawrence Erlbaum Associates.

Scherer, K. (Ed.). (1988). *Facets of emotion: Recent research.* Hillsdale, NJ: Lawrence Erlbaum Associates.

Stubbs, M. (1983). *Discourse analysis.* Chicago: University of Chicago Press.

Tomkins, S. S. (1962). *Affect, imagery, consciousness: Vol. I. The positive affects.* New York: Springer.

Tomkins, S. S. (1963). *Affect, imagery, consciousness: Vol II. The negative affects.* New York: Springer.

Tomkins, S. S. (1991). *Affect, imagery, consciousness: Vol. III. The negative affects: Anger and fear.* New York: Springer.

Turner, R. (1972). Some formal properties of therapy talk. In D. Sudnow (Ed.), *Studies in social interaction.* New York: The Free Press.

6 The Logical and Extrinsic Sources of Modularity

Thomas Bever
University of Rochester

MODULARITY AND LANGUAGE

For a number of years, researchers on language behavior have believed that it involves the interaction of different kinds of partially autonomous systems of general and specific knowledge. That is, language is a modality, a natural kind of mental organization. The differentiation of such modalities as *language, vision, taste,* is pre-theoretically satisfying, but requires scientific explanation. How is it that they coalesce and emerge? How does the child know that aspects of his or her early experience are interrelated together and which motor patterns are related to them?

There are corresponding questions about the organization of information within a modality. For example, successful language behavior involves the appropriate interaction of systems of phonology, syntax, semantics, discourse, pragmatics, and world knowledge. Fodor (1983) sketched one proposal on the laws governing mental traffic between such systems. He crystallized a modern form of the old doctrine of "specific energy" of sensory systems, now coined, "modularity." Fodor's specific proposal is articulated and discussed elsewhere in this book. Certain intuitively appealing and widely believed aspects of this proposal are important for this discussion: Modules are architecturally segregated, that is, their internal processes cannot be mutually influenced; modules are neurologically distinct and reflect devoted innate neurological predispositions; modules utilize processes and forms of memory unique to each, that is, principles of "general cognition" either do not exist or exist outside of cognitive modules in the system of general intelligence, the "central processor."

In this chapter, I sketch an alternative framework for a research program on the interaction of mental systems underlying language behaviors, and some current results that support that program. I argue that language behavior recruits a heterogeneous set of distinct capacities and neurological structures, each of which has intrinsic constraints on how it can interact with others. Furthermore, I raise the possibility that the differentiation of cognitive processes is general, cutting across types of behavior. These facts and constraints can result in modular-like properties of certain aspects of language without being unambiguous evidence for an innate and architecturally distinct module for language, nor for modules within the language modality.

A currently fashionable form of demonstration of the modularity of language is to show that computation of linguistic knowledge proceeds independently of other kinds of belief. I argue that such demonstrations may only reflect the necessary computational incompatibility of different kinds of information. Thus, the current experimental evidence for modularity actually follows from the fact that distinct levels of representation have distinct internal computational languages.

The preceding is in part a point of logic, not fact. Arguments do not require facts to be interesting, but they do require facts to be convincing. Accordingly, I also explore a kind of fact about some general cognitive bases for processes used in language, based on the isolation of biologically coded individual differences. I show that logical distinctions among kinds of cognitive processes used in language are reflected in different cognitive strategies used in biologically distinguishable populations. Such biological variation suggests that language processes do not rest on an isolated innate module, but rather, at least in part, are drawn from a set of generally available cognitive mechanisms.

ARE WE MAKING MOUNTAINS
OUT OF MODULES?

The background assumption underlying the modularity hypothesis is that mental life is computations—it involves the transmission and transmutation of symbols as inputs and outputs of operations. This assumption partially defines the necessity of some sort of modularity because specific transformational systems have correspondingly specific input and output schemata. The corresponding property of a module is that it resists all but a specified set of inputs and has a specified set of possible outputs. There is an intuitive ordering of such systems; the most plausible are those clearly based on physiologically tuned input/output systems; less plausible are "modules" defined only in terms of function.

Sensory Systems

The classic module is sensory, based on isolatable physiological constraints: The doctrine of the specific energy of sensory systems reflects the existence of specialized sense organs that normally are sensitive only to specific kinds of stimulation. The output of such a system is fed into a particular modality, regardless of the input: A classic and often cited example is that pressure on the eyeball is partially perceived as light. The isolation and analysis of such modules rests on clear phenomena, with clear neurophysiological explanations offered in current theories. Modules of this kind are not controversial, and set the guidelines as to what to look for as modules in more complex behavior.

The Whole Iguana

Much of complex behavior, such as object recognition, appears to operate as though it were a sensory/motor system or instinct, even though it is implausible to argue that it is completely innate. Claims that there are modules at this level of organization are the most interesting because they are also the most controversial. A major argument in favor of their existence in perception is that there must be some boundary between what we are perceiving and what we expect to be perceiving. To paraphrase an argument from Fodor (1983), if I believe there are no lions in the room, and there are, it would be dysfunctional (and an evolutionary failure) to have a lion-perception system totally dominated by my beliefs. Hence, the processing of complex percepts (e.g., lions), must proceed with some autonomy from other sources of belief.

Language lies in this range of phenomena. On the one hand, it is an elaborate system of behavior and knowledge that interacts with many of our thoughts and precepts. On the other hand, like lion-perception, it must be potentially autonomous from beliefs, or we would never learn anything unexpected from linguistic information. Accordingly, the claim that language behavior is modular is often taken to be an empirical claim about the insensitivity to contextual knowledge of ongoing language processing: For example, it is generally claimed that there is an "architectural" barrier between meaning and syntax processing—the syntax processor must complete its work before semantic context can be involved. Semantic discourse effects can occur, but only after syntactic structure is assigned to sentences.

A brief consideration of how this proposal is expressed in psycholinguistic practice illuminates the difficulty of studying modularity in general. A typical example of such empirical controversy comes from the work of Marslen-Wilson and Tyler (1987), researchers who believe that language comprehension is not modular, in the sense that contextual information of all kinds plays a role at each point in processing. They attempt to show that an on-line task sensitive to local syntactic processing can be influenced by semantically based information. For example, if a subject hears a sentence fragment and then must quickly read aloud a word that appears on a screen, local syntactic agreement between the end of the sentence fragment and the word influences reading time. Thus, reading time for "is" is faster following the fragment in (1a) than that in (1b), whereas just the reverse is true for reading time for "are."

    1a. Finding support ...
    1b. Talking mothers ...

This effect is taken to show that the syntactic relations between a verb form and the following noun are computed quickly enough so that a verb agreement expectation is set up immediately. Marslen-Wilson and Tyler then asked the question, would context preceding an ambiguous sequence like (1c) determine the reading time effect? That is, would the sequence in (2a) lead to faster reading times for "is" than "are," and would the opposite result pattern occur following (2b)?

    1c. Visiting relatives ...
    2a. When it becomes a duty, visiting relatives ...
    2b. When they stay too long, visiting relatives ...

Marslen-Wilson and Tyler showed that contexts did have such effects, and they concluded that the modularity hypothesis for syntax processing is false because clearly the contextual information was guiding the syntactic processing. There are a number of responses to this, but the empirical one is most revealing. Townsend and Bever (1982) noted that Marslen-Wilson and Tyler characteristically had only singular verbs and nouns in the contexts like (2a) and plural verbs and nouns in contexts like (2b) (also noted by Coward, 1982). Thus there might have been a word-to-word facilitation of "is" and "are," rather than a semantically mediated effect on the syntactic processing. Townsend and Bever tested for this and indeed found such a direct lexical associative effect. That is, regardless of whether the semantic context influenced the expectation of a singular gerund or a plural phrase, the word reading time for "is" was facilitated by the presence of a singular noun in the context, and time for "are" by a plural noun. The results also showed some (weak) semantic context effects, but only for facilitating the reading time of "is" after contexts like (2a), not of "are." Townsend and Bever argued that the context effect is limited to the gerund because the gerund form (as in 1a) maintains the canonical English phrase order, in which a verb precedes its object, the sequence can be recoded immediately and given a semantic interpretation: This contrasts with the adjectival interpretation (like 1b), which is not a complete proposition. Townsend and Bever argued that the reason that semantic context can have an immediate effect on the singular gerund interpretation is that it has an immediate semantic analysis that can interact with the preceding context, whereas the adjectival analysis is not yet available in the form of a complete proposition at a semantic level. Thus, the modularity of processing between levels is a function of when each level of representation has a complete unit available. Semantic context can influence new semantic units as they are processed, but semantic context cannot influence the choice of a syntactic unit except when there is a complete semantic unit to which the syntactic unit has been linked.

This exemplifies an important distinction between two kinds of modularity. The classic claim about research like that of Townsend and Bever is that modularity is "architectural," that higher level semantic processes cannot influence lower levels. The cases studied by Townsend and Bever show that the mediator of such interaction is the form of information itself. That is, temporal discontinuities in the use of semantic information from outside a sentence occur because of discontinuties in the formation of semantic units inside the sentence. This brings us to a point of logic underlying the necessity of modularity when different kinds of representational systems are concerned: If the computational language of two systems differ, one cannot affect the internal operation of the other. This does not necessarily demonstrate an architectural boundary between them, because their mutual computational opacity would lead to such discontinuities of influence anyway.

Consider a cross-modal example as an extreme, say the matching of pictures to words. At first, this would seem to be an obvious example of two distinct modules at work, separated architecturally. Operationally speaking, to demonstrate their modular independence one would want to show that if the perception of a word was facilitated by a corresponding picture, it was only after the word was initially sensed. That is, a picture of an iguana can not directly facilitate perception of the isolated letter sequences, I, or IG, or IGU, or IGUA, but only of a representation of the word, IGUANA. Such facts, if true, would support the assumption that picture processing and word finding are architecturally distinct modules. But in fact, the results show something weaker. It is empirically reasonable that the computational language of object recognition is not expressed in letter sequences: It follows logically that object recognition cannot inform word recognition. That is, the picture of the iguana cannot constrain the word-finding process to search for words beginning with I, or IG, or IGU, or even IGUANA: It can only constrain the word-finding process to find words with semantic structure related to that of iguanas. Of course, the word-finding process itself may quickly provide the information that the most important word semantically related to iguanas is "iguana" and they constrain its visual expectation for that word. But that constraint does not interact with letter recognition directly, only via conceptual and lexical levels of representation (see Schwartz & Schwartz, 1984).

This logical point makes it necessary to be cautious about any evidence for architectural modularity between different sources of information relevant to language behavior. Because there are empirical reasons to believe that the internal computational languages of nonlinguistic knowledge, semantics, syntax, and phonology all differ, we must expect on those grounds alone to find discontinuities in the apparent influence of information from one system on another.

THE CENTRAL PROBLEM AND THESIS

With this background, consider more closely the nature of the claim that language is a module. One essential component other than architectural segregation of processing is that it utilizes behavioral principles that are unique to it. This uniqueness is presumably related to specific neurological bases, such as the left-hemisphere superiority for language. There appear to be appropriately distinct components of linguistic knowledge, such as that between the syntax and lexicon—the former represents computational knowledge, while the latter includes associative information between words and concepts. Finally, the child's discovery of grammar is viewed as depending on unique innate mechanisms. In brief, the claim that language is a module involves the following associated claims:

1. the unique neurological bases for language account for its localization in the brain.
2. the different kinds of linguistic knowledge are uniquely represented within the language capacity.
3. grammar is acquired via unique learning mechanisms.

In this chapter, I outline the thesis that modular-like properties of language may have an initial source in prelinguistic subcortical mechanisms. I then argue that each of the three unique properties just outlined may be an expression of general properties of cognition. I argue further that the relation of those properties to biologically defined groups suggests that they are innate at a general cognitive level, not limited to language.

Perceptual/Motor Instinct and the Early Segregation of Modalities

The apparent existence of general modalities is evidence for neurological prefiguring of knowledge domains. An increasing number of researchers are concluding that the young child has a specific set of innate knowledge domains. Their domains include "naive physics," "naive biology," "naive interpersonal psychology," "language," "person recognition" (see Baillergeon, Spelke, & Wasserman, 1985; Carey, 1987; Keil, 1989; Leslie, 1987; Wellman, 1990). Each of these domains appears early in childhood, partially segregated from the others: The set of domains partitions experience and knowledge in ways that are functional for an adult world, and that are the basis for module-like systems in the adult world.

At first blush, the child's ability to segregate his or her world into mentally relevant packages would seem to demonstrate an innate modular structure at the cortical level for each of those systems. Clearly, something must be innate to enable the infant to parse the world into experiences relevant to the acquisition of distinct mental systems. The question is: How can such constraints be causally relevant to the cortex, before the cortex is fully operational? The answer may lie in the existence of postnatal perceptual schemata and motor reflexes, which have autonomous characteristics. For example, the infant in the first 2–3 months of life has many highly tuned perceptual abilities (see Mehler & Dupoux, 1990, for a review). The infant can isolate critical aspects of his or her species—specific behavior (e.g., verbal input, faces); the infant also has perceptual and motor schemata responsive aspects of the physical world (Baillergeon et al., 1985). At the same time, the infant engages in apparently higher social functions such as facial mimicry, smiling, and reaching outward (Maratsos, 1982; Meltzoff & Moors, 1983; Murray & Trevarthen, 1986). These highly adaptive behaviors are the basis for the child's first lie, in the sense that they convey to adults the belief that the child has a functioning, physical, psychological, and social personality, but they occur based on subcortical and automatically functioning neural substrates. Such behaviors may depend on instinct because the learning structures of the cortex are not fully operational at birth, or simply because the newborn lacks experience from which to extract physically and socially functional behaviors. On either interpretation, the functional role of such autonomous structures is clear; it provides the precortical infant with a repertoire of physical, perceptual, and socially functional behaviors. These structures in turn shape the cortical organization as it emerges. This idea must be true, at least in part, because the innate schemata themselves give specific organization to what the emerging cortex experiences: The child cannot help but learn to segregate kinds of experiences as they are grouped by the schemata the child is born with. In this way, an initially unorganized cortex can be trained to parse the world in accordance with the shape and grouping given to initial experiences by the set of early innate sensory/motor schemata. That is, the child's first successful lie, that it is actually a functioning mind, succeeds because the instincts themselves have been selected to survive in the physical world and fool the adult world. But in surviving and fooling the world, they also package experiences for the emerging cortex into the rudiments of an adult-like organization in modalities.

It is clear that an innate repertoire of precortical instincts relevant to worldly physics, species recognition, and species-typical behavior is functional for the infant at birth. If cortical computational mechanisms are not yet functional, precomputational instincts can carry the infant through the first few months of life while the cortex matures and accommodates to experience. In the meantime, innate physical perceptual/motor mechanisms save the child from corporeal disaster; species-recognition mechanisms orient the child toward caregivers; species-typical motor behaviors encourage the child's caregivers to treat the child as a human. But the innate mechanisms have a further consequence; they shape and partition experience into mentally natural kinds. Thus, the presence of such mechanisms before experience has interacted with cortical structures, must constrain the infant to divide the world into mentally natural modalities. This hypothesis offers an explanation of the innate basis of such functional modalities as "language," "naive physics," " naive psychology" without assuming an innate cortical computational module underlying them. Rather, the infant's set of innate socially adaptive mechanisms channel cortical experiences such that general computational processes operate on appropriately grouped activities. On this view, the functional modalities indeed have innate bases; infantile sensorimotor organizational instincts, selected to promote early survival in a physical, psychological, and social world, before more complex systems are available.

Evidence for Processing Dimensions in Cognition

The modularity hypothesis is most naturally related to the fact that mental life appears pre-theoretically to have distinct modalities. But, there is also a direct approach to the discovery of mental computational boundaries—the study of biologically differentiated processing systems. There are two important ways to show evidence for a direct relation between brain structures and particular cognitive processes: Study distinct behaviors in clinical populations with specific neurological damage; study different behaviors of brains in normal populations that can be biologically differentiated. I concentrate on what can be learned from differences in normal populations because of the obvious limitations of clinical data. Brain lesion studies are not experimentally controlled; the patients' overt behavior must be taken as an adaptation to the loss of a structure, not necessarily the direct expression of that loss. Similarly, genetically abnormal brains have the opportunity to adapt to their abnormality over a lifetime. I am not suggesting that nothing can be learned from such investigations; but the discovery of the isolation of an overt cognitive process in a clinical population requires a complex interpretation involving not only an explicit hypothesis about the lost process, but also about the nature of compensatory mechanisms contributing to the overt behavior (see Mehler, Morton, & Jusczyk, 1984; Shallice, 1984).

It may seem eccentric to expect that normal population variation can illuminate fundamental dimensions of cognitive processes. But, in fact, it is a direct consequence of our growing theoretical success in correctly distinguishing the dimensions of cognitive processing. Suppose the following:

1. cognitive processes are differentiated in part because of neuro-logical differences.
2. those differences are in part innate.
3. the genetic code for such differences is complex, leading to relevant co-variation with other genotypes, and consequently phenotypes.

Then if we distinguish cognitive processes correctly, we may find that populations differentiated on the basis of biologically superficial phenotypic traits may also have characteristic differences in cognitive processes. In brief, the better our theoretical cognitive science, the more likely it is that theoretically distinct cognitive processes will appear differentially in biologically coded groups.

Much progress in understanding the physiology of sensation, perception, and cognition has depended on the study of normal populations: A rationale for such a study is that isolation of the component processes intrinsic to a behavior guides the search for relevant physiological bases. A frequent method has involved the theoretical and empirical study of behaviors in terms of pairs of opponent processes. Color vision is a well-known example: The study of such phenomena as contrast effects, adaptation effects, and afterimages, supported a theory that color vision depends on the interaction of two sensitive systems, one sensitive to a blue/yellow dimension, the other to a red/green dimension. Within each system, activation of one of the dimensions inhibits the other. Thus, blue is the behavioral opposite of yellow, and red of green. The behavioral isolation of these linked systems was an indicator of a physiological dimension. Of course, the physiological distinction between these systems was ultimately confirmed and the chemical basis for the apparent processes became a topic of study.

The existence of opponent processes defines modularity in two different ways. First, opposition of processes implies a dimension that connects the two processes, linked by activating mechanisms (e.g., the red–green system). Second, each of the processes is distinct from the other, and hence is potentially a distinct subsystem of its own. In the following discussion, I apply the technique of isolating linked opponent processes to cognition. I first describe a formal distinction between a pair of processes, single and multiple, then offer some empirical evidence that the theoretical distinction is genetically coded in the biological substrate for three aspects of cognition—that is, the expression of the formal distinction in each of these domains is respected in the behavior of biologically distinguishable brain systems. The results support the validity of physiological relevance of the formal distinction: They also support the view that the associated specific properties of language are a reflection of corresponding general properties of cognition.

COMPUTATIONAL MODULARITY—PROCESSING SINGLE VERSUS MULTIPLE REPRESENTATION

The concept is quite simple: Certain computational activities within a modality are opaque to each other, because of differences in the kind of mental action they involve, rather than differences in modality, architectural, or informational boundaries. Activities can involve one representation or several. For example, recognition that two right angles are identical is a direct process that involves one representational type. This contrasts with recognizing the part–whole configurational relation between a right angle and a square. Understanding the sentence "dogs chase cats" as a function of interlexical associations is a direct process, which contrasts with computing the formal semantic relations from the word order and inflectional information. Acquiring an abstract hypothesis via successive refinement of it based on evidence, contrasts with successive replacement of it by an internally generated hypothesis.

Learning to negotiate a known neighborhood in terms of an angular relation to a memorized local landmark is a different kind of process from learning to use a cognitive map that sets several landmarks in relation to each other.

These differentiations of mental activities by a number of representations is formal, and may not correspond to a dimension along which mental activities are actually arrayed physiologically. The following empirical discussions show how this distinction is in fact reflected in differences between distinct populations. First, the left hemisphere may be more computationally powerful than the right: This results in its specialization for so-called relational processing while the right hemisphere is specialized for comparatively simple processing. Second, the representation of associative knowledge in right-handers from left-handed families may be more diffuse than for pure right-handers: This results in relatively better differentiated associations in left-handed familials and hence, more reliance on local lexical knowledge during language processing. Third, female humans and rats use local and episodic knowledge to navigate, whereas males use motor and vector representations in spatial behavior. Fourth, the abduction of an abstract representation of an artificial language in female humans may depend primarily on single hypothesis refinement, whereas in males it depends more on competition between hypotheses. There are also some formal and empirical similarities between the population variations in spatial and artificial language learning. In particular, there are similar interactions between gender and familial handedness: In each case, the gender differences in performance are larger for subjects with left-handed families. Such similarities suggest the possibility that a single cognitive dimension underlies both types of behavior.

It is important for our conception of modularity that the three process dimensions are general. That is, they cut across modality domains. If this differentiation is borne out by further research, it will lead to a formulation of modularity in which behavioral modules draw on shared general cognitive capacities.

THE GENERALITY OF THE PROCESSING DIFFERENCES IN THE CEREBRAL HEMISPHERES

The difference in function between the left and right hemisphere can be taken as an existence demonstration that certain kinds of computational processes can occur in isolation from others. The most stable finding is the relative vulnerability of language to damage in the left compared with the right hemisphere. This fact is consistent with the view that language is a module, given the apparent special location of its neurophysiological bases. Indeed, numerous researchers have suggested that some special property of the left hemisphere may be the critical biological cause of humans' linguistic capacity (Calvin, 1982; Gazzaniga & Hillyard, 1971; Gazzaniga & Sperry, 1967; Hewes, 1973; Kimura, 1976; Le Doux, 1983; Levy, 1988). For a number of years, it was thought that there was a general partition of modalities between the hemispheres—language and logic to the left, music, vision, and art to the right (Kimura, 1976). Typical supporting experimental evidence was the fact that words are better perceived in the right ear. Typical examples of right-hemisphere superiority were superior recognition of an angle in the left visual field or superior recognition of short melodies in the left ear (Kimura, 1964).

The unique relationship between the left hemisphere and language might instead be due to a general computational property of language, which is better processed in the left hemisphere. Considerable evidence that this is true has accumulated over the last two decades. Language processing is peculiarly dependent on relational compositional processes: The formation of phonological, syntactic, and semantic levels of representation involve setting components into relation with each other. The left hemisphere excels at meeting this computational demand: Hence, language is most strongly represented in the left hemisphere (Bever, 1970, 1975, 1980; Levy, 1969).

A clear way to demonstrate that the left hemisphere is dominant for relational processing in general is to show the corresponding feature for nonlinguistic behaviors. For example, the right visual field (left-hemisphere) is dominant for visual tasks involving relations between images: When a square is followed by a right angle, the decision time that it "contains" the right angle is faster in the right visual field (Hurtig, 1982, see also Kosslyn, 1987, for related demonstrations). The perception of music provides another crucial test case. On the one hand, like language, music is serial and can involve higher-order integrations. On the other hand, basic melody perception is a classic example of holistic gestalt organization, as evidenced by the ease with which transposed melodies are recognized as identical. Various studies have shown that becoming musically sophisticated involves shifting from perceiving melodies as gestalten to perceiving them in terms of isolatable motifs and relations between motifs (Tan, Aiello, & Bever, 1981; Werner, 1948). Many other studies have shown that musicians also process melodies more actively in the left than right hemispheres (Bever & Chiarello, 1974; see Bever, 1980, for a literature review). That is, as the way one processes music shifts from direct to relational the hemisphere dominance shifts from right to left. This does not mean that an entire modality shifts, only the specific relational activities in it. Even though musicians' melody perception is dominant in the left hemisphere, their recognition of two-note intervals is better in the right hemisphere (Kellar & Bever, 1980).

The hemispheric differentiation of processing styles might be fundamentally caused by a more specific asymmetry. For example, it might be that the left hemisphere has innate structures that are the critical cause for language. In this view, other compositional activities become better processed in the left hemisphere because of that initial predisposition, which generalizes to other tasks (Chomsky, 1965; Gleitman, 1981; Lanneberg, 1967). Other hypotheses suggest that the left hemisphere is innately dominant for integrated motor behaviors (Kimura, 1973); in this view, language becomes dominant in the left hemisphere because speech requires intricate motor behaviors.

It is difficult to disentangle these hypotheses from one based on a fundamental difference between the hemispheres in processing style.

Certainly, adult humans intentionally mediate many complex tasks by language, and language involves both compositional and motor integrations. The potential causal basis, however, for asymmetries is important for this chapter. If the ultimate cause is the presence of an innate neurological module for language in the left hemisphere, then the different language behaviors of the hemispheres is not fundamentally a developmental result of general computational modularity, but rather has a linguistically specific neurological base. Clearly, there must be some asymmetry between the hemispheres: The question is, how specific is that asymmetry? For analytic purposes, we can contrast a modular asymmetry against an asymmetry in computational power (Bever, 1980). Consider the following assumptions:

1. the left hemisphere is computationally more powerful than the right.
2. there is complementary inhibition between the hemispheres.
3. relational tasks arc computationally more demanding than associative tasks.

The third assumption is logically necessary: A relational task involves processing the relations between entities. A unary task involves direct processing of a single representation. Thus, relational tasks presuppose unary actions, and are more complex (for some otherwise undifferentiated computational engine). Assumption 2 is widely documented: Activity in one hemisphere inhibits activity in the corresponding area of the opposite hemisphere. If the first assumption is true, then during childhood, the left hemisphere would tend to take over relational activities such as language. This predicts further that unary activities would become asymmetric at a later age because only after language and other compositional tasks are specialized in the left hemisphere would there be pressure to represent the simpler tasks asymmetrically. The relative late appearance of asymmetries for simple tasks has been noted by various researchers. This hypothesis also explains why it is possible for children with surgically removed left hemispheres to learn language at all (Dennis & Kohn, 1974, 1975; Newman, Lovett, & Dennis, 1986). There is some evidence that their performance is not as skilled as in children with only a left hemisphere, but that difference, as well, is explained on the view that the fundamental difference between the hemispheres is raw computational power.

One way to gain further perspective on the basis for hemisphere asymmetries is to examine their nature in other mammals, for whom natural language is not a theoretically corrupting influence. A recent review suggested that apes have a consistent asymmetry in favor of the right paw for tasks requiring intricate or forceful action, and the left paw for simple and passive actions (McNielage, Studdert-Kennedy, & Lindblom, 1987). This is consistent with the general nature of handedness and asymmetries in humans. Several experimental studies give more particular support. First, we showed that rats learn to recognize tone sequences better in the right than left ear: This difference increases as the length of the sequence increases (O'Connor, Roitblat, & Bever, in press). Such results are consistent with the findings with humans, but leave open the question of whether it is sequencing as such, or complexity of relations that brings out the superiority of the left hemisphere. A separate study with a dolphin suggests that the critical factor is not sequencing as such, but rather whether the task involves relational processing (Morrell-Samuels, Herman, & Bever, 1991). A dolphin had been trained to respond to hand signs, following a set of ordering constraints (Herman, Richard, & Wholz, 1984). There were three kinds of sequences involving several verbs and numerous objects: (3a) single signs involving only the dolphin's action; (3b) two-sign sequences involving an action by the dolphin on an object; (3c) three-sign sequences involving an action by the dolphin setting two objects into a particular relation to each other.

3a. Jump
3b. Hoop tail-touch
3c. Hoop frisbee bring (different meaning from 'Frisbee hoop bring')

Herman, Morrel-Samuels, and Pack (1990) had shown that the dolphin would respond to videorecordings of signs, presented on a 13-inch television through a window in its tank. This allowed us to control which eye could see a sign and to time the speed of the response. We found a significant superiority in the left eye for those sign stimuli that involved only the dolphin or the dolphin and a single object. We found a right-eye superiority for the sign stimuli involving two objects in relation to each other. Unlike humans, the dolphin's eye is completely connected to the contralateral hemisphere. Thus, we can conclude that the dolphin's left hemisphere is superior for the relational sign stimuli, and the right hemisphere is superior for the stimuli involving at most a single object. The fact that the two-sign sequence is superior in the right hemisphere shows that the superiority of the left hemisphere for the more complex stimuli is not a function of it being a sequence as such. Rather it is a function of a sequence in which the named object's words have a structured relation to each other.

This range of studies suggest that the left-hemisphere superiority for language in humans may not be a reflection of a unique linguistic ability of the left hemisphere. Rather, the specific difference between the hemispheres reflects the logical distinction between relational and unary processing. This difference between the hemispheres holds for language behaviors and nonlanguage behaviors in humans, and for some behaviors in some other mammals. All the phenomena can be explained as the result of a difference in computational power between the hemispheres, which interacts developmentally with the logical distinction between the two kinds of processing. The conclusion here is that we do not have to postulate a left-hemisphere bound linguistic module to explain the presence of language in the left hemisphere of humans. Language is better handled by the left hemisphere because of what language is, but the unique *cause* of what language is lies elsewhere.

FAMILIAL HANDEDNESS AND VARIATION
IN KINDS OF LINGUISTIC KNOWLEDGE

Within language behavior there is a distinction between local-associative and global-computational knowledge. Understanding the sentence "cats sleep" involves accessing the associative and conceptual knowledge connected to the individual words "cat" and "sleep"; it simultaneously involves organizing the words into phrases with global thematic interrelations. Thus, using language involves both accessing lexical information about the reference and association of individual words, and organizing phrases in relation to each other at several levels of representation.

Various modular theorists have canonized this distinction into a claim that there are distinct lexical and syntactic modules that operate independently of each other. Accordingly, the role of lexical knowledge in sentence processing is an important factor in developing empirical evidence for or against modularity of linguistic components. The distinction turns out to be reflected in a general difference in the way two groups of people process language. It is a common supposition that in normal people there is a large degree of homogeneity in the way language is organized neurologically and processed psychologically. The only exception to this generality is the general acceptance that left-handed people may have some differences in the neurological organization of language. There are also clinical reports that right handers with left-handed family members have relatively more linguistic involvement of the right hemisphere (Brown, 1976, 1978; Brown & Hecaen, 1976; Hecaen, 1976; Subirana, 1958, 1969). Our recent research suggests that the familial handedness of normal right-handed people also influences how language is organized and used (Bever, 1983; Bever, Carrithers, Cowart, & Townsend, 1989). The dimension that differentiates right-handed people with left-handed family members (LHFs) from those with only right-handed family members (RHFs), is exactly that between local lexical knowledge and global syntactic organization. LHF right-handers access local lexical knowledge more directly, whereas RHF right-handers are more immediately sensitive to grammatical knowledge.

The distinction between accessing local and global linguistic information runs through a number of experimental investigations. For example, LF subjects read computer-displayed short discourses about 10% faster when they are presented word by word, than when presented one clause at a time; RHFs read whole-clause presentations about 10% faster than word-by-word presentations. This follows from the view that LHFs naturally give emphasis to individual word recognition, whereas RHFs emphasize overall grammatical structure. This is also true of the behavior when understanding sentences. For example, Carrithers (1989) used a word-by-word reading time measure and had subjects read active and passive sentences: It is traditionally reported in the psycholinguistic literature that passive sentences are more complex, presumably because analyzing their meaning involves a computational step not needed for active sentences. Carrithers confirmed this finding: The reading time for final words was longer for passive than active sentences. This result, however, was true only for RHF readers. LHF readers showed no difference in response to the structural difference between passives and actives.

The difference between RHFs and LHF in sensitivity to local versus global information also effects the processing of single words. This can be shown in a priming lexical decision paradigm that differentiates associative from semantic relations between words. In this paradigm, subjects must decide as quickly as possible whether or not a briefly presented letter sequence is a word. On critical trials, the target word is preceded by a word that has a specified kind of relation to the target word, either associative or semantic. For example, the relation between a target word "rose" and a prime word "thorn," is associative, that is, the prime word has a real-world connection to the target world; in contrast, the prime word "flower" has a linguistically specified relation to "rose," namely being its category. This distinction appears strongly in the different performance of LHFs and RHFs (Bever et al., 1989). LHFs show a strong priming effect of associative relations between words, and a moderate effect of linguistically semantic relations. In contrast, RHFs show a stronger priming effect for semantic relations and little for associative relations. The significance of this kind of result is that the task involves relations between isolated words, but differentiates between local linguistic and global extralinguistic information about the single words: RHFs are specifically more sensitive to linguistic relations and less sensitive to extralinguistic relations.

Other heterogeneous studies of these two groups confirms the distinct way in which they access information about language (see Bever, Straub, Shenkman, Kim, & Carrithers, 1990). As in the case of cerebral asymmetries, there are several points that follow from this discovery. First, it gives construct validity to the distinction between local-associative and global-structural knowledge about words and sentences. It suggests further that the organization of these kinds of knowledge is related to general innate variables.

This leads us to the question of mechanism: What might differ in the brains of RHF and LHF people that would account for this different behavior in language? One answer derives from the hypothesis that left-handedness is the result of an overexposure of testosterone during gestation (Geschwind & Galaburda, 1987). The idea is that the testosterone exposure occurs and slows all cerebral growth just during the period when the left hemisphere would otherwise be in a growth spurt relative to the right hemisphere. The result is that the hemispheres end up more equipotential, with a greater chance of left-handedness ultimately emerging. The details of this hypothesis and the evidence for it are not critical for this discussion. What is critical is the idea that familial left-handedness may be a marker for a uterine condition, which often, but now always leads to explicit left-handedness. On this view, right-handed people from left-handed families have more equipotential hemispheres at critical stages, but end up right-handed through chance factors. Although right-handed, these people have more bilaterally equal capacity than those from pure right-handed families: This may result in more right-hemisphere representation of lexical association and/or more widespread representation within the left hemisphere. Either way, lexical associative knowledge would be represented more diffusely in LHFs.

Several facts support the idea that LHFs have a more bilateral representation for language than RHFs. For example, LHFs show a greater incidence of crossed aphasia (aphasia resulting from an injury to the right hemisphere; Joanette, Lecours, LePage, & Lamoureaux, 1983; Luria, 1947). Second, although processing language tasks, LHFs show more bilateral evoked potential activity (Kutas, Van Petten, & Bessen, 1988; Kutas & Klueder, personal communication, May 5, 1991). Our results suggest that this bilaterality reflects a more widespread representation of associative linguistic information in familial left-handers. On this interpretation, computational linguistic knowledge must be represented in the left hemisphere regardless of familial handedness because it is so heavily dependent on relational processing. But associative and referential linguistic knowledge can be represented more widely when there is less general asymmetry between the hemispheres.

On this view, left-handed familials can access their associative and conceptual knowledge about individual words with associative processes relatively distinct from grammatical processing: Accordingly, left-handed familials can make more distinct use of associative information connected to individual words, separate from their role in grammatical relation to other words. The research on familial handedness discussed so far is limited to the language domain. The fact that there is consistent variation in how different aspects of linguistic knowledge are accessed demonstrates that the neurological foundations for a linguistic module are not monolithic. However, it remains to be shown that familial handedness mediates behavioral differences in local versus global processing in non-linguistic domains. I return to this later.

BIOLOGICAL VARIATION IN MODES OF ABDUCTION

The previous two case studies involve distinctions between component mental processes (direct vs. relational) and levels of detail of representations (local-associative versus global–syntactic). A third formal distinction speaks to the way in which humans go about forming abstract concepts, the process Pierce (1957) referred to as *abduction*. Abduction occurs in simple conceptual activities like learning a simple concept, such as "dog"; it also occurs in the learning of more complex abstract structures, such as the grammar of a language or a mental map of a neighborhood. Abduction is the process (neither induction nor deduction) through which internally generated hypotheses interact with data as a person arrives at a correct abstract structure. Pierce noted that there are two contrasting forms of the interaction of data and internalized abstract hypotheses: In one method, new data can be used to refine an existing hypothesis; in the other, the data can be used to choose between competing alternative hypotheses. Each of these methods can be reduced to an extreme form of the other, but they represent important differences in focus and emphasis. Consider a child developing the concept of what a "dog" is as opposed to a "cat," when presented for the first time with a small dog, such as a Chihuahua. Hypothesis refinement would extend the previous generalization of the distinction between "dogs" and "cats." Hypothesis competition would replace the previous hypothesis (e.g., "cats are small, dogs are big"), with a new one (e.g., "cats meow, dogs bark"). The net result of both procedures is ultimately the same, but hypothesis refinement involves changing a single internal hypothesis, whereas hypothesis competition involves generating a new hypothesis and choosing one of them.

The distinction between the two kinds of abduction raises an interesting question concerning the learning of grammar. Do children emerge with a correct grammar by successive hypothesis refinement or by hypothesis competition? Linguists tend to assume the latter because grammars appear to them to be too complex to be formed gradually; psychologists find hypothesis refinement more compatible with the notion of "learning." It would seem likely that grammar acquisition should rest on the use of both kinds of abductive strategies, but first one must show that the formal distinction corresponds to a mental one. Following the general thesis in this chapter, if we can show that language may be learned by different strategies that correlate with population variables, it will suggest that the abductive procedure for language learning is not univocal within a single language-learning module. Rather, it rests on a general difference in abduction style that itself may cut across different cognitive domains.

To study this, I and my colleagues used the study of population differences in the same way described in the previous cases: We designed a situation in which hypothesis refinement would be a more natural way of acquiring an abstract structure, in contrast with a situation in which hypothesis competition would be more natural. We then found that performance in the two different structure learning conditions indeed corresponded to a biologically coded difference in the subject population. We take this to be a demonstration of the construct validity of the distinction, as well as a result that leads to new ways of thinking about the formation of abstract representations. [1]

We used an artificial language learning study, taken in part from the

---

[1] The new experiments reported in this chapter are all being presented more fully in other publications. All the results reported are statistically significant on standard statistical measures. Co-workers on these studies include, Dustin Gordon, Ralph Hansen, Pietro Michelucci, Ken Shenkman.

literature on what structural properties of languages make them easy to learn. The language we used was a verb-final language, close to that used in studies of artificial language by Meier and Bower (1986). This language allows for the description of arrays of geometric figures displayed in quadrants of a computer screen. The language uses English lexical items, but its own grammatical order, and it has one grammatical morpheme, "te," which is roughly a relative clause introducer. Typical sentences in the language are:

1. triangle circle striped below
   (the triangle is below the striped circle)
2. triangle striped te circle above square left-of
   (the striped triangle that is above the circle is to the left of the square)

Previous studies of artificial language learning typically present subjects with sequences and ask them to learn to discriminate between those that are grammatical in the language and those that are not. This seemed to be unnecessarily artificial: Natural language learners are learning to use a language, to understand and be understood in the language. Accordingly we changed the usual procedure by focusing on situations that force subjects to learn to use the language. For example, in the "production" task, subjects were trained to take as input a geometric array, and produce as output a grammatical sequence that describes that array. The subject was provided with a button for each "word" (e.g., "blue," "triangle," "right-of"); on each trial, the subject typed a sequence as describing the geometric array presented on that trial. If the sequence was correct, he or she was told that; if the sequence was incorrect, the subject was shown a sample of correct sequences. There were 48 different trials with this procedure. Every 12 trials, the subject was stopped and given a forced-choice grammaticality judgment test, in which he or she was to indicate which member of each of 12 pairs of sequences was "grammatically correct" in the test language. These pairs were constructed to give information about a range of structural types of sentences.

A separate procedure involved learning "perception" of the language, in which subjects were given a correct sequence as input and were asked to "draw" the geometric array that the sequence described (we pre-trained subjects in the use of a simple graphics package, designed for this purpose). In this case, the geometric arrays were exactly those used as input to the production version of the study; also, every 12 trials, subjects responded to the "grammaticality" judgment task.

In a third version of the study, subjects were given "two-way" training both perception and production training, alternating from trial to trial. Every 12 trials, subjects responded to the "grammaticality" task. Our initial expectation was that subjects would learn the grammar of the language best in the task that alternated between production and perception because it most closely approximates the child's situation in learning a natural language. At the same time, we noted a fundamental conceptual difference related to the two kinds of abduction, between the two-way condition and the other conditions, each of which was "one-way." The two-way condition naturally stimulated subjects to build up separate mental systems to relate meanings with sequences, one for production that maps meanings onto sequences, and one for perception, which maps sequences onto meanings. If it had any effect at all, two-way training would tend to emphasize the hypothesis competition model of learning, at least because it stimulates subjects to develop separate models that relate meaning and sequence. Each of the one-way conditions would tend more to emphasize the hypothesis-refinement strategy of learning because only one model of the meaning–utterance relationships is required. Hence, we were in a position to find a contrast between subject groups that find hypothesis competition more conducive to learning an abstract structure, and subject groups that find hypothesis refinement more conducive to learning.

To this end, we controlled subject groups stringently on a number of variables. First, they all fell within the same narrow range of verbal and math SAT scores, age, and socioeconomic status. They were all native speakers of English. Gender and handedness background were part of the experimental design, so that we could examine the effects of each. There were 144 subjects who were run in slightly varying versions of the study. The dependent measures were success in grammaticality judgments, and success in the actual mapping tasks.

The results were complex and rich, and I discuss only part of them here, primarily those having to do with the grammaticality judgments, because, *prima facie*, they reflect the formation of an abstract grammar. There was a clear gender difference in the impact of two- versus one-way training. Males learned to discriminate the grammaticality task about 10% better in the two-way condition, than the one-way conditions; females show the exactly opposite pattern. These effects are quite large and statistically reliable. They are not due to differences in handedness background (which were balanced) or SAT scores (which were restricted in range, but which we also co-varied in our statistical analyses).

The first impact of these differences is to support the construct validity of the distinction between the two strategies for abduction. The results suggest that males are more likely to form an abstract structure when learning distinct hypotheses that bear on that structure. Females are more likely to form an abstract structure when learning a single model that applies the structure. Another way of describing the difference is that females do best at abstracting a structure out of a single model for its use, whereas males do best at abstracting a structure from competing models for its use. Gender is a biologically coded difference, and it would be tempting to argue that this finding shows that the different kinds of abduction may themselves be biologically coded. However, unlike familial handedness, gender is a biological variable with immediate social consequences. It is possible that the different social roles for males and females are expressed in the formation of distinct learning strategies. It is difficult to formulate a specific hypothesis as to how such a socially based differentiation does, or could occur, but the complexity of the social patterns makes us cautious at this point about claiming that the abduction difference is directly biologically caused. The data in the next sections of this chapter strengthens the biological interpretation of these differences.

SPATIAL LEARNING: TWO WAYS
TO GET THERE FROM HERE

The strength of these results made us turn to other areas in which the cognitive performance of the genders might differ in a way related to the different styles of abduction. Both anecdotes and research have supported the claim that women are not as adept as men at reading conventional maps (Maccoby & Jacklin, 1974). Yet there is no evidence that this reflects or causes a fundamental difference in the ability to negotiate familiar and novel neighborhoods. Our first study is a laboratory demonstration of these two observations. We asked 20 men and 20 women to learn to get from one point to another in a set of corridors arranged in a digital-style figure 8. The subjects were started at a colored flag in the middle of a corridor at the top or bottom of the figure 8, and told to wander through the system until they found the differently colored goal flag; the goal flag was located at the middle of the corridor at the opposite end of the figure 8. Subjects were always started in one clockwise or counterclockwise direction by the presence of a "barrier" to the left or the right of their start position (on alternate trials, the starting barrier was on different sides). Several configurations of additional barriers were arranged so that the middle cross corridor of the figure 8 always turned out to be a blind alley: Subjects could turn into the middle corridor, but discovered barriers as soon as they exited at the other end of the middle corridor. Thus, what subjects had to learn was to walk on the perimeter of the figure 8, starting in the direction allowed by the initial barrier, and to avoid the middle alley. Between each trial, subjects were blindfolded and brought to their starting flag in a wheelchair. Subjects were run for four trials. At the end of the experiment, we asked subjects to choose from a set of 8 prepared stick drawings, the one that depicted the exact arrangement of the corridors and flags (excluding barriers).

Males were significantly better at choosing the correct drawing of the corridor arrangement (87.5% correct for males, 25% correct for females). Overall running performance on the maze task, however, was identical, with respect to average number of turns made and the total time taken on each trial of the maze. This is consistent with the apparent fact that males and females can learn to negotiate a new neighborhood equally well. If that is true, why are the two genders reported to be so different at using a configurational representation of that neighborhood?

Recent investigations of the cognitive components of mental maps in humans and animals casts light on this question. The most consistent use of mental maps in nature is to provide a mechanism that allows an individual to leave a home base and return to it as directly as possible (Gallistel, 1990). For example, a bee leaves its hive and may forage in an irregular path until it finds some food. At that point it makes a beeline back to its hive rather than retracing its exact steps. This can occur when the home base is well out of sight. This clearly shows that the animal has an ability to "dead-reckon," to calculate from local cues where it is in relation to its home base. This computational ability resolves into two kinds of abstract representation: (a) episodic knowledge of individual landmarks and how they look from from different angles in relation to the home base, and (b) configurational knowledge of the spatial relationship between the landmarks. Each of these kinds of knowledge is sufficient in the limit to represent in behavior knowledge of an area: An exhaustive list of landmarks and their angular relation to home base can allow for navigation within the area, as can a list of landmarks and their angular relations to each other and home base. However, although extensionally equivalent, these two kinds of map representations emphasize different aspects of spatial knowledge.

A map is an abstract representation of a space independent of how that knowledge is used—it serves for spatial behavior the same representational function as that served by a grammar for language behavior. Furthermore, how one might best learn the two kinds of spatial knowledge corresponds to the two forms of abduction. Consider the impact on one's current spatial knowledge of an additional landmark location. Learning by hypothesis refinement is naturally suited to respond to the new information, by simply adding it to the existing list of landmarks. Learning through hypothesis competition is better suited to the exchange of active sets of configurations: If new information to a spatial array is represented in terms of angular relations between locations/landmarks, then adding a new location to elaborate an existing array involves learning a complex set of new angular relations. It is a more direct method to replace the old array of locations with a new one—that is, to replace the previous map with a competitor.

I am arguing that the theoretical differentiation of two computational components of mental maps is like the differentiation of the two modes of abduction. This might resolve the difference in spatial abilities between males and females to the same source as that in artificial language learning. In particular, females may access episodic landmark-based spatial knowledge compared with males, relatively more easily than they access configurational knowledge. If the computational distinction is coded genetically in this way, it serves as a confirmation of the construct validity of the distinction. It suggests that the distinction is genetically represented; it offers an explanation of gender differences in using particular kinds of maps. The remainder of this section is directed at showing the gender difference indeed corresponds to the computational distinction between the two kinds of information involved in using mental maps.

Prior research has shown that females recognize photographs of areas in known neighborhoods better than males (Golledge, 1988). This is consistent with the hypothesis that females have richer access to landmarks from different perspectives in their home territory. The corridors and corners in our study using the figure 8 maze were visually similar, so we did not use such a test. Instead, we varied the reliability of cues for deciding what turns to make by running some subjects in opposite directions on different trials. That is, half the subjects were returned in the wheelchair to their original starting flag for each trial, and always learned the maze in one direction; the other half of the subjects were brought in the wheelchair to what had just been the goal flag, which was now treated as the start flag for the next trial. Accordingly, the latter subjects were exposed to the maze, going in both directions. Because the maze was symmetrical, the actual turns to be made were the same for both sets of subjects.

Our prediction was that the one-way condition would be easier than the two-way condition for females, whereas the opposite would be true for males. This prediction follows from the fact that in the one-way condition, each landmark had a univocal meaning about directions and turns to take; in the two-way condition each landmark has two opposite meanings, depending on one's running direction. Consequently, one-way training, in which landmarks have consistent meaning, should be easier for females, whereas two-way training, which discourages reliance on separate landmarks alone, should be easier for males. The results were consistent with these predictions. Performance on the first trial revealed large individual differences in number of turns and total running time. Because the first trial was the same for all subjects, it served as a baseline to scale relative performance on the subsequent trials. There were three relative measures: (a) improvement in number of turns made; (b) improvement in time taken; and (c) improvement in the time for each turn. These measures show that females' performance actually deteriorated during the study in the two-way condition, while improving on several measures in the one-way condition. Males' performance became slightly better in the two-way than one-way condition on all measures. (The interaction between running condition and gender was significant on various measures.)

In the corridor study, subjects were free to extract a wide variety of individually idiosyncratic information about local cues. To gain more experimental control over such variables, we implemented a computerized version of the figure 8 maze. In this maze, the walls and floor are displayed in a forced three-dimensional projection on a computer screen; the walls and floor are scored with lines to enhance the perspective effects of movement, but there were no local cues to differentiate one choice point or wall from another. The only unique markings were a dark triangle and a light triangle on the floor in the middle of the top and bottom corridors of the figure 8, corresponding to the start and goal flags in the original study. Subjects could see these triangles only when they were three or fewer steps from there. Subjects stepped forward, backward, right, and left, using the standard cursor movement arrows on a computer keyboard. The design was as before, crossing gender of the subject and one-way versus two-way running conditions. We ran 48 subjects on this paradigm. The results confirmed the corridor study. Females performed better in the one-way than two-way running conditions. We ran 48 subjects on this paradigm. The results confirmed the corridor study. Females performed better in the one-way than two-way condition, whereas males performed better in the two-way than one-way condition. This is consistent with our hypothesis and confirms the reliability of the original corridor study. Most impressive in this case is the fact that all choice points in the maze are visually identical for all subjects (the start and goal diamonds on the floor receded from sight before the first corner is reached). This means that the effect of the one-way/two-way variable on choice points was entirely a function of what each subject thought he or she was doing, not the actual visual configuration.

The conclusion from these studies is first a confirmation of the construct validity of the different mechanisms involved in spatial learning.

The conceptual distinction between relying on the configural location of local cues, and relying on a more global map is reflected in the differential performance of males and females: A genetic difference corresponds to a difference in cognitive style. The mechanism for the transmission of this difference to individuals is unclear: As in the case of the difference in style of learning an artificial language, we do not now whether the difference is a direct function of neurological differences, or one mediated through social interactions. In this case, however, we can consider whether there are corresponding differences in other mammals. In fact, it is the case that female and male rats differ in the kinds of cues they use in spatial learning. In a series of elegant studies, Williams has shown that female rats rely on nearby cues when learning a maze, in contrast, male rats rely more on configurational cues (Williams & Meck, 1991).

We studied this difference in rats further, using a real figure 8 maze, similar to the one we used with humans. As with humans, we had a one-way procedure, in which the animal always ran in the same direction; we contrasted this with a two-way procedure, in which the animal ran in both directions, on different trials. The learning performance of male and female rats in these mazes has the same relative difference as what we found in humans: Male rats perform relatively better right away on the two-way maze; female rats initially perform better on the one-way maze. The neurological basis for such differences awaits further research: It is certainly the case that male and female neonatal brains differ in the distribution and relevance of hormonal receptors (Christensen & Gorski, 1978; Clark, MacLusky, & Goldman-Rakic, 1988; Dawson, 1972; Dawson, Cheung, & Lau, 1975; Juraska, 1984; Linn & Petersen, 1986; Maccoby & Jacklin, 1974; MacLusky, Clark, Naftolin, & Goldman-Rakic, 1987; McGlone, 1980; Plaff, 1980). One can also construct after-the-fact sociobiological stories to "account" for the females' relative dependence on local cues and the males' on configurational knowledge—given that there is a gender difference at all in spatial learning (Gaulin & Hoffman, 1987). For our purposes here, however, the difference in rats serves the same validating function as does the existence of cerebral asymmetries in nonhuman mammals. It suggests that the difference found in humans reflects a fundamental biological property of mammals in general.

THE RELATION BETWEEN ABDUCTION
AND SPATIAL MECHANISMS

Returning to the data from humans, the question arises as to whether there is more than an abstract theoretical relation between the two modes of abduction and the two corresponding ways of forming mental representations of spatial knowledge. The finding that there are corresponding gender differences in each domain is suggestive that there is a common basis, but requires more elaboration. We have further evidence on this point from an analysis of the relation between performance and handedness background in relation to gender. Our interpretation of the handedness background variable as expressed in language behavior was that it differentiates local/lexical processing from global/syntactic processing. That is, right-handers from left-handed families (LHFs) tend to process natural language in smaller units than right-handers without left-handed family members (RHFs).

Suppose this difference generalized to other tasks, in particular artificial language learning and spatial learning, what would one predict? If LHFs divide problems into smaller subunits they should tend to exaggerate the effects of other variables (i.e., LHFs should show larger gender differences than RHFs on both the artificial language learning task and the spatial learning tasks). This is exactly what our initial results suggest: The one-way/two-way learning difference between males and females was larger in both kinds of tasks.

Accordingly, the previous two cases suggest that there may be some intrinsic variable that underlies a dimension for both the abstraction of a grammar and the formation of a mental map. Of course, the apparent similarity of the gender variation in both kinds of learning may be misleading: It could be due to a third factor, which itself is related to gender, whereas the learning variations are not. Further research is necessary on this point, in particular to test subjects on both kinds of tasks, as well as other assessments of variables that might be relevant.

In the meantime, however, we can speculate about the bases for the co-variation with gender in the two kinds of learning. One possibility is that different styles in abduction underlie the formation of abstractions, be they in language or spatial representations. The alternative is that spatial representation underlies certain aspects of the representation of abstract systems in general. This hypothesis has been recently advanced in a number of different forms (most notably in the writings of Roger Shepard, 1984; see also Talmy, 1988). Shepard, for example, argued that there has not been enough time for the evolutionary development of a new set of mechanisms for advanced skills such as music, and suggests that language as well, may make use of spatial mechanisms. These arguments are buttressed by consideration of the spatial basis of space terms such as prepositions.

It is hardly surprising to learn that the references of spatial words are conditioned by the mental organization of spatial knowledge. And it is hard to see how that confluence could explain our discovery that gender seems to correspond to similar kinds of variation in learning grammars and maps. Elissa Newport and I are pursuing a more structural interpretation of the relation between spatial mechanisms and grammar that would explain this relation—in particular, we are developing the hypothesis that spatial mechanisms of representation are deployed in the representation of grammatical mechanisms directly. For example, we are investigating the possibility that laws governing apparent motion are structurally homologous to linguistic constraints on long-distance dependencies in language. This and other data may become the basis for the claim that human abstract knowledge in general recruits spatial representational mechanisms (see also Deane, 1990).

CONCLUSION AND SUMMARY

In this chapter, I have reviewed some different interpretations of the concept of *modularity*. I pointed out that modular separation of capacities rooted in sensory or motor systems is not controversial. The modularization of cognitive skills such as language is controversial just because their neurological roots are difficult to determine. Furthermore, insofar as such skills assume the interaction of distinct kinds of levels of representation, impenetrability between levels occurs by definition. This follows from the fact that each level has its own internal computational language that is immiscible with that of other levels. Hence, experimental investigations may show modular-like segregation of levels of representation, results that would follow from their informational opacity, not necessarily from architectural segregation.

The lack of an unambiguous argument for the innately determined architectural modularity of skills like language, opens up the possibility of finding more general sources of modalities and their internal structure. One source is developmental. At the outset, postnatal sensorimotor mechanisms regulate much behavior in ways that anticipate normal adult categories of behavior: This has the natural consequence that immediate postnatal cortical experience is packaged in arrays that correspond to adult modalities. This has the natural consequence of shaping and organizing early experience for an otherwise undifferentiated cortex in ways that lead to learning adult modalities. Thus, the basic segregation of natural kinds of knowledge may rest on innate subcortical mechanisms, not specific pre-tuned cortical areas.

A second source of structure within apparent modalities follows from the view that cognitive processes are arrayed in a set of pairs, along dimensions that themselves are innately determined. Processes can be paired in a general sense according to whether they involve single or multiple representations. The interaction of this pairing with different aspects of language define pairs of representational and processing options that correspond to variables found in nature. Thus, the contrast between relational and unary processing is coordinated in a general way with the difference between the left and right hemispheres, which may explain why language is ordinarily primarily represented in the left hemisphere. The contrast between a strategy of accessing global computational and local associative information about words is correlated with familial handedness, which may reflect a relative symmetry of the representation of associative information about language in people with left-handed families.

The correlation of the previous two contrasts with general biological variation gives them construct validity, and also allows for direct speculation as to how the genetic basis for the dimensions and variation within them lie outside the capacity for language. In addition, our studies suggest that learning an abstract system such as a grammar calls upon a general system of abduction, which can vary in emphasis across a biological dimension—gender. The existence of this systematic variation again lends validity to the construct, and suggests that the ability to discover grammar calls on abduction capacities not limited to language. A similar gender differentiation in how spatial learning in humans and animals occurs, suggests (but only suggests) that the difference in abduction strategies may be quite general. This in turn, supports the argument that the abduction of grammar in particular calls on general learning mechanisms not unique to language.[2]

In brief, I am arguing that there are regularities in general cognition, independent of modality, and that those regularities are genetically coded. I have isolated three cognitive dimensions along which biologically

---

[2] The study of cognitive differences between genetically coded groups in the normal population is just one method to reveal cognitive distinctions that correspond to genetically coded neurophysiological differences. This method must be used with great social and political responsibility: The goal is not to 'scientifically' define cognitive differences in general abilities, which are based in political and social facts. Rather, the goal is to partition general capacities into natural subsets that can differ along genetic lines. As I show in this chapter, careful attention to the distinct multiple cognitive components in an apparently undifferentiated behavior can actually explain an apparent group difference in ability as the result of a group difference in cognitive style. Thus, our research has shown that the previously alleged superiority of males in spatial learning may be a function of how the learning task is presented.

As our theories of the mind and the brain improve, it is not impossible that we will find an increasing number of cases of difference in cognitive style associated with biologically defined differences in populations. We must squarely face the possibility that such discoveries, like all of science, can be misused for political ends: In particular, differences associated with biologically defined groups could be used to justify a form of scientific racism. I hope I have shown by example in this chapter, that such political misuse of population differences is also scientifically corrupt for several reasons.

based populations differ. I have suggested possible mechanisms that might underlie the bases for each of those dimensions. The hypothesis that there are modules for natural kinds of complex behavior is not imperiled by such proposals, but it must be somewhat modified (Shallice, 1984). Stipulating the framework I have outlined for cognition in general, there still may be specific neurological mechanisms that are responsible for recruiting general cognitive capacities in ways specific to each modality. I have suggested the postnatal instinctive mechanisms are certainly such mechanisms: Nothing I have said demonstrates that there are not corresponding higher-order mechanisms as well.

My focus here has been to outline a research program, not to claim its definitive success. Little has been conclusively proven. I have outlined a program aimed at exploring how a complex domain such as language could come to be a modality without resulting from an innately architecturally delimited cortical module. The goal at the least is to show which aspects of language can be explained from general principles and facts about behavior and learning: Those that cannot be so explained become the basis for more specific hypotheses about what is truly uniquely innate to language.

First, while group differences in cognitive style can be isolated experimentally, there is no direct implication for the social role of such distinctions. There are atomic differences between steel and aluminum, but either can be the material for an excellent armchair. Groups may differ in the way they tend to solve a problem, but have functionally equal abilities.

Second, the range of differences between groups is generally the same along each cognitive dimension: The difference lies in a group average. Such differences are scientifically instructive, informing us as to how cognitive dimensions are differentiable biologically, in specially constructed experimental situations. But they are socially useless distinctions because they tell us nothing about an individual.

Third, racism is not a scientific concept and can never be supported by scientific investigation. Racism is a political doctrine. In this regard, claiming that one biologically defined group is politically different from another is like the claim that a republic is better than a democracy: There is no scientific domain in which to test such a claim.

Finally, in fact, if science speaks to racism at all, it is to discredit it and show further that it is political in nature. Science can offer us correct ways to redress uniformed racism: Insofar as we discover cognitive differences in biologically defined groups, we will be better able to decide how to make those differences socially and politically unimportant

REFERENCES

Baillargeon, R., Spelke, E. S. & Wasserman, S. (1985). Object permanence in five month old infants. *Cognition, 20,* 191–208.

Bever, T. G. (1970). The cognitive basis for linguistic structures. In R. Hayes (Ed.), *Cognition and language development* (pp. 277–360). New York: Wiley.

Bever, T. G. (1975) Cerebral asymmetries in humans are due to the differentiation of two incompatible processing mechanisms: Holistic and analytic. In D. Aaronson & R. Rieber (Eds.), *Developmental psycholinguistics and communication disorders* (pp. 76–86). New York: New York Academy of Sciences.

Bever, T. G. (1980). Broca and Lashley were right: Cerebral dominance is an accident of growth. In D. Kaplan & N. Chomsky (Eds.). *Biology and language* (pp. 186–232). Cambridge, MA: MIT Press.

Bever, T. G. (1983). Cerebral lateralization, cognitive asymmetry and human consciousness. In E. Perecman (Ed.), *Cognitive processing in the right hemisphere* (pp. 1939). New York: Academic Press.

Bever, T. G., Carrithers, C., Cowart, W., & Townsend, D. J. (1989). Language processing and familial handedness. In A. Galaburda (Ed.), *From neurons to reading* (pp. 331–360). Cambridge, MA: MIT Press.

Bever, T. G., & Chiarello, R. J. (1974). Cerebral dominance in musicians and non musicians. *Science, 185,* 1317–139.

Bever, T. G., Straub, K., Shenkman, K., Kim, J. J., & Carrithers, C. (1990). The psychological reality of NP-trace. *Proceedings of the 1989 Meeting of the Northeast Linguistic Society,* 48–64.

Brown, J. W. (1976). The neural organization of language: Aphasia and lateralization. *Brain and Language, 3,* 482.

Brown, J. W. (1978). Lateralization: A brain model. *Brain and Language, 5,* 258.

Brown, J. W., & Hecaen, H. (1976). Lateralization and language representation. *Neurology, 26,* 183.

Calvin, W. H., (1982). Didn't throwing stones shape HOMINID evolution. *Sociobiology, 3,* 115–124.

Carey, S. (1987). Conceptual change in childhood. Cambridge, MA: Bradford Press.

Carrithers, C. (1989). Syntactic complexity does not necessarily make sentences harder to understand. *Journal of Psycholinguistics Research, 18,* 75–88.

Chomsky, N. (1965). *Aspects of the theory of syntax.* Cambridge, MA: MIT Press.

Christensen, I. W., & Gorski, R. A. (1978). Independent masculinization of neuroendocrine systems by intercerebral implants of testosterone or estradiol in the neonatal rate. *Brain Research, 146,* 325–340.

Clark, A. S., Maclusky N. J., & Goldman-Rakic, P. S. (1988). Androgen binding and metabolism in the cerebral cortex of the developing rhesus monkey, *Endocrinology, 123,* 932–940.

Cowart, W. (1982). Autonomy and interaction in the language processing system: A reply to Marslen-Wilson and Tyler. *Cognition, 12*(1), 109–117.

Dawson, J. L. M. (1972). Effects of sex hormones on cognitive style in rats and men. *Behavioral Genetics, 2,* 21–42.

Dawson, J. L. M., Cheung, Y. M., & Lau, R. T. S. (1975). Developmental effects of neonatal sex hormones on spatial and activity skills in the white rate. *Biological Psychology, 3,* 213–229.

Deane, P. D. (1990). *Grammar in mind and brain: Explorations in cognitive syntax.* Unpublished manuscript, University of Central Florida, Orlando.

Dennis, M., & Kohn, B. (1974). Selective impairments of visuo-spatial abilities in infantile hemiplegics after right cerebral hemidecortication. *Neuropsychologia, 12*(4), 505512.

Dennis, M., & Kohn, B. (1975). Comprehension of syntax in infantile hemiplegics after cerebral hemidecortication: Left-hemisphere superiority. *Brain and Language, 2*(4), 472–482.

Fodor, J. A. (1983). *The modularity of mind: an essay on faculty psychology.* Cambridge, MA: MIT Press.

Gallistel, C. R. (9190). *The organization of learning.* Cambridge, MA: MIT Press.

Gaulin, S. J. C., & Hoffman, H. A. (1987). Evolution and development of sex differences in spatial ability. In M. Borgerhoff-Mulder, L. Betzig, P. Turke (Eds.L), *Human reproductive behavior. A Darwinian perspective* (pp. 129–152). Cambridge, JA: Cambridge University Press.

Gazzaniga, M. S., & Hillyard, S. A. (1971). Language speech capacity of the right hemisphere. *Neuropsychology, 9*(3), 273–280.

Gazzaniga, M. D., & Sperry, R. (1967). Language after section of the cerebral commisures. *Brain, 90,* 131–148.

Geschwind, N., & Galaburda, A. M. (1987). *Cerebral lateralization.* Cambridge, MA: MIT Press.

Gleitman, L. R. (1981). Maturational determinism, *Cognition, 10,* 103–114.

Golledge, R. G. (1988). *Integrating spatial knowledge.* Santa Barbara: Geographical Press.

Hecaen, H. (1976). Acquired aphasia in children and ontogenesis of hemispheric functional specialization. *Brain and Language, 3,* 114.

Herman, L. M., Richard, D. G., & Wholz, J. P. (1984). Comprehension of Sentences by Bottle-nosed Dolphins. *Cognition, 16,* 129–219.

Herman, L. M., Morrell-Samuels, P., & Pack, A. A. (1990). Bottlenosed colphon and human recognition of veridical and degraded video displays of an artificial gestural language. *Journal of Experimental Psychology: General, 119,* 215–230.

Hewes, G. W. (1973). Primate communication and the gestural origin of language. *Current Anthropology, 14,* 5–24.

Hurtig, R. (1982). Cerebral asymmetry in the strategies used in processing random line stimuli. *Cortex, 18,* 337–343.

Joanette, Y., Lecours, A. R., LePage, Y., & Lamoureux, M. (1983). Language in Right-Handers with Right Hemispheric Lesions: A preliminary study including anatomical, genetic and social factors. *Brain and Language, 20,* 217–248.

Juraska,J. A. (1984). Sex differences in developmental plasticity in visual cortex and hippocampal dentate gyrus. *Progressive rain Research, 61,* 205–214.

Keil, F. C. (1989). *Concepts, kinds and cognitive development.* Cambridge, MA: Bradford Press..

Kellar, L. A., & Bever, T. G. (1980). Hemispheric asymmetries in the perception of musical intervals as a function of musical experience and family handedness background. *Brain and Language, 10,* 24–38.

Kimura, D. (1964). Left-right differences in the perception of melodies. *Quarterly Journal of Experimental Psychology, 16,* 355–358.

Kimura, D. (1973). The asymmetry of the human brain. *Scientific American, 228,* 70–78.

Kimura, D. (1976). Intrahemispheric interaction between speaking and sequential manual activity. *Neuropsychologia, 14*(1), 2333.

Kosslyn, S. (1987). Seeing and imaging in the cerebral hemispheres: A computational approach. *Psychological Review, 94*(2), 148–175.

Kutas, M., Van Petten, C., Besson, M. (1988). Event-related potential asymmetries during the reading of sentences. *Electroencephalography and Clinical Neurophysiology, 69,* 218–233.

Le Doux, J. E. (1983). Cerebral asymmetry and the integrated function of the brain. In A. W. Young (Ed.), *Functions of the right cerebral hemisphere* (pp. 203–216). New York:

Academic Press.

Lenneberg, E. H. (1967). *Biological foundations of language.* New York: Wiley.

Leslie, A. M. (1987). Pretense and representation: The origins of "Theory of Mind." *Psychological Review, 74,* 412–426.

Levy, J. (1969). Possible basis for the evolution of lateral specialization. *Nature, 224,* 614–615.

Levy, J. (1988). Individual differences and cerebral hemisphere asymmetries; theoretical issues and experimental considerations. In H. Jerison & I. Jerison (Eds.), *Intelligence and evolutionary biology* (pp. 157–173). New York: Springer-Verlag.

Linn, M. C., & Petersen, A. C. (1986). A meta-analysis of gender differences in spatial ability: Implications for mathematics and science achievement. In. J. S. Hyde & M. C. Linn (Eds.), *The psychology of gender* (pp. 67–101). Baltimore, MD: Johns Hopkins University Press.

Luria, A. R. (1947). *Traumatic aphasia: Its syndrome, psychopathology and treatment.* Moscow: Academy of Medical Sciences.

Maccoby, E. E. & Jacklin, C. N. (1974). *The psychology of sex differences.* Stanford, CA: Stanford University Press.

MacLusky, N. J., Clark A. S., Naftolin, F., & Goldman-Rakic, P. S. (1987). Estrogen formation in the mammalian brain: possible role of aromatase in sexual differentiation of the hippocampus and neocortex. *Steroids, 50,* 450–465.

Maratsos, O. (1982). Trends in the development of immation. In T. G. Bever (Ed.), *Regressions in mental development.* Hillsdale, NJ: Lawrence Erlbaum Associates.

Marslen-Wilson, W. & Tyler, L. K. (1987). Against modularity. In J. L. Garfield (Ed.), *Modularity in knowledge representation and natural-language understanding* (pp. 37–62). Cambridge, MA: MIT Press.

McNeilage, P. F., Studdert-Kennedy, M. G., & Lindblom, B. (1987). Primate handedness reconsidered. *Behavioral and Brain Sciences, 10*(2), 247–303.

McGlone, J. (1980). Sex differences in human brain asymmetry: A critical survey. *Behavioral Brain Science, 3,* 215–264.

Mehler, J., & Dupoux (1990). *Naitre Humain [Human nature].* Paris: LaRousse.

Mehler, J., Morton, J., & Jusczyk, P. W. (1984). On reducing language to biology. *Cognitive Neuropsychology, 1,* 83–116.

Meier, R. P., & Bower, G. H. (1986). Semantic reference and phrasal grouping in the acquisition of a miniature phrase structure language. *Journal of Memory and Language, 25,* 492–505.

Meltzoff, A. N., & Moore, M. K. (1983). Newborn infants initiate facial gestures. *Child Development, 54,* 702–709.

Morrel-Samuels, P., Herman, L., & Bever, T. G. (1991). *The relation between processing demands and cerebral asymmetries in a dolphin.* Unpublished manuscript, University of Michigan, East Lansing.

Murray, L, & Trevarthen, C. (1986). The *infant's* role in mother-infant communications. *Journal of Child Language, 13*(1), 15–29.

Newman, J. E., Lovett, M. W., & Dennis, M. (1986). The use of discourse analysis in neurolinguistics: Some findings from the narratives of hemidecorticate adolescents. *Brain and Language, 30*(1), 63–80.

O'Connor, K. N., Roitblat, H. L., & Bever, T. G. (in press). Auditory sequence complexity and hemispheric asymmetries of function in rats. In H. L Roitblat (Ed.), *Study in animal behavior.* Hillsdale, NJ: Lawrence Erlbaum Associates.

Pierce, C. S. (1957). The logic of abduction. In C.S. Pierre (Ed.), *Essays in the philosophy of Science* (pp. 235–255). Boston: Liberal Arts Press.

Pfaff, D. W. (1980). *Estrogens and brain function.* New York: Springer-Verlag.

Schwartz, M. F., & Schwartz, B. (1984). In defense of organology. *Cognitive Neuropsychology, 1,* 25–42.

Shallice, T. (1984). More functionally isolable subsystems but fewer "modules?" *Cognition, 17*(3), 24–252.

Shepard, R. N (1984). Ecological constraints on internal representation: Resonant kinematics of perceiving, imaging, thinking, and dreaming. *Psychological Review, 91*(4), 417–447.

Subirana, A. (1958). The prognosis in aphasia in relation to cerebral dominance and handedness. *Brain,81,* 415.

Subirana, A. (1969). Handedness and cerebral dominance. In P. J. Vinken & G. W. Bruyn (Eds.), *Handbook of clinical neurology* (Vol. 4, pp. 248–272). Amsterdam: North Holland.

Talmy L. (1988). Force dynamics in language and cognition. *Cognitive Science, 12*(1), 49–100.

Tan, N., Aiello, R., & Bever, T. G. (1981). Harmonic structure as a determinant of melodic organization. *Memory and Cognition, 9,* 533–539.

Townsend, D. J., & Bever, T. G. (1982). Natural units of representation interact during sentence comprehension. *Journal of Verbal Learning and Verbal Behavior, 21,* 688–703.

Wellman, H. W. (1990). *The child's theory of mind.* Cambridge, MA: Bradford Press.

Werner, H. (1948). *Comparative psychology of mental development.* New York: International University Press.

Williams, C. L., & Meck, W. H. (1991). The organizational effects of gonadal steroids on sexually dimorhic spatial ability. *Psychoneuroendocrinology, 16*(1), 155–176.

7 Beyond Modules

Jacqueline Goodnow
Macquarie University

The several chapters in this volume have established a convincing case for the presence of modules of specialized—and possibly segmented—areas of knowledge and skill. I wish to start from the assumption that modules or constraints exist, and to ask: What follows? The specific three questions I raise have to do with (a) criteria for the inference of separate or dissimilar areas of knowledge or performance; (b) the nature of relations or connections among segmented areas; and (c) the implications of a concept of modules, constraints, or segments for developmental theory in general.

THE QUESTION OF
DEFINITIONS AND CRITERIA

This question is the final form of a concern that arose early in the volume and went through several forms. My initial concern was with the meanings of several terms—*constraints, specificity, domains, modules*—and the overlaps between them. This initial concern began to diminish in the course of Michael Maratsos' opening argument that these several concepts may be regarded as independent of one another (each does not imply the other). It shrank a little further with Ellen Markman's (chapter 3) use of "constraint" in the sense of a bias or predisposition, altering the probabilities of particular responses, Tom Bever's (chapter 6) analysis of various kinds of modules, and the several criteria offered by Carol Malatesta-Magai and Bruce Dorval (chapter 5), and Laura Petitto (chapter 2) for determining whether various forms of communication or ways of thinking about the world one encounters (Keil, chapter 4) were alike or not.

At a certain point, then, I set some of my definitional concerns aside and started from an acceptance of a proposition that seemed to cut across all chapters. Suppose we all agree that there is not a single form of ability, not a single mode of communication, not a single way of thinking about, learning about, or exploring the world. There is, instead, some segmentation, some early specialization in the response made to various kinds of information or various kinds of problems. One may use a variety of labels for these segments (predispositions, systems, constraints, modules, modes of construal, stances, and so on), but the baseline is the presence of segments that are different from one another.

My first question then becomes: Among the criteria that may be used for deciding whether segments are different or separate from one another, rather than alike, *is there a preferred order, a hierarchy?* If there is, what is the basis of preference? And what place in any hierarchy would be occupied by a criterion such as the presence of a neurophysiological basis?

Let me start with the first and second parts of that three-part question. The issue of preferred criteria first became a concern for me in the course of noting the several criteria that Petitto offered for her decision that words and gestures were not similar, making it unlikely that gestures could be regarded either as a precursor for word acquisition or as stemming from the same capacity. The issue came up again when Malatesta-Magai and Dorval offered several criteria for arguing that language and affect were similar systems, when Bever listed a set of criteria for deciding whether something was or was not a module, and when Keil offered another set for determining whether children took different "stances" toward objects as compared with biological organisms.

I was, in short, awash with criteria. Surely there must be some order here, some kind of preference for one kind of criterion rather than another. Preference certainly seems close to the surface in Petitto's material. She lists, for instance, a number of criteria for her decision that words and gestures are not similar to one another. To take some of these: The two do not show the same developmental course. One (words) displays "syntax," the other does not. The two show a different order for the emergence of comprehension and production (the former earlier for words, the latter apparently earlier for gestures). In addition, gestures violate boundaries in ways that words do not. They violate, for instance, the mutual exclusivity principle that Markman finds so powerful in early word learning (no two words for the same object). Words may be overextended or underextended, but they never violate the boundaries of objects, events, properties, or locations, in the way that gestures do when the one gesture is used for example, to indicate the actions of closing or opening a jar, the jar itself, or the contents of the jar.

Petitto invites us to reflect on the question: *How many* similarities allow the inference that two ways of operating belong to the same system? At the same time, she invites us to consider the possibility that some criteria (some "telltale differences") are more important than others. The really essential difference appears to be the way that gestures violate boundaries that words do not.

Let me take as a second example Keil's account of thinking about organisms rather than about objects. He again gave us a list of intriguing differences between machines or tools and living things. The latter, for instance, reproduce. They have a complex internal structure (if you chop them up, the pieces are not identical). They grow. Some internal base seems to regulate their appearance and their growth. Their properties— their color, size, shape, for instance—seem to serve some useful purposes. Attention to any of these properties might mark the drawing of a distinction between organisms and objects. Of all these possibilities, however, the one that appeared to be the favored criterion was that children asked a kind of question about living things that they did not ask about objects. For the former, they asked about purpose, about what various properties (color, pincers, etc.) were *for*. For the former, they also regarded, as "better," explanations that were in terms of purpose rather than in reductionist terms that could apply to either living or nonliving things. In Keil's phrase, children take a "design stance" toward living things that they do not take toward the nonliving. I was again interested in the suggestion of a preferred criterion, and again interested in further comment on the question: What would be the basis for the preference?

Locating preferences and their bases, I should add, is not an idle interest on my part. I suspect that data about them would help make explicit some assumptions about the nature of behavior and of development. I think they would also enable me to reflect on two proposals from Bever that still give me pause: (a) that associative and relational "modes of construal" are different from one another, and (b) that ways of thinking about verbal and spatial arrays may be similar, with the former possibly a subclass of the latter. At the moment, I find it difficult to put together the separation in the one proposal and the possible merger in the other.

The final part of my concern with criteria has to do with a criterion that seems to have a preferential status in many discussions of domains or modules. A system or a way of acting or thinking seems to be regarded as separate from others if it can be shown to be "hard-wired," "genetically coded," differentially affected by damage to some particular area of the

216

brain. I find brain-behavior connections always intriguing, and I am happy to consider these connections as one of several criteria for arguing for segmented or separate skills or ways of thinking. I am far less happy, however, with any implication that these connections should have a favored place in any set of criteria.

That kind of concern is fueled, on my part, by uncertainty about the implications of a term such as *genetically coded* and by Bever's own apparent ambivalence about genetic coding as a criterion for whether a segment is or is not a module (in a possibly "throwaway" line, he commented in his chapter that whether being genetically coded makes something a module is perhaps "a political question"). It is fueled also, I must admit, by comments made by people more knowledgeable about neurophysiology than I am. In Charles Nelson's view, for instance, psychologists and neurophysiologists may be proceeding in different directions. Psychologists, for example, seem to be emphasizing the discreteness and possible localizations of functions. Neurophysiologists, in contrast, still talk about localization of function, but are embracing more and more concepts like neural networks and parallel distributed processes (Nelson, personal communication, October 25-27, 1990).

In short, I see the need for further thought about preferences within the criteria one may use for separateness, similarity, or difference, and about the bases for preference.

THE QUESTION OF
RELATIONS AMONG SEGMENTS

Let me turn to a second question. Suppose we accept the notion of segments, in whatever form. Now we need to face the question: *How are these segments related to one another?* Let me call the segments simply X and Y, and start by concentrating this time on Markman's material (chapter 3).

In principle, Segments X and Y could be interrelated in several ways:

- *X may have priority over, or take precedence over, Y.* X may be the first response to be tried, then Y may take over. If I extend Markman's "default assumption," this could be when X does not work well, when X has served its purpose, or conceivably when X is well established and "the mind" can afford to turn to considering some elaborations or alternatives.
- *X could inhibit Y.* Giving a name to an object, for instance, makes it unlikely that a young child (or a novice learner of any new language?) will readily learn another label for the same object.
- *X could facilitate Y.* This possibility emerged in the course of a

question about the ways in which young children acquire number names and apply them to objects which already have label names. One possibility, Markman suggested, was that a way of proceeding that is in strong contrast with one already in place may be more easily learned by virtue of the contrast.

- *X may become connected to Y,* especially over time. This possibility cropped up in the course of several chapters. X may "bind" or become "co-assembled" with Y (Malatesta-Magai and Dorval, chapter 5), or X and Y may "interpenetrate" one another, losing some of their earlier more "encapsulated" state (Bever, chapter 6).

At the moment, it seems best to keep all possibilities open and to concentrate on asking about the conditions under which various kinds of effects across systems will occur, and the processes that give rise to various effects. For developmental purposes, one would certainly want to entertain at least the two possibilities that emerge in Markman's and Keil's material. In the former case, a mutual exclusivity approach on the child's part seems to provide a strong account of the way that early word learning proceeds. It seems indeed highly likely, as Markman suggests, that a narrow hypothesis — one word for each object—will speed up the initial acquisition of a number of words. There will be no stumbling, for instance, over a lamp being called both a lamp and a light, over a chair being called a chair, a seat, or a piece of furniture. At some point, however, the constraint will lose its functional value. In contrast, there seems in everyday life to be no gain attached to a shift away from what Keil has called a "design stance" toward nonliving objects. The categories based on a sense of "essences" (e.g., living/not-living, male/female) seem to have a very firm hold and to be retained over time. Both kinds of development—change and remain in place—need to be considered as developmental possibilities. My search is for some principles or guidelines that would help me anticipate when one form of development is the more likely to occur than the other.

The same kind of search applies when we turn to the possibility that change may take the form of segments becoming interconnected. During the course of this symposium I collected several suggestions as to what may be involved.

Frequency of Association. This is the basis that Malatesta-Magai and Dorval mention as forging a link between the emotion of shame and the emotion of fear. The argument is that shame often tends to occur in situations where fear is also felt, leading the two emotions, originally distinct, to "bind" with one another.

The Quality of Information. One of Bever's proposals is that the form of response—the associative or relational "mode of construal"— is determined, at least in part, by the source of the information (e.g., its presentation to the left or right ear and accordingly its being dealt with by the right or left hemispheres). Another possibility, mentioned in the discussion, goes beyond quality in the form of source. It considers instead variations in the form of the degree of structure contained in what is presented or what is already known. The suggestion, as I heard it, is that segments (modules in this case) may more readily interlock with one another when the information in both cases is organized to a comparable degree. It may be easier, one imagines, for two bodies of knowledge to link together when both are organized—even if the organization is based on different principles—than when one is well-structured and the other is amorphous.

The Quality of the Processor.   I have abstracted this possibility from Markman's material although it is implied also in Keil's concern with age differences. It certainly seems necessary to make allowance for some type of developmental change in the capacity to cope with a variety of hypotheses or a multiple set of relationships.

Some Interaction Between the Quality of the Information and the Quality of the Processor or of the Predisposition.   This is a possibility that has surfaced less often in the course of the volume than one might have expected. Perhaps because a theory of predispositions is in some ways a "cognitive version of affordance theory" (Keil), the nature of the information "out there"— especially the social input—has received short shrift in the course of establishing that specific predispositions, rather than simply some all-purpose readiness to make sense of the world, existed and took some documentable forms. The time now seems ripe, as both Bob Siegler (chapter 8) and Michael Maratsos (chapter 1) suggested, and as most schema theories would advocate, to give some further thought to the way that we selectively pick up some pieces of information rather than others, protecting our biases by discounting what does not fit until some moment arises when an alternative way of thinking about events comes to seem not only possible but natural.

THE QUESTION OF IMPLICATIONS

The third and last question is one I deal with briefly, although it is of more importance than the space I give may suggest. It takes the form of asking about implications for general developmental theory.

I indicated earlier that the reason for asking about preferred criteria and their bases is that some general assumptions are implied: assumptions about the nature of behavior and of development. I now wish to place the issue of general assumptions and implications in the center of the stage.

The first implication has to do with the kinds of activity in which an organism is likely to engage. If we took constraint theory at its current level of development as an endpoint (which it clearly is not), then it seems to me that we would be proposing an organism that was largely *reactive*. Information comes to the organism, and predispositions give rise to its being attended to and processed in some ways rather than others. Only in Keil's presentation was there a mention of children as likely to seek out events or information that would be of a particular kind: Would confirm or test, for instance, the hypotheses that a "design stance" suggests. The proactive aspects of cognition or learning now seem to warrant further attention.

The more general implication takes me back to one of Maratsos' opening points. We pay attention to constraint proposals, he proposed, and are surprised by them, because they run counter to the view that we are possessed of a single general capacity that changes from one overall level or stage to another. The concept of minds ready and able at the start to process some kinds of information rather than others, and to do so in particular ways, runs counter to this model. We are then prompted to think of capacity in a different way from before. In similar fashion, the notion of segments of any kind, as an initial state, pushes us away from a developmental model that sees everything as integrated at the start and then differentiated. On the "old " model, for instance, specific categories might be seen as emerging out of some general undifferentiated mass. With the "new" model, where segmented thought may be the starting point, development may need to be thought of as more in the nature of integration (with perhaps, in some cases, a maintenance of separateness). Words and categories that were initially distinct, to repeat the example, now need to be blended or cross-connected. Both models are present within the history of developmental theory, but the former (initial differentiation) now seems to be achieving a new strength. I would be eager to learn more about other broad implications contained in proposals about constraints, modules, or domain specificity. Now that constraint theorists have solved one problem—now that the documentation for some degree of initial specificity is relatively firm—I look forward to seeing a new round of questions, together with further challenges to assumptions we have come to take for granted but should examine.

8 What Do Developmental Psychologists Really Want?

Robert S. Siegler
Carnegie Mellon University

I recently read a particularly incisive description of the goals of developmental psychology. It included the following description:

The eventual goal of developmental psychology is to provide a single theory that describes the whole of development. However, the approach most scientists actually follow is to separate the problem into two parts. First, there are the laws that tell us how the child changes with time. (If we know what the child is like at any one time, these laws tell us how it will look at any later time.) Second, there is the question of the initial state of the child. (pp. 10–11)

Actually, the original text did not read quite this way. It used the term *science* rather than *developmental psychology* and *universe* rather than *child*. The substitutions that I made were necessary because the passage was written not to describe the goals of developmental psychology, but rather the goals of astrophysics. The statement came not from any book on child development, but rather from Stephen Hawking's (1988) *A Brief History of Time*. Nonetheless, the description captures the deepest goals of our field as well as Hawking's. The two fundamental properties we would like to see in a theory of development are a characterization of the child at the beginning of development and a characterization of the laws that govern changes after that point.

Selection of "modularity and constraints" as the theme of the Minnesota Symposium attests to the prominence these constructs have assumed within developmental psychology. I suspect this prominence reflects in large part the promise of the constructs for moving us toward the two main goals cited earlier. They promise to tell us both about the

221

innate organization of the mind and about how this organization produces development by promoting appropriate interpretations of experience.

The chapters in this volume include a number of intriguing theoretical ideas relevant to these constructs and a great deal of informative data regarding language and conceptual development. My discussion of these ideas and data is organized around four central issues: rootedness, change, evidence, and method. Rootedness and change correspond to the two fundamental requisites for theories of development; evidence concerns the types of data that can help us build such theories; method concerns how we can obtain such data.

ROOTEDNESS

One goal of theories of development is to explain why changes take place when they do. We would like to know why the vocabulary explosion occurs so consistently at around 18 months (Smith, 1926), why 30-month-olds so rarely and 36-month-olds so consistently succeed in using scale maps to locate hidden objects (DeLoache, 1987), why 5-year-olds almost never and 10-year-olds almost always understand conservation of liquid quantity (Piaget, 1952), and so on. The external environment does not appear to change in ways that are obviously relevant to producing such changes. For some changes, such as the vocabulary explosion, relevant experiences (hearing words in context) are present long before the change. For others, such as mastering scale maps and liquid quantity conservation, neither older nor younger children seem to encounter directly relevant experiences, and indirectly relevant experiences abound at all ages. Seen from another angle, it is unclear that anyone who only had knowledge of children's environments, not of children themselves, would predict that these changes should occur when they do.

A broad range of developmental psychologists would like to better understand how these changes are rooted in the child's biological endowment. Much of the appeal of stage theories reflects their attempt to anchor changes in this way. They at least try to explain why changes occur regularly at particular ages. Numerous criticisms have been leveled regarding how well they accomplish this goal. The internal changes (in logicomathematical structures, optimal level of functioning, M-space, etc.) that are said to underlie the behavioral shifts are often only vaguely defined; their relation to the behavior is often unclear; what causes the explanatory factor to change is often left unspecified. Nonetheless, because the main alternative theories (behaviorist, information processing, contextualist) have rarely provided any account of why changes should regularly occur at particular ages, many have regarded the stage theories as the lesser evil.

The appeal of constraints approaches stems in large part from their promise of achieving this anchoring function, while at the same time being better defined, more specific, and more closely linked to data than the mechanisms proposed in stage theories. Precisely because language and conceptual development usually flow so effortlessly and successfully, it is easy to ignore how remarkable they really are. By explicitly recognizing how children could interpret their experiences in ways that are logically possible but totally at odds with the understanding of the surrounding community, advocates of the constraints approach have brought to the fore a critical problem for developmentalists to consider. By proposing specific constraints that could allow children to overcome problems of induction, advocates of this approach have started to address the problem.

The chapters in this volume advanced the discussion of constraints in a number of ways. One was to place the discussion in a more reasoned, less warlike, context. As Maratsos (chapter 1) noted, the issue is not whether development is constrained; few, if any, investigators think that development is an unbiased reflection of environmental input. There is little disagreement, for example, that short-term memory capacity and a variety of encoding biases constrain the information children take in. Instead, the main issues on which people disagree are ones of *definition* (what are constraints?); *representation* (are constraints represented explicitly or are they emergent properties of more basic processes?); *scope* (are there constraints unique to word learning?); and *origins* (are constraints innate or learned?).

Markman (chapter 3) has consistently been a leader in the constraints movement. Her contribution to this volume reflects continued progress in her thinking and clarifies her stances on several important issues. In particular, she amplifies her view, also stated in Woodward and Markman (1991), that constraints are best thought of as default assumptions, to be used when consistent with other evidence and to be overridden when necessary. This view echoes the conclusion reached by Merriman and Bowman (1989) after an extensive review of the literature on the mutual exclusivity constraint, and represents a much more plausible interpretation than the view of constraints as rigid and exceptionless that has been attacked in the literature (MacWhinney, 1989, 1991; Nelson, 1988, 1990).

It is understandable, however, how the view of constraints as rigid, exceptionless entities arose. The term *constraints* itself has some connotation of rigidity within the everyday language. Putting people into constraints limits their movement in a rigid, not a flexible, manner. Chomsky's prior use of the term reinforced the connotation of rigidity for psychologists and linguists. Even Markman's own uses of the term have varied, sometimes within a single sentence. For example, in Woodward and Markman (1991), which was written in part to clarify what constraints are, a main theoretical position is summarized as follows: "It is hard to see how children could acquire language as rapidly as they do without *biases* that enable them to *rule out* many alternative hypotheses for the meanings of a word" (p. 139, italics added). "Biases" implies a probabilistic process; "rule out" implies determinate exclusion. Which is the intended position?

I cite this sentence not to quibble but rather to underscore the need for more precise and consistent characterizations of what is meant by constraints. The large number of charges and countercharges in recent articles about who said what and who meant what about constraints (e.g., Behrend, 1990; Gathercole, 1987; Kuczaj, 1990; MacWhinney, 1989, 1991; Merriman, 1991; Merriman & Bowman, 1989; Nelson, 1988, 1990; Woodward & Markman, 1991) stems in large part from uses that are inconsistent within as well as between investigators. Such ambiguity almost guarantees arguments about what different investigators meant, because different readers will focus on different uses. Specification of how cognitive development is rooted within the organism demands precision concerning exactly what is being said to be rooted.

This problem is not limited to discussions of constraints. The same objections could be raised about the related constructs of "theories," "principles," and "modules," which have been around for years, as well as the newer constructs of "affinities," "resonances," and "modes of construal," which also received attention in this volume, particularly by Keil (chapter 4). These terms are rich in meanings, and have a variety of interesting connotations. Which meanings and connotations are meant and which are not intended by any given investigator is extremely hard to determine, however. Reading about children possessing such rich, multifaceted, competencies is exciting, but it also places an extra burden on investigators to be especially clear about what they mean.

To avoid ambiguity and resulting confusion, the following set of questions needs to be addressed for constraints, modules, resonances, and other rich cognitive constructs. How clearly we can answer them is a good measure of how far our understanding of the construct has progressed.

1. How is it defined?
2. What evidence indicates its presence or absence?
3. To what range of phenomena does it apply?
4. When and through what processes does it originate?
5. How does it operate?
6. How does it interact with other processes to give rise to behavior?

Markman's chapter includes a good example of a move toward the type of specification that I think is needed. This example involves the discussion of the domains of applicability of the taxonomic, whole-object, and mutual exclusivity constraints. Before encountering this discussion, I had always assumed that these constraints applied only to word learning. Markman's examples of how the approach could apply to areas of conceptual understanding other than those involved in word learning promises to bring together previously disparate areas of research. It also clarifies what she means by these constraints.

Refinement of answers to these questions feeds on itself, in that it exposes vaguenesses that were difficult to perceive previously. For example, now that it is clear that a variety of investigators equate constraints with default assumptions, it becomes critical to clarify the choice mechanisms through which children choose whether to follow them in particular cases. Work reported in Markman's chapter and elsewhere (e.g., Au & Glusman, 1990) concerning what children do when two constraints conflict is a positive step in this direction. The work should provide a database for the critical next step of proposing mechanisms that produce the choices of when to behave consistently with a constraint and when to violate it.

CHANGE

In addition to rooting development in characteristics of the organism, approaches that emphasize constraints also provide an appealing framework for thinking about change. I think of this framework in terms of a visual metaphor. Children are born in an ocean and need to swim toward a destination of mature competence that lies somewhere beyond the horizon. Constraints function as a channel that helps them avoid swimming off in unproductive directions. The children can swim around rocks and sharks if they need to, but the constraints provide persistent guidance that helps keep them on course.

Keil's chapter represents progress beyond previous work in this area in that it explicitly recognizes that associative knowledge, as well as constraints, principles, and causal concepts, contributes to this channeling process. For example, Keil describes a series of elegant experiments that demonstrate that from early on, children's understanding of biology contains a mix of causal concepts and associative knowledge. The associative knowledge provides a kind of cutting edge, in that it subsumes much of the most recently acquired information, especially information that is not fully grasped. The causal concepts are said to gradually encompass a broader and broader range of phenomena, with previous associative knowledge being progressively incorporated into the causal understandings. In a sense, the associative knowledge provides the raw materials for extension and reworking of the causal network. Thus, the process is open ended; development can occur throughout life, as people acquire more and more associative knowledge and recursively extend their causal models to encompass it.

These interpretations represent substantial progress from the often-expressed view that children progress from early associative or exemplar-based understandings to later theory-governed ones. As Keil notes, it is not at all clear what mechanisms could produce such a qualitative shift in the representation. If, on the other hand, children are always forming causal concepts as well as associations, the need for a mysterious process that would transmute a set of base associations into an explanatory network is eliminated.

Particularly noteworthy is Keil's proposal that young children recognize not only mechanistic and psychological (intentional) causes but also functional ones. That is, they believe that teleological causal explanations apply to biological entities in a way that they do not to inanimate natural objects. Thus, children believe that the color of an animal can be explained in terms of its adaptive quality, but that the color of iron cannot. As Keil notes, such construals provide footholds into acquiring more specific beliefs, and thus facilitate learning about biological entities.

Although it seems reasonable to view early as well as later knowledge as a mix of causal and associative information, adopting such a view is only a first step toward understanding change. The hard problem of specifying the mechanisms that produce the change remains. How exactly is the causal knowledge extended so as to incorporate the associative information? Do separate local causal structures coalesce and become united? Do other causal structures begin as a single structure and later divide into separate ones? If so, what triggers these changes, why do they occur when they do, and how are they effected?

Understanding mechanisms demands understanding of not only properties of the child but also of the input that the child encounters. The value of sophisticated analyses of input for understanding language development can be seen in MacWhinney, Leinbach, Taraban, and McDonald's (1989) connectionist model of how children acquire the German article system. This is a classic problem in psycholinguistics. As Maratsos (1982) noted, the relation between German nouns and the articles that accompany them is complex and far from intuitive. Maratsos concluded that phonological and semantic cues are insufficient to predict which article will be attached to a given noun, and that correct use of the article system therefore implied reliance on purely syntactic cues.

Other investigators, however (e.g., Kopcke & Zubin, 1983), argued that phonological, semantic, and case cues within typical German input do allow accurate prediction of which article will accompany the noun. The

MacWhinney et al. simulation indicated that this latter position was correct, that the cues in the input were sufficient to allow accurate prediction. The first part of the test involved presenting to the simulation 102 common German nouns. Each noun was presented in a variety of case and number contexts. The simulation would predict which article would accompany the noun in that context, and would then receive feedback on which one actually did.

After encountering such experience, the simulation accurately predicted not only the examples it had encountered in particular case and number roles, but also the article that would accompany that noun in unfamiliar case and number roles and the articles that would be chosen for the 48 most commonly used German nouns that had not been encountered in any role previously. The simulation's learning pattern also was like that of children, both in the overgeneralizations that it generated and in the particular article–noun combinations that were the most difficult to learn. As MacWhinney et al. concluded, many changes may prove to be attributable to increasingly accurate identification of subtle regularities in the input, rather than to constraints within the child.

Another lesson that may be drawn from the MacWhinney et al. research is the usefulness of simulation models for studying change. Without such a simulation, it is not clear how arguments could ever have been resolved concerning whether the available semantic and phonological cues were sufficiently strong to support learning of the article system. A similar situation is arising as work progresses on constraints, modules, and related constructs. How much of the burden of learning can these constructs carry? Some, such as Behrend (1990), claim they reduce the task of learning to manageable proportions. The task obviously is manageable (children do learn word meanings), but without a formal model, it is difficult to evaluate the individual and joint contributions of constraints to the process. How exactly would the child know when to rely on a default assumption and when to abandon it? If relatively specific constraints are necessary for word learning, how does the child learn verbs and adjectives, where mutual exclusivity and other postulated constraints clearly do not apply? What more general cognitive processes must work with the hypothesized constraints or causal models in order for word learning to occur? Simulations could yield more refined ideas both about how these constructs function and about how they contribute to change.

EVIDENCE

Progress in understanding constraints has been limited by uncertainty concerning what evidence would indicate absence of a constraint. Nelson

(1988) and Merriman and Bowman (1989) evaluated constraints against the strict criterion that any deviation from them would count against their being present. Markman, in this volume and in Woodward and Markman (1991), argued that such deviations were not necessarily evidence that the constraint was absent. The deviations might just indicate that other influences led children to deviate from the default rule.

Although viewing constraints as default assumptions represents important theoretical progress, it also makes it difficult to know what evidence would disconfirm the claim that a constraint is present in a particular child or age group. It reduces, and perhaps eliminates, the possibility of falsifying such claims. What exactly would constitute evidence that a constraint was not present? The problem is exacerbated by the lack of precision in many discussions of what a constraint is. People are biased in extremely large numbers of ways. Does each of these constitute a constraint? For example, when I raise my arm, snap my fingers, and ask "What's this?", most people would assume that the snapping was what I had in mind. But within the standard Quinean riddle-of-induction logic, it could be any number of possibilities: raising my left arm, making a perpendicular angle with it, having my left arm above my right, touching my thumb and middle finger, and so on. Does every response tendency represent a constraint, and if not, what evidence distinguishes those that do from those that do not?

A related evidentiary issue involving constraints might be labeled the "compared to what" issue. The phrase "fast mapping" has frequently been used to characterize children's word learning. In one or two trials, quite young children can gain at least a fairly accurate impression of what a new word means (e.g., Carey & Bartlett, 1978). This pattern is often contrasted, as in Markman's chapter, to the slow rate of learning in classic concept formation, hypothesis testing, and scientific reasoning studies (e.g., Levine, 1966; Wason & Johnson-Laird, 1972).

The contrast may not be as meaningful as it first appears, however. Classic concept formation and hypothesis-testing tasks were chosen precisely because they allowed extended observation of concept formation strategies and hypothesis-testing patterns. Where the relevant concept is "red and/or square" or "Line above Capital X," there is no way for subjects to induce it at anything other than a slow pace. Lacking ESP, the best that they can do is to eliminate half of the logically possible alternatives on each trial. Fast mapping does not appear on such tasks because it cannot appear.

The process by which scientific reasoning problems are chosen for study reflects similar considerations. Such problems are often selected because subjects are known to be biased against the correct answer. This is reflected in the entire area often being referred to as the "misconceptions literature." The same argument applies to Piagetian reasoning problems, such as those involving conservation, class inclusion, and proportionality. It is not just that children do not know the answers to such problems. They also have a strongly preferred alternative that conflicts with the correct one.

To further complicate the issue, fast mapping is also found in many areas that have nothing to do with acquisition of word meanings or language. The example of snapping fingers just alluded to is one such case. Children also are quick to learn how to build with blocks, how to play video games, and how to annoy their parents. Do all competencies that children acquire rapidly reflect fast mapping? If not, what is the critical evidence?

A third evidentiary issue involves the role of physiological data. Evidence concerning the contribution of neural to cognitive development has become much stronger in recent years. One striking example is the work of Banks and Shannon (in press), documenting how changes in the size of the eye and in the density and shapes of cones in the fovea, together with optical laws, account for many aspects of early visual development. Another is Diamond's (in press) work on how the development of the frontal cortex, in particular the development of inhibitory influences, contributes to acquisition of object permanence. Nelson's (in press) work on how development of the frontal cortex contributes to development of recognition memory in infancy is a third good example. Evidence relating neural and cognitive changes seems likely to prove invaluable in anchoring the development of concepts and word meanings.

METHOD

Through what methods can we obtain high quality evidence relevant to the many issues involving constraints, modules, and related constructs? Recently, I have become convinced that microgenetic methods may be especially valuable for generating such evidence. Because the term *microgenetic* has been used in a variety of ways, I should briefly define what I mean by "microgenetic methods." I am referring to methods that have the following three qualities: (a) observations span the entire period from the beginning of the change of interest to the time at which it reaches a relatively stable state; (b) the density of observations is high relative to the rate of change of the phenomenon; and (c) observed behavior is subjected to intensive analysis, with the goal of inferring the processes that give rise to the change. This approach can illuminate both qualitative and quantitative aspects of change, indicate the conditions under which changes occur, and yield otherwise unobtainable information about short-lived transition strategies. (See Siegler & Crowley, 1991, for a review of the contributions of such studies to date.)

Laura Petitto's chapter (chapter 2) illustrates a number of the benefits that can be gained by using this approach. Petitto studied hearing children who were in the process of acquiring spoken and sign language, hearing children who were acquiring only spoken language, and deaf children who were acquiring only sign language. She observed and tested them monthly, from ages 8 to 26 months. Thus, the observations spanned the entire period of the rise and decline of gestures as a primary means of communicating. The monthly sessions were sufficiently frequent to closely track changes in use of signs and spoken language. The videotapes that were made in each session allowed intensive examination of production and comprehension of words and gestures.

The method yielded a number of findings regarding the development of oral and gestural language that would otherwise have been unlikely to have been obtained. One example was the discovery of the signing equivalent of babbling at the same age at which verbal babbling occurred in the hearing children. This suggests that the verbal babbling is probably not entirely due to motoric difficulty in producing speech, as is often assumed. The method also allowed Petitto to contrast the lack of increase in the length and complexity of gestures over time with the increasing MLU that typifies speech in this period and to establish the rarity of her category of symbolic gestures at all points in the period.

All this is not to say that such microgenetic methods produce research that will not spark disagreement. For example, I find unconvincing Pettito's claim that children's gestures are nonsymbolic. She acknowledged that children produce gestures such as stretching their arms upward when they wished to be picked up, but says that "the form does not 'stand for' the 'pick up' — it is literally part of the activity involved in being picked up." But how literal is the similarity between thrusting one's arms upward and being picked up? Why does the mother take the gesture as a signal to pick the child up, rather than as a signal to thrust her own arms upward? After all, when a child signals "bye-bye" through touching her fingertips to the heel of her hand two or more times, the mother responds by literally repeating the gesture, not doing something else. It is not clear why saying "up" should be viewed as symbolic, but gesturing skyward should not be.

The microgenetic method also could allow insights into many other issues that arose in this symposium. Consider how it might enrich our understanding of how word meanings are acquired. Studies of fast mapping sometimes give the impression that after one or two trials, the child has constructed a meaning for the new term that exactly coincides with the meaning that adults have. Bowerman's (1982) descriptions of her daughters' acquisition of the meanings of such terms as *kicks* call into question how close the early mapping is, however. Her observations suggest that the early meanings overlapped but did not coincide with adults' usage. Dense sampling of a word's meaning from the time a child first encounters it to the time when the meaning closely resembles that of the surrounding linguistic community may provide exactly the kind of data base we need to make progress in understanding the word learning process—data about the initial state of understanding and the changes that occur beyond that initial understanding. Put another way, it may lead to the kind of theory and data that developmental psychologists really want.

ACKNOWLEDGMENTS

Preparation of this chapter was supported in part by grants from the National Institutes of Health (HD-19011), the Spencer Foundation, and the Mellon Foundation.

REFERENCES

Au, T. K., & Glusman, M. (1990). The principle of mutual exclusivity in word learning: To honor or not to honor? *Child Development, 61,* 1474–1490.

Banks, M. S., & Shannon, L. (in press). How optical and receptor immaturities limit the vision of human neonates. In C. E. Granrud (Ed.), *Visual perception and cognition in infancy.* Hillsdale, NJ: Lawrence Erlbaum Associates.

Behrend, D. A. (1990). Constraints and development: A reply to Nelson (1988). *Cognitive Development, 5,* 313–330.

Bowerman, M. (1982). Starting to talk worse: Clues to language acquisition from children's late speech errors. In S. Strauss (Ed.), *U-Shaped behavioral growth* (pp. 101–146). New York: Academic Press.

Carey, S., & Bartlett, E. (1978). Acquiring a single new word. *Papers and Reports on Child Language Development, 15,* 17–29.

DeLoache, J. S. (1987). Rapid change in the symbolic functioning of young children. *Science, 238,* 1556–1557.

Diamond, A. (in press). Frontal lobe involvement in cognitive changes during the first year of life. In K. Gibson, M. Konner, & A. Petersen (Eds.), *Brain and behavioral development.* New York: Aldine Press.

Gathercole, V. C. (1987). The contrastive hypothesis for the acquisition of word meanings: A reconsideration of the theory. *Journal of Child Language, 14,* 493–531.

Hawking, S. W. (1988). *A brief history of time: From the big bang to black holes.* New York: Bantam.

Kopcke, K., & Zubin, D. (1983). The cognitive organization of knowledge of gender of the one syllable noun of German everyday language. *Zeitschrift fur germanistische Linguistik, 11,* 166–182.

Kuczaj, S. A. (1990). Constraining constraint theories. *Cognitive Development, 5,* 341–344.

Levine, M. (1966). Hypothesis behavior by humans during discrimination learning. *Journal of Experimental Psychology, 71,* 331–336.

MacWhinney, B. (1989). Making words make sense: Commentary on Merriman and Bowman. *Monograph for the Society for Research in Child Development, 54 (Serial No. 220),* 124–129.

MacWhinney, B. (1991). A reply to Woodward and Markham. *Developmental Review, 11,* 192–194.

MacWhinney, B., Leinbach, J., Taraban, R., & McDonald, J. (1989). Language learning: Cues or rules? *Journal of Memory and Language, 28,* 255–277.

Maratsos, M. P. (1982). The child's construction of grammatical categories. In E. Wanner & L. R. Gleitman (Eds.), *Language acquisition: The state of the art* (pp. 240–266). Cambridge, UK: Cambridge University Press.

Merriman, W. E. (1991). The mutual exclusivity bias in children's word learning: A reply to Woodward and Markman. *Developmental Review, 11,* 164–191.

Merriman, W. E., & Bowman, L. L. (1989). The mutual exclusivity bias in children's word learning. *Monographs of the Society for Research in Child Development, 54* (Serial No. 220).

Nelson, C. A. (in press). Neural correlates of recognition memory in the first year of life. In G. Dawson & K. Fischer (Eds.), *Human behavior and brain development.* New York: Guilford.

Nelson, K. (1988). Constraints on word learning? *Cognitive Development, 3,* 221–246.

Nelson, K. (1990). Comment on Behrend's "Constraints and Development." *Cognitive Development, 5,* 331–339.

Piaget, J. (1952). *The child's concept of number.* New York: Norton.

Siegler, R. S., & Crowley, K. (1991). The microgenetic method: A direct means for studying cognitive development. *American Psychologist, 46,* 606–620.

Smith, M. E. (1926). An investigation of the development of the sentence and the extent of vocabulary in young children. *University of Iowa Studies in Child Welfare, 3,* 5.

Wason, P. C., & Johnson-Laird, P. N. (1972). *Psychology of reasoning: Structure and content.* London: Batsford.

Woodward, A. L., & Markman, E. M. (1991). Constraints on learning as default assumptions: Comments on Merriman and Bowman's "The mutual exclusivity bias in children's word learning." *Developmental Review, 11,* 137–163.

Author Index

Subject Index

A

Abduction: abstract concept formation, 197-200, 206
 differences in male and female, 200
 hypothesis competition, 197, 202
 hypothesis refinement, 197, 202
 in grammar acquisition, 197
 spatial learning, 201-205
  configurational knowledge, 202
  episodic knowledge, 202
  gender differences, 201-205
  in rats, gender differences, 204-205
  use of mental maps, 201
Affect theory, 141-143
 affiliation, 144
 biases in, 143
 communicative interchange, affective analysis of, 144
 density of affective communication, 147
 emotional expression, frequency and type 146(t), 148(t)
 language and affect, 142
 language and emotion, 142
 primary emotions, according to Tomkins, 144
 sequential patterns in, 149-150(t)

B

Beliefs, intuitive biological, in children, 106-107, 185-186
Biological bases of language development, 28-30, 54-55
Biological constraints, 59, 60

Biological thought
 acquisition of, 104
 children's beliefs and disease agents, 123-125(f), 126
 children's beliefs and patterns of biological contagion, 119-121(f), 122(f)
 children's intuitive beliefs, 106-107
 developmental changes in, 112-119
 domain specificity, 131-132
 emergence of, 135
 teleology and, 127-131

C

Cerebral hemispheres, processing differences in, 190-197
 asymmetry in animals, 193
 familial-handedness and variations of linguistic knowledge, 194-197
 left hemisphere and language, 190
 local lexical processing vs. global syntactic processing, 207
 relational vs. unary processing, 192-194
Chomsky's model of linguistic structure, 12-15
 modules in, 12(f)
 transformational grammar in, 13(f)
 limitations of, 140
 see also: Fodor's model of cognitive structure, 15-19
Co-orientation, linguistic and affective, 159
Cognitive structure, Fodor's model of, 15-19
Computations, mental life as
 and linguistics, 180
 in modularity hypothesis, 180
 input-output systems, 180